FRENCH OPERA

FRENCH OPERA

Its Development to the Revolution

by

Norman Demuth,

Professor of Composition, Royal Academy of Music, London
Membre correspondant de l'Institut de France
(Académie des Beaux Arts)

THE ARTEMIS PRESS

SUSSEX : MCMLXIII

Printed and made in Great Britain
by A. Wheaton & Co. Ltd., Exeter, Devon.

FOREWORD

Some years ago I tried to find an English book dealing exclusively with French Opera and with Opera in France. I sought in vain. The subject seemed to warrant such a volume, and I decided to attempt the work.

I had no idea how far my enquiries would take me, or to what extent I should find French Opera bound up with the social history of France. The first step lay in the accumulation of a considerable library of French books, none of them devoted solely to Opera, followed by many fascinating hours spent in libraries and museums. The sociological study proceeded for some time before I touched the music, and when I eventually reached the point of examining innumerable scores of operas of all kinds, I had penetrated the mysteries of ancient *Privilèges*, Laws and Regulations. All these not only stimulated my interest and enjoyment, but lured me into many barely relevant enquiries.

I have yielded to the temptation of introducing some of these matters, hoping that they will add general interest to the book without disrupting its continuity. Others I have been forced to omit. It would have been easy to drift into Ballet at the expense of the main subject. Similarly, certain authenticated facts that I chanced upon might have gone far to disprove the theory so vehemently expressed by my late friend Dr. Percy Scholes that, whoever may have written the tune for the English National Anthem, it certainly was not Lully.[1] I now believe that there is every reason for regarding the great Florentine as the composer, but unfortunately the details do not belong in this book.

The French sociological writers are refreshingly unanimous over the facts. They differ, however, on the matter of precise dates, though not on the years. Where necessary, I have adopted the 'majority view', and consider it over-meticulous to quote divergences of days.

To maintain smooth reading, I have kept footnotes to a minimum, and not given sources and authorities for every statement, nor quoted gramophone records unobtainable in this country. I have, however, mentioned the sources of certain episodes and occurrences which might otherwise have been ascribed to my imagination (flattering though this would have been). The biblio-

---

[1] God save the Queen - (O.U.P.), pp. 208, 291-6.

graphy is sufficiently comprehensive to satisfy the most exacting student, although I have omitted the obvious dictionaries.

In France, opera and the theatre have always evoked an enormous amount of writing, but the English list is distressingly thin. English literary and historical studies treat music with scant courtesy. Lytton Strachey in his *Landmarks of French Literature* devotes considerable space to Molière without once mentioning Lully or the *raison d'être* for many of Molière's works, while W. H. Lewis in *The Splendid Century* disposes of Lully and the *Académie royale de musique* in a short paragraph, likening the works and their production to musical comedy.

I have refrained from translation in most cases because the old French is more apposite than an English version can ever be, and the old spelling and phraseology are too interesting to ruin. Where no acknowledgement is made, the translations are my own.

I should state that Professor Girdlestone's *Rameau* appeared at the time that I was writing the corresponding section of this book and I have refrained from reading it.

Little of the music discussed in this volume can be bought except in second-hand shops and bookstalls. One occasionally comes across vocal scores of Lully and his contemporaries in the *Editions Michaelis*, but these are rare and often expensive. Prunières' edition of Lully remains incomplete, and the modernised versions of Rameau are out of print. However, there is rich treasure to be found in the British Museum, and in the *Bibliothèques Nationale, de l'Arsenal, du Conservatoire,* and *de l'Opéra.* In the last there is a wonderful collection of scores of all works produced by the Paris Opera under its various appellations.

I hope that the musical wanderer in Paris who reads this book will derive as much enjoyment from evoking the scenes and events related in its pages as I have. An ordinary street can become instantly alive by its associations, and houses cease to be anonymous shells. Should he be in the fortunate position of having a cheque to cash in the *Banque de France,* he may reflect that he is doing so in a building which once housed the Paris Opera.

I began the writing of this book in Paris, and conclude it with this Preface in the same place as that in which I made my final decision and collated the results of my first day's research.

NORMAN DEMUTH

Hôtel du Danube,
rue Jacob,
Paris VI.

ACKNOWLEDGMENTS

Once again I must thank my wife for her help and encouragement during the periods of research and writing.

I am also deeply grateful to Mlle. Béatrice Piettre for the final verification of authorities and references; to M. V. Fédorov, Librarian of the Paris Conservatoire, for granting her special facilities; and to Mr. W. Stock, Librarian of the Royal College of Music, for suggesting several improvements after checking the proofs.

My ex-pupil Miss Christine Hardwick has cleared up many points relating to the recorded music, and M. Theodore d'Erlanger provided some very valuable data.

CONTENTS

Part Two:　Jean Baptiste Lully

To my friend Jacques Chailley,
Professor of Musicology at the University of Paris

CHAPTER ONE

DRAMATISED LITURGY — LITURGICAL DRAMA — MYSTÈRE —
LES CONFRÈRES DE LA PASSION — LES CLERCS DE LA
BAZOCHE — LES ENFANTS SANS-SOUCY — ITINERANTS —
FOIRES DE SAINT-LAURENT ET SAINT GERMAIN-DES-PRÉS —
LE THÉÂTRE DE LA FOIRE — JEUX — CHANSON DE GESTE —
CHANTE FABLE   —   FÊTES DE COUR   —   MASCERADES
(NAUTIQUES) — RONSARD — BEAUCHAMP — ECLOGUES —
BAÏF — ACADÉMIE DE POËSIE ET DE MUSIQUE — SAINT
BARTHOLOMEW'S EVE — GELOSI

OPERA originated in Italy. Its roots lie in the primitive dramatisations of the Liturgy and in the later, more elaborate, Liturgical
Dramas. In France, it had similar French roots, but the actual
idea of an entirely musical drama came from Italy.

It would be begging too many questions to state that opera
originated entirely in these early dramatic manifestations. Although
they contained what became recognised as certain operatic elements, other factors, to be found in ordinary theatrical writing and
production, were also present. In a study of this evolutionary
process, it is necessary to consider, in some detail, the social circumstances in which clergy and laity lived.

The derivation of Opera, therefore, can be traced to that
dramatisation of the Liturgy which the early Christian clergy
found more effective as a lesson to their unruly, and mostly
illiterate, congregations than the simple reading of the Gospel
and the use of a formalised ritual. The Faithful, knowing no Latin,
grasped little of what was said in the Sanctuary. Any doctrinal
instruction given from the pulpit went mainly unheeded if, indeed,
much of it was ever heard. There was neither reverence nor

discipline. The preachers were applauded, or hissed; badinage passed between the members of the congregation, arguments and fights were rife and comments were shouted by all and sundry. Sermons were regarded rather as the twentieth century regards political meetings, and the behaviour of the congregation in general foreshadowed that in the later, secular theatre.

The dramatisation of the Liturgy reached its climax on Good Friday and Easter Day. The Resurrection was acted in its entirety, each actor declaiming the words of the Gospel 'in character', and with action. The three Marys were played by Priests in dalmatics or by Clerks in tunicles, the amices being pulled over their heads to represent the female coif. (Here can be seen an early instance of stage costume.) The scenes were enacted as elaborately as each particular church could afford. Similar dramatisations took place at Christmas and at the Epiphany, the crib being simple and always covered with gifts. Each dramatic representation concluded with a Festival *Te Deum*.

Much of the trouble lay with the abuse of the Right of Sanctuary which created undue familiarity between clergy and refugees. This Right of Sanctuary had long since ceased to be a question of affording shelter in a church to the casual fugitive from justice or oppression. On March 23, 431 Théodore le Jeune passed a law widening Sanctuary to the entire precincts of Abbeys. In this way room was made for hundreds of people fleeing their creditors, and for those whose poverty forced them to seek alms, but whose pride prevented them from doing so openly for fear of being arrested as vagabonds. They moved their goods and chattels into the precincts, and took up residence. They treated the clergy with no ceremony and the nobles among the refugees, regarding the vestry, refectory and living quarters in general as an extension of their own châteaux, thought nothing of purloining wine and food that was intended for the clergy. The men diced, drank and wenched as they would have done in the ordinary way. Murders were committed, but the murderers claimed the Right of Sanctuary and escaped punishment. The Abbey, therefore, became a town within a town. Small wonder then that there was no respect for the clergy or their calling, for their preaching or their praying. The only thing to be said for the system is that there was complete democracy in the Church itself. Those out of Sanctuary were quite unabashed by the magnificence of those living inside it.

As time went on, the simple dramatisations of the Gospel stories became more elaborate. The *mise en scène* moved from the Sanctuary to other parts of the building, and, from these small and centralised dramatisations of the Liturgy, there grew the Liturgical Drama which was at once more mobile and more comprehensive. Strictly speaking, it was not fully liturgical since it did not adhere closely to the words of the Liturgy; but these formed the bases of the drama, and specially-written lines in Latin, called *tropes*, allowed considerable elasticity. In due course it became the custom to speak the whole drama in the language of the province.

The principal subjects were the Resurrection and the Nativity, in that order of importance. The stories were unfolded between a Prologue and an Epilogue consisting of the episodes immediately preceding and succeeding the principal subject. Thus, the Resurrection was preceded by the purchase of the ointments for burial and was followed by the appearance of Christ after His Resurrection. Eucharistic vestments gradually gave place to stage costume.

The music consisted mainly of the liturgical melodies. When the actual words of the Liturgy were not in use, the liturgical music was fitted as far as possible to the new text, not the text to the music. When this was not practicable, and an experienced composer was available, original music was used. This was monody of the most primitive kind, of a plainsong character, either metrical or non-metrical. It was sung by chorus or soloists.[1]

The process of moving about the church eventually took the proceedings to the West Door, the onlookers moving through the porch on to the square. Here there were no restrictions either in space or time, and the originally simple-minded and practical liturgical dramatisation broadened out into the *Mystère* of the

---

[1] *Quem quaeritis in sepulchro?* (Lament from *Daniel*) – H.M.V. History of Music, HLP 3.

13th, 14th and 15th centuries. The productions became elaborate, complex, and extremely spectacular. The subjects widened in scope, but music always played a secondary supporting role.

Time was no object.

The *Mystère des Actes des Apostres par personnages* consisted of sixty thousand verses. It was performed on a tiered stage, the highest being reserved for Paradise (and the singers), the middle one for Earth, and the lowest one for Hell. When the instrumentalists were not playing they handed their instruments to angels, who held them in those static poses which can be seen in any Renaissance painting. The effect was that of a stained-glass window. The sacredness of the subjects, though frequently overlooked to maintain the interest of the illiterate and the ribald onlookers, was never entirely forgotten.

The whole population of the town took part, filling the dual roles of stage-crowd and audience – in relevant costumes. Preparations began many months in advance. Everything was taken most seriously. Once the stage had been set (the 'sets' consisted of towers, temples, gates etc.) and the population duly positioned, nobody dared move. Many concerned had a bird's-eye view of the proceedings, which sometimes put the players in a quandary. While perched on the summit of a tower in the *Mystère de Saint-Christophe*, one Claude Chevalet looked down and suddenly saw his wife behaving very improperly with a male stranger in his own house. He could not decide whether to go and stop them and thus create a disturbance during the performance, or to look the other way. Eventually he came to the conclusion that by the time he reached the spot the damage would have been done – so he looked the other way.[1]

The libretti were coarse and direct, serious moments giving place to farcical ones at which the crowd roared with laughter, regardless of the proprieties. At Beauvais, when the Blessed Virgin entered on an ass, the clergy intoned an *Introit*, followed by the *Kyrie*, *Gloria* and *Credo*, concluding with a loud nasal inflection 'hin han', to imitate the braying of the ass, which the crowd took up with unquenchable zest. Unconscious humour appeared at

---

[1] *La Vie au Moyen Age* – Jacques Castelnau (Hachette) p.281.

serious moments. In the *Passion* by Greban, the following conversation took place:—

L'ANGE: Père Eternel, vous avez tort,
Et devriez avoir vergogne;
Votre fils bien aimé est mort
Et vous dormez comme un ivrogne.

DIEU LE PÈRE: Il est mort?

L'ANGE: Oui, foi d'homme de bien.

DIEU LE PÈRE: Diable emporte qui n'en savait rien.

The incompetent physician was one of the main sources of amusement, and there is no doubt that Molière found the basis here for some of his situations.

The production itself was meticulously detailed and literal. In the *Mystère du Vieil Testament*, Heaven and Hell were depicted in an uncompromising manner. 'Adonques se doit mentrer ung beau paradis terrestre le mieulx et triomphamment fait qu'il sera possible et bien garny de toutes fleurs, arbres, fruicts et autre plaisances, et au milieu l'arbre de vie le plus excellent que tous les authres'. The standard set for Hell appears to have been 'essentiellement composé de trois éléments; une tour de forteresse, sur le plan de celles dont étaient flanquées les villes du Moyen Age; un puits où Jésus ayant brisé les portes d'enfer jette Satan, et une entrée généralement en forme de gueule passage aux diables. Il faut ajouter un parloir ou place oy les diables tiennent à la vue du public souvent au-dessus de la porte, ou sur une des platesformes de leur forteresse, leurs orageuses assembles.' The 'gueule' left nothing to the imagination and it sometimes happened that the principal actors lost their lives when Hell's flames got out of hand.

Miracles had to be convincing. When Judas Iscariot hanged himself, the line in The Acts of the Apostles stating that 'all his bowels gushed out' was represented by the splitting of a bag of blood and animals' entrails hidden on the actor's person. When Saint Barthelmy was burnt at the stake, an image was substituted for the actor under cover of smoke and flames, the latter illuminating only a skeleton. There were, no doubt, some conjurors available and, having no inhibitions, the producers must have enjoyed themselves.

Stage machinery was used, the Almighty being shown seated among stars which circled round Him, while thunder and the noise of battle were supplied by real gunfire.

No work was done during the period of performance. The opening was signalled by a procession through the town, with pipe and tabor. Shops were closed; clock towers and church bells were silent. The four hundred and eight actors in the *Mystère des Actes des Apostres*, the hundred and fifty-two in the *Mystère de Saint-Martin*, the four hundred and seventy in the *Passion*, played only static roles, occupying the same positions throughout, so that, at the end, they all went mad, as well they might, having been present in the arena for perhaps forty days from six until eleven in the morning, and then again from one till six. Pent-up energies were allowed full play.

From these *Mystères* dates the tradition of the spectacular drama, a tradition which has never waned and which was to rise to even more complex heights as time went on. The *Mystères* rank as the genuine 'Operas' of the Middle Ages. In course of time the principal actors became known as 'Comédiens', a title which has remained.

In Paris the *Mystères* were performed by 'Les Confrères de la Passion', who gave their performances in the Trinité, but in 1402 Charles VI gave them permission to act in public, the Letters-Patent reading 'afin qu'un chacun *par devotion* se puisse et doibve adjoindre et mettre en leur compagnie à iceux maistres, gouverneurs, et confrères de la Passion Nostre-Seigneur'. The complete Privilège was issued in 1407, and is one of the oldest in French history (Appendix One). In 1539, the Confrères moved to the Hôtel de Flandre and remained there until 1543.

There were *Mystères* at, among other places, Rouen, Angers, Le Mans, and Metz. The forty-day *Mystère des Actes des Apostres* of 1440 has already been mentioned. In 1486, Jean-Michel d'Angers produced the *Mystère de la Passion* in his native city, repeating it in Paris in 1507. This performance continued for twelve days and covered the entire life of Christ. Its episodes included those of Marie-Madeleine at her toilet surrounded by ladies-in-waiting, a full description and enactment of the suicide of Judas Iscariot, with 'effects', and the Crucifixion, the actor remaining on the cross for three hours. Other *Mystères* were *La Grande Diablerie*, produced in 1500 by Eloy d'Amernal, Priest and Master of the Choristers at Béthune; *L'Homme juste et l'Homme mondain* by Simon Bougouin, valet de chambre to Louis XI (1508); *L'Apocalypse de Saint-Jean en rime françoise* by Louis Chocquet (1540); and the *Mystère de la Nativité* (1547) by Barthelmy Aneau de Bourges, a Lutheran who found fame by dropping a large stone on the priest who was carrying the Holy Sacrament in an outdoor procession. This work was described as being composed 'en imitation verbale et musicale.' Nothing, however, appears to have surpassed the *Mystère de la Passion* of 1490, which took place at Angers by order of Conrad Bayer, 75th Bishop of Metz. This was decorated in the most lavish manner by the best available painters and machinists and contained singing, dancing, poetry and spoken prose dialogue. The performances were preceded by High Mass celebrated on the stage, Vespers being delayed in order that the singers might assist in the service; the performances ended, as was usual, with a solemn *Te Deum*.[1]

Meanwhile, two other bodies outside the Confrères de la Passion had come into being. The first of these was formed by the Clercs de la Bazoche, under Philippe le Bel. They performed 'moralitez, farces et soties', the last being political satires. The plays had to be sanctioned by Parliament. Their musical force consisted of a drum, four trumpets, three oboes and a bassoon. They were abolished in 1478, owing to abuses which had crept in among the company, and not performed again until the veto was removed by Charles VIII. Louis XII established the 'Liberté des Théâtres', 'pensant aussi apprendre beaucoup de choses qu'autrement il lui serait impossible de savoir'. The Bazochiens gave their performances on a marble table in the Grande

---

[1] Modern *Mystéres* include *Jeanne d'Arc au bûcher* (Honegger) and *Lucifer* (Delvincourt), while d'Indy's *La Légende de Saint Christophe* contains many of the genre's qualities and elements. It is becoming increasingly popular among 20th century French composers who find that it gives more scope to inventiveness and variety than opera.

Salle de Paris until, on March 6th, 1618, the Salle was burnt down.[1]

The other body, called 'Les Enfants Sans-Soucy', consisted of young people of family who enjoyed the art of living without following any strictly moral code. Their Privilège was granted by Charles VI, their leader, Gringoire, calling himself the 'Prince des Sots'. Taking as their motto 'Tout par raison, raison partout, partout raison', they exercised a considerable critical faculty in the choice of their plays, and eventually became associated with the Confrères de la Passion. Earlier, they had compromised with the Bazochiens to the extent of permitting the latter to play 'soties'; in return for this favour, they were themselves allowed to produce 'farces et moralitez'. Louis XII held them in high esteem. He granted them the privilege of criticising freely all the faults of any individual, including himself, or any group of individuals. Mention of the Queen, however, was proscribed.

In 1548 the Confrères took over part of the Hôtel de Bourgogne, but within three weeks of doing so a parliamentary decree, issued on November 17th, forbade them to perform plays based on sacred subjects. At the same time, it gave them the sole right to perform those on profane and secular subjects. For a time they made full use of this Privilège, eventually engaging outside actors, to form what became known as 'Les Comédiens du Roi'. The edict proclaimed that all the plays were to have 'sujets profanes, licites et honnêtes'.

The seamy side of the matter, however, played a part which was not without influence upon the future. Europe was full of itinerant musicians, clowns, jugglers, tumblers, mountebanks, conjurors and quack doctors, all known as 'jongleurs', a word meaning deceivers, tricksters, and cheats. They earned a precarious livelihood by entertaining casual parties at inns and taverns (where they literally 'sang for their supper') and by placing themselves at the disposal of any person wanting a private entertainment on the spur of the moment. They eked out this living in the market squares and at street corners.

Poets offering their skill (it could hardly be called their art) to anyone requiring a love sonnet engaged musicians to accompany

---

[1] The first chapter of Victor Hugo's *The Hunchback of Notre Dame* gives a vivid picture of one of these *fêtes*.

its reading outside the window of the recipient, and it thus became an unwritten law that each 'art' should assist the others whenever the opportunity offered. In this way, there arose a species of *esprit de corps* among these vagabonds which was admirable, if somewhat misdirected, since it worked the 'wheels within wheels' system. It is not known if the employer extorted any commission from the employed.

Life, if curtailed by dirt and disease, was at least full of incident and a good deal of colour. In the 13th century, the itinerants became impossible to control and Philippe Auguste (1180 – 1223) ordered them out of the realm of France as being prejudicial to public morality. Saint Louis IX removed this ban.

In 1321 the itinerants demanded a Charter for themselves, with a view to forming a Corporation. This was granted, and the new Corporation was placed under the patronage of Saint-Julien-des-Meneztriers. It soon split into bands, one of jongleurs and one of musicians, the latter divided into two groups, singers and instrumentalists. Life was difficult for them. They were forbidden to sing or talk politics, to mention the King, the Pope, the Lords, or the Church. This left them very short of material and they were consequently driven, if 'driven' be the right word, to bawdry. At the end of the century the musicians severed their connection with the jongleurs and became an autonomous body forming an integral part of all State and Civic functions. They regarded themselves as a 'kingdom', and their President adopted the regal title. On each Epiphany the real King was given presents by his quasi-cousin who received, in his turn, a substantial reward for doing so (Appendix Two).

The itinerants and their confrères were the life and soul of the *Foires* which, in Paris, took place during August and September at Saint-Germain-des-Prés and Saint-Laurent. The scum of Paris mingled with the more or less respectable citizens and traders, while *Vaudevilles* entertained the onlookers as much with their humour as with their lewdness. The King and courtiers liked to mix incognito with the crowd, cracking a pate here and there when provoked. Courtiers unpopular with the mob were severely handled when they were recognised.

The Théâtre de la Foire, the cesspool from which the *Opéra-*

Comique arose very much later, is remembered in two weighty volumes of plays. The most casual glance at these reveals, on almost every page, a monotonously similar vein of humour. English Restoration drama, with its accent on sexual intrigue, seems, by comparison, almost romantic. The following stage direction, taken at random, from *La Condemnacion de Baucqyet* by Nicholas de la Chesnaye, is typical of the contemporary humour:

> 'Pause pour pisser le Fol – Il prend ung coffinet en lieur de orinal, et pisse dedans, et tout coule par bas.'

This is but one extract from the play, and since it is described as a *moralité*, it is small wonder that on April 16th, 1641, Louis XIII issued a strongly-worded Edict (Appendix Three).

Not all theatrical performances, however, were of this nature. Noblemen of the time whiled away dull hours in their own châteaux by producing plays, known as *Jeux*. Many regard Adam de la Hale's *Jeu de Robin et Marion*[1], produced at Tournai in 1277 and performed regularly at Angers each Easter, as the first French Opera. This it certainly is not, as it is little more than a play with music.[2]

This work, together with the *Jeu d'Adam et Eve*, occurred in complete isolation, like the English *Sumer is icumen in*. It had no direct influence and its unsophisticated story and music are hardly sufficient to make it anything more than a small landmark.

Marion loves Robin, preferring him to a rich knight; that is all there is to it. The melodies are as simple as the verses.

Ex. 1ᴬ.

RO-BINS M'AI-ME, RO-BINS M'A   RO-BINS M'A DE-MAN-DÉ-E SI MA-RA

Ex. 1ᴮ

RO - BINS — M'AI - ME,   RO - BINS   M'A ;   RO - BINS

M'A —— DE - MAN —— DÉ - E,   SI M'A —— RA.
(IL M'AU —— RA.)

---

[1] *Le Jeu de Robin et Marion* – (11/54) Archive Production APM 14018.
[2] A French radio announcer described this work as 'the First Opéra-Comique' (January 3rd, 1959). This seems a reasonable point of view.

The verses continue:

Robins m'acata	Robin m'achêta
Cotele d'escarlate	Cotillon d'écarlate
Bone et bele	Bonne et belle,
Souskranie	Souquenille
et	et
Chanturele	Centurie
a leur ivaz.	a leur iva.
Robins m'aime	Robin m'aime
Robins m'a	Robin m'a
Demandee	Demandée
Si m'aura.	S'il m'aura.

The second song, called *Le Jeu du Berger et de la Bergère*, is equally simple-minded and pastoral in what became the accepted sense of that musical expression.

Ex.2

Between the two strophes the following dialogue clinches matters:

ROBIN: Magotte, veux-tu plus de moi?
MARION: Oil en no Dieu. [Oui, au nom de Dieu.]

Perhaps it was not quite as unsophisticated as all that.

The work has some of the elements of the early *Pastoral* (or *Eclogue*) which was to appear presently and shine in the hands of Ronsard.

The *Chanson de Geste* and *Chante Fable*, typified in *Aucassin et Nicolette* and *L'Histoire du Roi Florus* were the work of the Troubadors (Southern France)[1] and Trouvères (Northern France)[2] – Adam

---

[1] Ventadorn, Bernat de (c.1150 – 1195) – *Lemcon vel la olha* – Archive Production APM 14068. *Quant val l'aloete mover* – H.M.V. History of Music, HLP 3.
[2] Brule, Gace (12th century) – *Je ne puis pas si loing fuir* – H.M.V. History of Music, HLP 3.

de la Hale was one of the latter and Richard Coeur de Lion one of the former, although they were in a class different from that of the itinerant jongleurs. These *Chansons* and *Chantes* consisted of a plot, a few lines of music, spoken dialogue and mime, but there was not sufficient to warrant their being classed as anything but plays with music, certainly not as incipient operas, even if one can see certain connecting links.

The *Jeux, Mystères* and *Vaudevilles* of the Théâtre de la Foire bypassed the Court, but out of the splendours of the *Mystères* and the elaborate Italian *Mascherata* there arose the *Fêtes de Cour*. These were entertainments on a lavish scale and consisted of dancing, ballets, tourneys (both 'à pied' and 'à cheval' – ballets were sometimes 'à cheval'), fireworks and *Mascerades nautiques*. On a less extravagant scale, there were the evening entertainments when, after supper, ladies of the court danced ballets in the style of the Italian 'Brando'. They entered on a chariot, grouped to display their charms to the fullest advantage, and then carried out evolutions upon geometrical figures. It was not until the end of the century that men took part in these dances and their role was, usually, either obscene or grotesque. The gentlemen of the court, however, entertained the ladies with feats of wrestling and other masculine contests. There was always some kind of fundamental subject running through the proceedings, and they were not unlike the modern charade.

The *Mascerade nautique*, however, was no hasty improvisation. It entailed the construction of a great number of mechanically driven 'strange sea monsters' of enormous size, sufficiently distorted and bizarre to make a brave and startling show. At one time live animals played important roles in the *Fêtes champêtres*, and these could be, and sometimes were, a danger to all concerned, the preventive measures amounting only to a few armed men at likely danger points. This practice had its origins among the Ancient Greeks and Romans, where the actors were drawn from condemned criminals who had to die some kind of violent death. If they succeeded in warding off the attacks of the animals, they were released.

The live element, however, was soon dropped in the *Fêtes de Cour* as so many of these took place indoors. Mechanical toys were substituted; and, where intense mobility was required, actors impersonated the animals.

The earliest record of a French *Fête de Cour* dates from François I (1515 – 1547). The Field of the Cloth of Gold was nothing more than such a production, though not, officially, so described. The genre became established when Henri II (1547 – 1559) married Catherine de Medici, for she brought with her, from Florence, a large number of her countrymen. She was determined to make the French Court the most splendid and opulent in the world, and succeeded in doing this through the Italian *Mascherata*, which took its French title of *Fête de Cour*. Under Henri II dancing became an integral part of court life. The King and his courtiers may be said to have lived a perpetual ballet, the sovereign being unable to move from one room to another except in procession, being handed on by successive groups of courtiers, from room to room.

The foremost contributor to the *Fêtes de Cour* was the poet Pierre de Ronsard (1524 – 1585). Deaf from the age of eighteen, he could still hear music, and he developed a great and lasting love for it. His poems move with a clearly defined musical impulse and rhythm, and in due course he wrote verses expressly for musical setting, the composers being Muret, Costerley[1], de la Grotte[2], Orlando de Lassus[3], Philippe de Monte[4], Jannequin[5], Certon[6] and Goudimel[7] (who was murdered during the St. Bartholomew Massacre).

Ronsard was serious-minded and at first regretted the frivolous superficialities of the new court life, but, before long, the *panache* of the Valois made a direct appeal to him and the charm of the

---

[1] *Allons au vert bocage* H.M.V. History of Music HLP 8; *En ce beau moys* Oiseau Lyre OL 50027; *Noblesse git au coeur – Mignonne allons voir* Brunswick AXTL 1048; *Je voy di glissantes eaux – Mignonne allons voir* Ducretet-Thomson mel 9007.
[2] *Quan je te veux raconter* Oiseau Lyre OL 50027.
[3] *Bon jour mon coer – Quand mon mary vient* Brunswick AXTL 1048; *Orsus filles, que l'on me donne – Un doux nenny* Archive APM 14055.
[4] *Benedictus – Agnus Dei* H.M.V. History of Music HLP 8.
[5] *Amour, la mort et la vie – Il estoit une filette – Las! pauvre couer* Oiseau Lyre OL 50027; *Au joli jeux – Chant des Oiseaux (Reveillez-vous) – Guerre – Ma peine n'est pas grande – Petite nymphe folastre* Archive APM 14042; *Ce Moys de Mai* Brunswick AXTL 1048.
[6] *Que n'est elle aupres de moi* Oiseau Lyre OL 50027; *Psalm 130* Nixa WLP 5058.
[7] *Amour me tue* Oiseau Lyre OL 50027.

court ladies stirred all the latent feelings of gallantry which lay beneath his somewhat austere exterior.

The geometrical figures constituting Ballet appealed to Ronsard's sense of form and symmetry. These had been devised by the King's Maître de Ballet, Beauchamp, who, as a pigeon-fancier, had been much struck by the figures unconciously made by his birds when they clustered round their feeding-bowls. The flexibility of Beauchamp's figures influenced Ronsard's verses, which became similarly flexible and plastic, and, in their musical setting, required a good deal of time-changing to ensure correct accentuation. Ronsard's composers fully realised the 'tyranny of the bar-line'.

Ronsard rhapsodised upon this flexibility in the Sonnet XLIX, Book II of his *Sonnets pour Hélène*. The accents and spelling are in conformity with the first printed edition (1578):—

Le soir qu'Amour vous fist en la salle descendre
 Pour danser d'artifice un beau ballet d'Amour,
 Vos yeux, bien qu'il fust muict, ramenerent le jour,
 Tant ils sceurent d'esclairs par la place respandre.

Le ballet fut divin, qui se souloit reprendre,
 Se rompre, se refaire et tour dessus retour
 Se mesler, s'escarter, se tourner à l'entour,
 Contre-imitant le cours du fleuve de Meandre:

Ores il estoit rond, ores long, or' estroit,
 Or en poincte, en triangle, en la façon qu'on voit
 L'escadron de la Gruë évitant la froidure.

Je faux, tu ne dansois, mais ton pied voletoit
 Sur le haut de la terre: aussi ton corps s'estoit
 Transformé pour ce soir en divine nature.

Ronsard's exquisitely polished verse, with its gracious musical subtleties, reaches forward over the centuries to Gabriel Fauré, whose music may be regarded as forming the 19th and 20th centuries' counterpart to Ronsard's 16th century poetry.

The *Fêtes de Cour*, however, were not simply domestic entertainments. They had a political purpose behind them, the general policy being to extol the qualities of the Royal Family under a mythological and allegorical guise. This custom was to remain in use for over a hundred years, reaching its peak in the operatic Prologues of Lully, and is to be found, indeed, at the back of much French drama. Ronsard, a poet first and then a courtier, avoided bombast and excessive flattery, although the correct technique was to achieve a flood of compliments, sometimes so fulsome as to be ridiculous.

The *Fêtes* were held mainly at Fontainebleau, the most notable occurring in the reign of Charles IX (1560 – 1574). Of these, three were outstanding: that held on the canal in 1563, the one in honour of the King's entry to Bar-le-Duc in 1564, and, particularly, one held in 1565, which consisted of a great number of spectacles, games, and *Divertissements*. Ronsard shared in the writing of the libretti, the chief characteristic being the primarily French *cartel* or 'Vers pour les personnages du ballet' which was printed and circulated to the onlookers.

The first of these three, *Les Sereines*, opened with a panegyric to the memory of Henri II, the King's father, and gradually drifted into a eulogy upon Charles IX himself:

Ainsi que nous, que depuis ce temps là
Que le malheur d'icy nous exila,
N'avions au Ciel monstré noz tresses blondes;
   Sinon de jour de long temps attendu,
Où Charles Roy de Henry descendu,
Vrais héritier des vertus de son pere,
Desur son peuple a maintenant pouvoir:
Et c'est pourquoy nous venons icy voir
Ce jeune Prince en qui la France espere.

The alexandrines continue for some while. They were probably recited to lute accompaniment.

The second was an allegorical *Mascerade* in which the four Elements and the four Planets extolled the King, Jupiter concluding with a judgement to confirm their opinions. Ronsard's share

finishes with some stanzas 'à chanter sur la lyre', anticipating the
visit of the Queen of Spain to Bayonne:

Soleil, la vie, et la force du monde,
Grand oeil de Dieu, Soleil pere du jour,
Monte à cheval, et tire hors de l'onde
Ton char qui fair pour nous trop de sejour:
Haste ton cours, et en France accompagne
L'autre beau jour qui reluit en Espagne.

The third included a comedy, *Guinèvre de l'Arioste*. Catherine
de Medici forbade tragedy for superstitious reasons. The music
for this production is known to have been composed by Nicolas
de la Grotte (1540 – 1587), the King's organist and a frequent
collaborator with Ronsard. It was performed by ladies of the
Court, and, as some fragments of it remain, it is possible to re-
construct a brief outline.

Love, armed with his bow, sings an air of eight strophes to
celebrate his invincibility. He then attacks the chariot of Chastity,
wishing to give battle and to conquer her. His arrows break in
pieces against the goddess' shield. Seeing him to be unarmed,
Chastity captures Love, leads him to her chariot, and sings a
Hymn of Victory.

Catherine herself always extolled chastity as a cardinal virtue.
She herself was proverbially chaste, even though she used unchaste
methods of worming state secrets out of unsuspecting courtiers
by means of her famous 'flying squad' of ladies-in-waiting.

Ronsard's contribution to the comedy consisted of *Le Trophée
d'Amour* and *Le Trophée de la Chastitée*, alexandrines of great charm
and elegance.

Fortunately, a little of the music has been preserved and it is
possible to compare two settings of Love's lines. The first is squarely
harmonic:

EX. 3

The second shows a little elasticity of movement,

while the following extract, concluding the same song, is an attempt at counterpoint:

It is interesting to see how far this early secular writing was below the sacred music of the time. It signified the change from polyphony to homophony, which was becoming steadily prevalent. The French style was beginning to formulate itself.

In the same year Ronsard wrote the first of a number of *Eclogues*, called, collectively, *Bergerie*, a popular form of entertainment again originating in Italy. It was a play with incidental music, but very little stage action. Its pastoral setting and casting at once became fashionable, as the authors were able to render oblique homage to the Royal Family by using thinly disguised, artificial characters, in this way:

ANGELOT:	Henri, duc d'Anjou (later Henri III)
MARGOT:	Marguerite de Navarre (formerly Valois)
NAVARRIN:	Henri de Bourbon (later Henri IV)
GUISIN:	Henri, duc de Guise
CARLIN:	Charles IX
HENRIOT:	Henri II

Catherine de Medici was given her own first name. At her age, it would have been considered an insult to disguise it.

Ronsard wrote five of these little plays. The third one was a long *Chant Pastoral* in honour of the 'Nopces de Monseigneur Duc de Lorraine, et Madame Claude, fille deuxième du Roy Henry II', which concluded with an Epilogue, *Le Cyclope Amoreux.*

The first one may be taken as representative of the genre. In addition to the principals mentioned above, there are two lutanists, a chorus of shepherds, a shepherdess, two travelling 'Pasteurs' and two others, who occupy a cave and represent the Queen and Madame Marguerite, Duchesse de Savoye. The alexandrines forming the Prologue were recited to the accompaniment of the first lutanist. Ronsard wrote that alexandrines were 'wonderfully suited for music, the lyre, and other instruments', implying that the flow of words combined well with a musical background. The verses intended to be sung are written in strophes.

The setting is a simple grotto, in which the twelve shepherds sit, six on either side. The Prologue explains the real nature of the actors:

> . . . . Ce ne sont pas Bergers d'une maison champestre
> Qui menent pour salaire aux champs les brèbis paistre,
> Mais de haute famille et de race d'ayeux:
> Qui tenans des Pasteurs le Sceptre en divers lieux
> Ont effroyé les loups, et en toute assurance
> Gouverne les troupeaux par les herbes de France.

At this point 'la première partie du coste dextre commence en chantant':

Si nous voyons entre fleurs et boutons
    Paistre moutons
Et nos chevreaux pendre sus une roche,
Sans que le loup sur le soie en approche
    De sa dent croche!

Si nous voyons la siècle d'or réfait
    C'est du bienfait
De la Bergère Catherine.

The shepherds sitting on the left take up the chorus:

Quand nous irons baigner les grasses peaux
    De moz trapeaux
Pour leur blanchir ergots, cornes, et laines,
Semant par tout des roses à mains pleines,
    Sur les fontaines,
    Et sur les eaux:

Lors nous ferons de gazons un autel
Tout convert de branche myrtine,
    Et de la Nymphe Catherine
Appellerons le grand nom immortel:
    Puis luy faisant hommage
Parmy son temple espandrons mille fleurs:
Car tant qu'Amour se nourrira de pleurs
Dedans le coeur nous aurons son image.

The Nymphs then join hands, singing and dancing:

Nous avons veu d'un Prince la jeunesse,
D'un Prince fils d'une grande Deesse,
Dont la beauté, le grace et les valeurs
Ornent noz champs, comme au matin l'Aurore
Orne le ciel, quand son beau front colòre
Tout l'Orient de perles et de fleurs.

    Au bon Carlin le ciel fasse la grace
De voir ça bas les enfans de sa race

c

Tout courbe d'ans des peuples adore:
C'est ce Carlin promis des destinées,
Sous qui courront les meilleures années
Du vieil Saturne et du siécle dore.

The Eclogue then proceeds in vaunting alexandrines between the
characters. 'Les Chansons des Pasteurs' are heard. There is no
text for these, but their quality may be gauged from the succeeding
comments:

Quel poignant crêve-coeur! quelle amère tristesse
Vous tenoit, O forests, quand la blonde jeunesse
Qui sont tousjours la Bise entre en son harnois,
Sainte crainte briganda le Sceptre des François?

More interminable dialogue follows between the principal regal
characters. The first travelling 'Pasteur' recounts his wanderings,
followed by the second in similar strain. 'L'autre Berger voyageur',
who is not mentioned in the list of 'Personnages', asks the
Shepherds:

Que faites vous icy, Bergers qui surmontez
Les Rossignols d'avril quand d'accord vous chantez?

———————

and the Shepherds reply in this exquisite chorus:

J'ay songe sur la minuit
      Ceste nuit
Quand le doux sommeil nous lie,
Que deux beaux Cygnes chantoient,
      Qui sortoient
Du coste de l'Italie.

———————

J'ay veu presque en mesme temps
      Le Printemps
Florir deux fois en l'année:
Dieu ces songes nous permet,
      Qui promet
Quelque bonne destinée.

'Le second joueur de Lyre' relates how two Shepherdesses turned out to be

> L'une mère de Roy, l'autre du Roy la tante,
> L'une venant de France et l'autre de Piemont.

The two 'Pasteurs' then carry on a long conversation in strophes, but it is not known if there was music during this recitation.

Finally, the chorus of Shepherdesses closes the work, reminding the audience of the prologue:

> Tout ainsi qu'une prairie
> Est portraite decent fleurs,
> Ceste neuve Bergerie
> Est peinte de cent couleurs.
> La Poete icy ne garde
> L'art de l'Eclogue parfait;
> Aussi la Muse regarde
> A traiter un autre fait.
> Pource Envie si tu pinces
> Son nom de broquars legers.
> Tu faux; car ce sont grands Princes
> Qui parlent. Cy non Bergers.
> Il mesprise le vulgaire,
> Et ne veut point d'autre loy
> Sinon la grace de plaire
> Aux grands Seigneurs et au Roy.

Such simple-minded entertainment did not hold the undivided attention of the court, and it served mainly to pass the time in an otherwise rather empty life. An eye was always open, however, for any forthcoming event likely to require a *Fête de Cour*. One presented itself in 1566, at Bayonne, where Catherine de Medici went to meet her daughter.

Ronsard was joined by Jean Antoine Baïf (1532 – 1589) as composer, and the two devised one of the most novel *Fêtes* hitherto produced. Poetry and Music were united as never before, but, nevertheless, in an incidental manner only. The music, alas, has disappeared.

This *Fête* consisted of spectacles of unusual magnificence, the *Mascerade nautique* forming the customary climax. On the river a whale and a gigantic turtle carried a group of Sirens, who extolled in song the graces of the Queen, while Orpheus, to lute accompaniment, recited the virtues of Philippe II. Jousts and tourneys occupied the days, Ronsard writing the *cartels*. The final moment came with the appearance of an enormous chariot, decorated with cloth of gold, moving through the clouds, drawn by four beautiful white 'hacquenées'. Venus sat enthroned between children dressed as Cupids who sang her praises. The chariot also carried the God of Love and a train of little Mercuries 'qui tous alloyant chantant et en faisant le tour de camp envoyaient pareillement aux dames et damoiselles les faveurs de celuy à qui estoit ledit chariot'.

Civil wars temporarily put a stop to this lavishness but, in 1567, Charles authorised Baïf to found an 'Académie de Poésie et de Musique'. It received its Royal Charter in 1570. Baïf was joined in this venture by Pybrac and Ronsard. Their aim was to restore music to its ancient splendour and to delve into the secrets of the antique drama, in which spoken dialogue was alternated with sung and danced ensemble movements. The deliberations of this Academy are shrouded in mystery. Charles IX, however, drew upon the Academicians, particularly Ronsard (who now began to write verses specifically intended to be set to music), for the necessary elements in his *Fêtes* and *Ballets*, the next of which took place in 1572. Much preparation was needed. It seems likely that the general plan of the *Mascerade* was drawn up a few years in advance, partly as an experiment on the part of the Academicians and partly to prepare for any eventuality. This *Mascerade* consisted of ballets and recitatives, sung or declaimed; writers of poetry, dramatic poetry, and music were called in to collaborate. It is not known with any certainty who they were, but it is assumed that they included Jacques Davy du Perron, who wrote verses for tunes composed by the Duke of Mantua, and Thibaut de Courville, the first composer of measured music. It is certain, however, that the greater part of the texts was written by Ronsard and Baïf.

On August 20th, 1572, four days before the Massacre of Saint Bartholomew's Eve, Catherine de Medici, with characteristic cynicism, arranged a ballet entitled *Le Defense du Paradis ou Paradis d'Amour*. This was part of the festivities which followed the wedding of Marguerite de Valois with Henri of Navarre. The performance took place in the Grande Salle du Petit-Bourbon (Appendix Four). On the right there was built an arch representing Paradise, reached by a flight of steps. The Champs Elysées could be seen through the arch, over which revolved a large wheel representing the Zodiac, illuminated by the seven Grand Planets and the stars. Twelve Nymphs, six naked and six dressed in the richest of garments, sat on the wheel. On the left was situated Hell, full of devils, instruments of torture, and other satanic paraphernalia (prepared, presumably, for the Huguenots). Charon rowed his boat along a stream representing the Styx which separated the two sites.

Paradise was guarded by Charles IX and his brothers, Hell by Henri of Navarre and his Huguenot friends. The latter attacked Paradise and, following the plan of the charade, were thrown back into Hell, which closed upon them – but not before the audience had relished their mimed destruction at the hands of the devils awaiting them.

Mercure (played by Etienne le Roy, a celebrated singer of the period) and Cupid descended from the sky on horseback. Mercure harangued the victorious defenders of Paradise, giving them permission, through Cupid (in the name of Love), to do what they liked with the Nymphs on the wheel as a reward for their courage and virtue. Both then returned as they had come, and the King and his brothers danced for an hour before the court, after which the defeated Huguenots were released.

Until this moment, the performance had merely been a series of symbolic gestures; their meaning was not lost upon the Huguenots, who began to wrestle in real earnest with the victors, with such success that the King and his brothers were well and truly beaten. This was not in accordance with the script.

The *Ballet* had a double meaning. It could be regarded either as a contest for the Paradise of Love (that is to say, for the Nymphs on the wheel) or as one for the Heavenly Paradise, which heretics could not hope to enter. Just so subtle was the mind of Catherine de Medici, and there can be no doubt which interpretation was put upon her ingenious design by the Huguenots.

Ronsard's share in the book consisted of two *cartels* addressed to Love, another to the King (in the character of Hercules), by Pluto when dragged into the royal presence, a Dialogue between a Masquer and Mercure, and a Monologue for Mercure, addressed to the ladies.

This *Mascerade*, conceived in the worst possible taste, ended with a firework display on the floor (*sic*) of the Salle, a train of gunpowder setting fire to a decorated pyramid. The dancers literally trod on fire. The general design of the work anticipated many of the elements which became features of the macabre 19th century Romantic Period.

After the massacre, the Court took on a more sober aspect and there were fewer *Fêtes*. The scenes of splendour, however, were revived in 1573 when the Polish Ambassador came to offer the crown of Poland to the duc d'Anjou (later Henri III).

Both *Mascerade* and *Eclogue* followed the tradition of wordiness established in the *Mystères*. The musical moments were inserted as relief from the continuous spoken dialogue. Many years later, Molière was to follow the same principle in his danced *Intermèdes*. These Valois presentations formed the original mixture of secular spectacle and drama, but the performances were rarely repeated. The costumes and décors, however, survived well into the 18th century.

Ronsard may be regarded as the first secular librettist both by virtue of his own musical sensitivity and because he wrote poems to be set to music. His works are a long way from opera since one or two musical movements do not constitute such a thing; but one may wonder if he and Baïf did not consider the possibility of a complete musical work during the deliberations of the Académie.

On the death of Charles IX, Henri III escaped from Poland at dead of night; but, once off Polish soil, he did not hurry himself. In 1574, he stayed for a short time in Venice, where he saw a tragedy performed by the Gelosi, the play being written by Frangipane and the music by Claudio Merulo. It was a mythological panegyric upon Henri III himself and was more in the nature of a Cantata than anything else. Henri invited the Gelosi to Paris where, on May 19th, 1577, they gave a performance before the Etats de Clois at the Petit-Bourbon. The name of the work has not come down to us, but Henri Prunières suggests that it may have been *Aminta* by Tasso, which the Gelosi had performed on July 31st, 1573, before the Duc de Ferrare.[1]

Their national arrogance and loose way of living made the Gelosi unpopular in Paris, and in due course they were forbidden to perform by the French Parliament. They were finally banished from the kingdom on the ground that they propagated only 'paillardises et adultères, du tenir escole de debauche à la jeunesse de tout sexe de la ville de Paris'. Apart from this there is no detailed record of their visit, and it had, in the end, no other effect than to provide a precedent for what came later.

---

[1] *L'Opéra italien en France avant Lulli* (Champion), p. XXXV fn.

CHAPTER TWO

"CIRCÉ OU LE BALLET COMYQUE DE LA ROYNE"
("CIRCÉ LA MAGICIENNE")

ON OCTOBER 15th, 1581, the Duc de Joyeuse married Mademoiselle Marguerite de Vaudemont-et-de-Lorraine with a splendour hitherto unparalleled. Joyeuse, La Valette, and d'O had taken the places of the assassinated favourites, Quélus, Schomberg, and Maugiron. D'Epernon's adversary, Bussy d'Ambois, had been murdered the night before the famous duel.[1] As usual, Catherine de Medici played a leading part in the organisation of the *Fêtes* and in the general control of the wedding, placing the musical responsibilities in the hands of Balthasar de Beaujoyeulx, who is better known as Baltazarini, his original Italian name.

This Italian violinist was sent to Catherine, in 1567, by the Maréchal de Brissac, Governor of Piedmont, and during his life at court served in the households of the Queen Mother, Marie-Stuart, Charles IX and Henri III. He brought with him a number of Italian violinists, who caused a sensation by playing on five strings – the French instruments still had only four. The Italians, therefore, were able to produce effects which, by their novelty, greatly impressed their French listeners and aroused the envy of their French colleagues.

A ballet upon a large scale was suggested by Catherine, who occupied herself with the smaller additional entertainments. Baltazarini gathered a team of collaborators round him, including Lambert de Beaulieu (of the Queen's Household), Jacques Salmon (Maître de Chapelle to Henri III), La Chesnaye (the King's Almoner and a member of the royal choir), who wrote the verses, and Jacques Patin (the King's Court Painter). In this way, the entourages of the Queen Mother, the King and the Queen all made their contribution. Baltazarini's share was to write the ballet scenarios and some of the music, while he acted as producer of the entire spectacle. Although it was found necessary to call in

---

[1] *Chicot the Jester* (Alexandre Dumas père) contains a vivid account of this event.

Ronsard and Baïf to help him, the credit must go first and foremost to Baltazarini.

The people of Paris were living in the direst poverty and squalor. As they had no money, they could not be taxed. The *Fêtes*, therefore, were financed by courtiers anxious to keep the royal favour; the money thus borrowed was never repaid.

Baltazarini chose the story of *Circé la Magicienne* and the production took place on Sunday, October 15th, the second day of the festivities. The complete celebrations consisted of a Banquet at the Louvre (Appendix Five), a *Mascerade nautique*, organised by the Cardinal de Bourbon at Saint-Germain-des-Prés (Appendix Six), *Circé*, at the Petit-Bourbon, and jousts at the Tuileries (Appendix Seven).

The title-page of the printed edition reads as follows:

BALLET COMYQUE

de la Royne, faict
aux nopces de Mon-
sieur le Duc de Joyeuse et
Mademoyselle de Vau-
demont, sa soeur[1]

par

Balthasar de Beaujoyeulx,

Valet de Chambre du
Roy et de la Royne, sa mère

à Paris,

par Adrien Le Roy et Mamert
Pattisson, Imprimeurs de Roy

M.D.LXXXII

The idea of *Circé* may well have been suggested by a tragedy with chorus of the same name, by Agrippa d'Aubigné, a production previously forbidden by Catherine on the ground of

---

[1] *i.e.* the sister of the Queen ('Royne').

expense. As this was not, on this occasion, a consideration, Baltazarini was given *carte blanche*. The entire musical and dramatic resources of the Court were placed at his disposal and, throughout the period of preparation and production, he reigned supreme.

Baltazarini fully explained the intention of his work in the preliminary dedication. '*Circé*', he said, 'is a poetic history of the King, the friend of well-being, who resists all the deleterious influences of passion and pleasure. He sits next to Jupiter in the midst of the Gods and exterminates vice. The name of Henri III will live for ever in an odour of virtuous sanctity.' It may be doubted if Henri III recognised himself in this eulogy. By 'vice' the author may have meant 'heresy', and, if so, he paid an oblique compliment to Catherine for her persecution of the Protestants.

Later in the same dedication, Baltazarini extolled Henri III as a paragon of all the virtues, a thing difficult to credit.

The ideas were fully elucidated. Ballet was defined in the old sense as a 'geometrical mingling of several people dancing together to the accompaniments of several instruments'. Baltazarini's idea was to fuse the elements of the disjointed *Mascerade* into one entity, making a perfect union of dancing, music, and poetry. The fact that he found it necessary to explain his aims and objects clearly indicates that he was attempting something new. The term 'comyque' he explained as implying 'comédie', and the full description of the work as a *Ballet comyque* was justified by the preponderance of dancing, the main purpose being to afford to the eye, ear, and intellect 'une jouissance également équilibrée'. *Circé* is a work of the highest importance. Not only was it the first of the *Ballets de Cour* which were to supersede the *Fêtes de Cour*, but it was the first work to hint at the potentialities of the later *Opéra-Ballet*, an essentially French genre although postulated, in this case, by an Italian. It is necessary, therefore, to study *Circé* in detail, since its apogee will be found in the *Opéra-Ballets* of Rameau and in those of the 20th century composers, such as Roussel, while the insistence on spectacle in its production forms the authority for the spectacular operas of the Romantic Era.

Circé consisted of long stretches of dialogue interspersed with songs, the entr'actes (or *Intermèdes*) being *Entrées de Ballet* or choruses. There were two orchestras. One, on the stage, was concealed by scenery, and consisted of oboes, horns, and trombones; the other, the main band, was composed of lutes, lyres, organs with wooden pipes, violins (the generic term for bowed instruments of all kinds), cornettes,[1] trombones, flutes and oboes, but no percussion. In addition, a small organ was hidden behind another piece of scenery. No full orchestral score is available, but the music is preserved in a part-book, with indications of the instrumentation. The performers were both professional and amateur, the latter being drawn from the courtiers.

The Royal Family (with the exception of the Queen, Louise, who was taking part) sat on a dais in the centre of the hall, surrounded by the foreign ambassadors. The audience sat in tiers behind the royal dais and in the galleries surrounding the hall. The décors were divided between the floor of the house and the stage which had been erected in the apse of the building, the archway forming a natural proscenium.

On the right hand side of the floor the home of Pan, God of the Shepherds, was set as a grove. Trees and glades were filled with Dryads. A brilliant grotto glittered like diamonds and was lush with flowers, among which played lizards and hares. One glade, however, was at first concealed by a veil which, later, disclosed Pan seated like a satyr, a crown on his head and a wand in his hand, with his pipes on the ground at his feet. Behind the grotto the small organ discoursed sweet music. Lamps shaped like ships hung from the trees.

On the King's left, a wooden canopy was hung with painted clouds. Behind them, there were six groups of musicians, revealed whenever the clouds were moved. In the centre, a bare space was topped with shining stars.

The stage in front of the King was dressed as an artificial garden, the Garden of Circé. This was overlooked by golden terraces, filled with flowers and fruit. Steps led to a château and behind it, on the backcloth, the open country stretched away towards a town set upon a mountain. On each side of the stage there were gilded arches, through which the dancers in the

---

[1] This instrument is in no way connected with the Cornet which did not appear until the nineteenth century, and became known as the 'Cornet à pistons'.

Intermêdes entered. A light curtain hung before the château of Circé, who was discovered sitting in front of the door, wearing a magnificent robe of cloth of gold, decorated with pearls, gold tassels and diamonds. A hundred wax torches lit the scene.

Such was the splendid scene which greeted an audience of more than ten thousand people,[1] and the performance lasted from ten o'clock at night until half past three in the morning, without pause or interval.

The tradition of *Circé* was never forgotten. The use of the floor of the house was dictated by the exigencies of space and it would not be altogether accurate to see in it any authority for bringing the actors among the audience or for placing the audience on the stage among the players.

The orchestra of oboes, horns, and trombones hidden behind Circé's château plays an Overture of which no trace now remains. This is a special instrumental force used for special effects, and it remains silent while those on the stage are playing.

A gentleman, played by La Roche of the Queen-Mother's Household, runs on to the floor of the house. He has escaped from Circé's château and to all appearances is in a state of panic. He explains that he had come to declare the reign of Peace and Liberty, but on the way had been seduced by Circé who offered him her Nymphs and her château if he would join her household. He succumbed to the temptation and was immediately changed into a lion, but for some unexplained reason he was then returned to his original form almost at once. He effected his escape while Circé was climbing the tower of her château to see if any of her Nymphs were running to find the King. Furious at her loss, Circé is trying to recover him and he implores the King's protection, saying that the Royal glory will blind her; at this moment Circé comes on to the floor of the house, uttering cries of vengance.

Thus ends the Prologue which, as had become customary, extolled the power, the might, and the glory of Henri III, King of France (and formerly of Poland), while at the same time forming an integral part of the work (later Prologues were to concern themselves with the former purpose alone).

---

[1] *Sic*, but we beg leave to doubt it.

Then follows the *Premier Intermède*. On Circé's retreat, three Sirens and a Triton, each with hair of gold, appear from beneath the lateral arches. Circé's servants sing a quartet devised in couplets, a refrain being repeated at the end of each. The message of the quartet is one of encouragement to the daughters of Achelous to follow the Triton. The last couplet draws attention to the fountain of Glauque, a piece of elaborate stage scenery.

In the fountain are seated twelve Naiads. These were acted by the Queen, the Princesse de Lorraine, the Duchesses des Marcoeur, Guise, Nevers, Aumale, Joyeuse, Retz and Archaut, and Mesdemoiselles de Pons, de Bourdeille and de Cypierre.

One part of the fountain represents the sea in which three sea-horses, controlled by three Tritons, swim round and round. The god Glauque and the goddess Téthys sit on golden chairs. Téthys accompanies her songs on the lute. Eight Tritons, chosen from the King's private choir, are ranged on both sides of the chairs, each Triton carrying a trident and some kind of musical instrument – a lyre, lute, harp, or flute. Behind them come twelve pages, in white satin embroidered with gold, each holding two white wax torches.

The fountain circles the hall and stops immediately in front of the King. A chorus in five parts, with instrumental accompaniment, follows. Glauque and Téthys take part in a kind of sung dialogue, the Tritons echoing the last two lines of each couplet. Glauque explains that he is in love with Scylla, whom Circé has changed into a sea-monster. He appeals to Téthys, but she, not being a Nymph, is unable to help him. Glauque then appeals to the Queen, knowing that the blood royal can accomplish anything and everything, both natural and supernatural. This interchange is an interesting example of early conversational music.

GLAUQUE: Et qui est cette nymph? Est-ce une nereide?

TÉTHYS: Non, car la mer n'a point telle concue.

GLAUQUE: Je sais bien, c'est Vénus!

TÉTHYS: Tu es encor déçu!

GLAUQUE: C'est donc Junon?

TÉTHYS: Ce n'est Junon;

C'est Louise, et son nom

Passe en pouvoir tous les noms de Junon.

This clearly shows the complimentary side of the whole principle of Court entertainment.

At the conclusion of the Duo, the Tritons repeat the opening music. Then follows the *Première Entrée de Ballet*.

The Naiads descend from the fountain, preceded by the violinists and followed by the twelve Pages. Headed by the Queen, the Naiads range themselves in three lines, three at the back, six in the middle, and three at the front. The most varied steps follow.

This *Première Entrée* consists of the twelve geometrical figures mentioned by Baltazarini in his Dedication. At the end of the last figure, Circé rushes from her garden and strikes the Naiads motionless with her wand. (Baltazarini describes Circé's dance as 'Son de la Clochette'. Neither Air nor Aria had as yet come into being and the verb 'sonner' was usually applied to all instrumental passages, the noun being applied to vocal entries.)

On Circé's disappearance, Mercure descends from the sky. His role was taken by du Pont, one of the King's gentlemen. In the traditional manner he announces who he is and what he intends to do.

He explains that it is his duty to guard people from the wiles of Circé, for which purpose he is armed with a charm, called 'moly', whose mythological origin is obscure (it may be described as 'wisdom contained in a bottle'). At a touch of this charm, the Naiads and instrumentalists return to life and recommence the Ballet. This is too much for Circé, who immobilises them again. She succeeds in seducing Mercure and touches him with her wand. Mercure, now completely powerless, enters Circé's garden. The 'moly' by itself is not strong enough to ward away danger; he must summon the aid of Pallas. Circé stands in triumph on the steps of her château, with Mercure at her feet; she is irresistible. In front of her passes a procession of animals (impersonated by actors), her ensnared human victims. The musical accompaniment for this is played by the special orchestra at the back of the stage.

Meanwhile, there is no respite for the audience. Almost before it has had time to absorb everything it has seen and heard, the scene is switched to the *Deuxième Intermède*.

Eight Satyrs enter the Hall, to the accompaniment of a gay March. (Their leader is Saint-Laurens, another of the King's choristers.) Alone among the huge cast the Satyrs wear traditional costume and not costly dresses. They sing another panegyric to the King and retire, being succeeded by the Dryads, who enter in a mechanically propelled coppice. They are immediately attacked by the Satyrs, who ask the King to help them win their prize – another curious example of what was expected from the royal omnipotence.

The coppice is shaped like a mound of earth. The trees, decorated with gilded garlands, are planted in rows; in the centre a rock supports a bush, whose branches mingle with those of the trees. The soil is covered with turf and flowers, upon which lizards and snakes lie sleeping. Four Dryads, dressed in cloth of gold, are seated round the rock. The Satyrs change the words, but not the music, of their chorus.

The Dryads are represented by Mesdemoiselles de Vitry, de Surgères, de Lavernay, and d'Estavay, all Ladies-in-Waiting to the Queen, the first appearing in the character of Opis. Her speech, addressed to the audience, ranges over a wide course of mythology and concludes with an invocation to Pan for help. The mechanical coppice moves away from the King to Pan's grotto, whose curtain falls to reveal him in person. Pan is acted by the Sieur de Juvigny, Huntsman to the King, a gentleman 'favoured by the Muses and by Mars'. He plays upon the flute, or flageolet, of which, according to the 'book', he is the inventor. He is softly accompanied by the organ placed behind him.

Opis brings her complaint to Pan, begging him to release Mercure from the toils of Circé. Mercure is heard groaning beneath the weight of slavery to which he has had to submit:

. . . . Cette servitude,

Qu'on rend à un indigne, est plus vile et plus rude.

Pan, however, is not enthusiastic. He replies that he will assemble his brothers in Circé's forest, but reminds Opis that the intervention of Pallas will be necessary. So far as he himself is concerned, rest and solitude are the only things which matter and he will not give them up until the last possible moment.

The Dryads leave their coppice and move to niches prepared for them in Pan's grotto. The eight Satyrs lie at their feet and sing the next chorus, which is similar to that sung at the entry of the Naiads. During the singing, the wood vanishes. Its place is taken by a vine-arbour, which moves in by mechanical propulsion.

The *Troisième Intermède* follows. This introduces the Four Virtues who, in gorgeous robes, enter in pairs, one pair singing to the lute accompaniment of the other. Pan answers them, but through the medium of the orchestra, as if he were replying from a distance and almost by suggestion. The song of the Virtues is in two parts, Soprano and Bass. The Virtues invoke the presence of Pallas, who enters in her chariot. This is constructed in the shape of a gigantic griffin, an animal of heraldic significance. Pallas, represented by Mademoiselle de Vaumont, carries a lance and an image of Medusa's head.

Her appearance is intended to flatter Catherine de Medici, whose age could hardly have warranted her presentation as a Nymph or Dryad. Pallas was a convenient form for adulation of the middle-aged and elderly, and it was quite in order for Baltazarini to address the Queen Mother in his Dedication as 'Cette Pallas de reine mère'. Mademoiselle de Vaumont, however, remained her true and charming self and did not make-up to fit her role. This would have been too pointed a dart. A hundred torches of white wax were fixed to the chariot, Baltazarini objecting to the more practical system of lamp-lighting.

The Four Virtues place themselves on each side of the chariot and follow it as it is drawn by an imitation dragon. The main orchestra, together with the voices, accompany its movements. The music grows in intensity and passion until 'qu'on eut dit qu'elle venait des cieux'.

Pallas, like Opis, addresses the King in a short lecture on mythology, reminding him that he traces his descent through the 'blood of the gods'. She makes the circuit of the hall, invoking Jupiter.

The King of Olympus descends from on high by means of a staircase which unrolls itself as it approaches the ground, enveloped by cloud.[1] The music grows louder as the deity nears. The text extols the wisdom of Jupiter (*i.e.* Henri III), under whose rule the people enjoy the benefits of peace. Jupiter is naturally clad in robes of the richest quality, reflecting the glory of his human counterpart.

Jupiter assures Pallas that all those metamorphosed by Circé will be restored to their natural state. The Olympian King condescends to mix with the mortals while his staircase is wound up into the sky. He and Pallas proceed towards the grotto. Pan rejoices at seeing them and plays upon his seven-tube pipe, again accompanied by the hidden organ. Pallas scolds him for having delayed the rescue of Mercure and accuses him of cowardice. Pan is indignant. Has he not gained a reputation for bravery? Has he not fought giants? There can be no object, however, in running unnecessarily into danger. He has already spoken to Circé and can do nothing for Mercure without the aid of Pallas herself. He then goes into the wood with the eight Satyrs, each of whom is armed with a stout cudgel. They salute the King as they pass him, and advance towards Circé's garden. Pan and his Satyrs head the procession, with Pallas and the Four Virtues behind them; Jupiter and the four Dryads follow.

Circé strikes a bell with her wand. Immediately the air is filled with the sound of dogs, lions, tigers, wolves and bears, uniting in a wild chorus not so much of anger at the intruders as of joy at the prospect of release. Circé explains that she is not afraid. The Sun is on her side and everything is in her power. She can alter the course of rivers; she can make the Moon descend to the Earth; she has conquered the Stars. She reminds Jupiter that she once changed him into a swan when he wished to lie with Leda. Her defeat would naturally redound to his credit, as in this way he would lend his aid to the only enemy she fears; this is, of course, Henri III, King of France and formerly King of

---

[1] This machine became so popular that it remained a standard 'prop' until the hey-day of the *Opéra-Ballet* of Rameau.

D

Poland. Her father, the Sun, would have to cede his eminence to the King and surrender the sky to him if she were beaten, while she herself would have to release all her prisoners. Thus does the flattery increase, at this point suggesting that even the Sun must retreat before the glory of Henri III.

The battle commences. Pan and the Satyrs attack Circé's château. Jupiter hurls a thunderbolt, the Dryads loose their arrows. Circé's Magic Circle, attacked by Pallas, gradually loses its power. Jupiter touches Circé with his sceptre and she falls at his feet. Jupiter, anxious to demonstrate the gift of mercy which is his, decides not to punish her. Pallas takes her by the hand, while Jupiter takes Mercure's arm. Pan, the Satyrs and the Dryads follow, and, after making the circuit of the hall, they come to a halt before the King.

Mercure now offers Circé's magic wand to the King, seating himself at his feet. Jupiter presents his children to his royal counterpart and they kneel to show their inferiority of rank. They do homage to the Queen Mother for 'her power, her wisdom, her eloquence', and, still more, 'for the son she has brought into the world'. Pallas congratulates the Queen on her modesty, her industry and her seriousness of purpose.

After this barrage of compliments, the Four Dryads climb back on to the mechanical coppice. Pan and the Satyrs return to the grotto, the procession reforms, and everything and everybody disappears through the garden. The hall remains empty for a few moments.

One might imagine, after all the long speeches, the dancing, the singing, and the instrumental music, that *Circé* had arrived at its conclusion; Virtue being now triumphant, the performance appears to have reached a satisfying end.

One would be mistaken. Everyone comes back, and this return constitutes the *Deuxième Entrée de Ballet*.

The violins play the introductory music and the Dryads move in line from Circé's garden. The Naiads, released from their enchantments, appear from all directions, the floor of the Salle du Petit-Bourbon having been prepared with trapdoors and other pantomimic accessories. The dancers advance to the centre of the hall in pairs, the procession being headed by the Queen and the Princesse de Lorraine. The Dryads and Naiads commence the *Petite Entrée de Grand Ballet*, which is composed of fifteen dance figures. The dancers find themselves facing the King, and, by the fifteenth figure, they have accomplished the circuit of the hall and have arrived close to him. The *Grand Ballet* itself is devised for sixteen dancers, in forty geometrical figures.

The hall has now the air of a fairy palace. The principal ladies of the court advance to the principal courtiers to offer their symbolical presents, this 'presentation of the gifts' being a characteristic feature of all marriage-ballets (Appendix Eight). As each presentation is made, the donor recites a line in Latin.

The Queen offers the King a Dolphin: *Delphinus et Delphinium rependat.*[1]

The Princesse de Lorraine offers Monsieur de Marcoeur a Mermaid (Siren): *Siren virtute haud blandior ulla est.*

Madame de Marcoeur offers Monsieur de Lorraine a Neptune: *Per mens invicta tridenti.*

Madame de Nevers offers Monsieur de Guise a Sea-Horse: *Adversus semper in hostem.*

Madame de Guise offers Monsieur le Marquis de Chaussin a Whale:[2] *Cui sat, nil ultra.*

Madame de Joyeuse offers the Marquis de Pont a Sea-Monster: *Sic famam adjungere famae.*

Madame la Maréchale de Retz offers Monsieur d'Aumale a Triton: *Commovet et sedat.*

Madame de Larchant offers Monsieur de Joyeuse a Branch of Coral: *Eadem natura remansit.*

Madame de Pont offers Monsieur d'Epernon an Oyster in the Shell:[3] *Intius meliora recondit.*

---

[1] This is a play upon the word 'Dauphin'.

[2] This gift was in doubtful taste, since the whale wore short horns.

[3] This was a back-handed compliment. D'Epernon was not noted for bravery and had earned a reputation for skill in hiding himself behind others and thus avoiding any direct contact with trouble.

Madame de Bourdeille offers Monsieur de Nevers a Sword Fish: *Sua sunt et militibus arma.*

Mademoiselle de Cypierre offers Monsieur de Luxembourg a figure of the astronomical Scorpio: *Vis non oblita suorum.*

It is now the turn of the four Dryads. Mademoiselle de Vitry, the first of these, gives an Owl to Monsieur le Bastard: *Artis vigilantia custos.*

Mademoiselle de Surgères gives the Comte de Saux a Roebuck: *Non teli secura usquam.*

Mademoiselle de Lavernay gives the Comte de Maulevrier a Deer: *Non periit victus assueta novari.*

Mademoiselle de Staney gives the Comte du Bouchaigre a Wild Boar: *Nusquam vis acrior urget.*

Pallas then offers the Queen Mother a figure of Apollo, with the words: *Linere et vincere suevi*; and Circé offers Monsieur le Cardinal de Bourbon a Book: *Fatorum arcana resignat.*

The donors now take the arms of those to whom they have presented gifts and proceed to the Grand Ball, the procession moving in the order of precedence in which the presentations were made, the orchestra playing the customary Pavane.

After the Grand Ball, the entire company dances Branles, and other dances of the moment, the festivities continuing without a break, until the royal party goes down to the river bank to witness a *Fête nautique* prepared by the Cardinal de Bourbon in Saint Germain-des-Prés.

A vast crowd has collected to see a host of mechanical fishes and sea monsters. They wait, and they wait; but something is wrong with the mechanism, and the sea folk decline to move. At seven o'clock in the morning the King and the Queens retire, their fatigue not unmixed with vexation and disappointment.

The collaborators in *Circé* were thoroughly satisfied with themselves. The King had sat patiently all through the performance and the Queen had appeared in person, as was the custom for 'nos rois et reines'. Baltazarini had taken no active part in the proceedings, since he deemed it stupid to dance himself when he had enough money to make others do it for him.

There was, however, a coda to the story.

The mechanical sea monsters may have refused to display their prowess before the King, but a far greater demonstration of his glory awaited him. At the end of three days' continuous festivities, which had included balls, tourneys, *Circé*, and a *Mascerade* written by Ronsard, a grand display of fireworks was held. These ran amok and a magnificent conflagration ensued, in which the immobilised sea monsters and most of the scenery and décors used in *Circé* went up in flames, as in a glorious *auto-da-fé*.

The mere detail of this production is almost overpowering. The audience might well, for instance, have dispensed with the *Intermèdes* and been allowed to refresh itself with silence and in other ways; but this was not yet the custom, nor was it to be for some years, during which time the complexities and complications of dramatic libretti increased in length and verbosity. It says much for the powers of resistance enjoyed by the people of the time. It also testifies to the royal stamina, for the King, metaphorically requiring no earthly physical support, sat on a stool with neither arms nor back-rest throughout the proceedings.

The music is interesting.

The choruses are square, and not very much more can be said for the ballets. There are, however, some curious harmonic progressions and false relations, such as these:

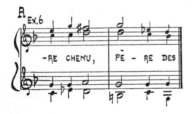 

This characteristic squareness adds a little piquancy to the *Son de la clochette auquel Circé sortit de son jardin*, which is presented thus:

There is a certain dignity about the choral invocations in the *Chant des Satyrs*, in Act II;

but, in general, the solos and ensemble numbers are superior. While it would hardly be accurate to describe these as being really 'lyrical', there is some freedom and looseness of line in them, and also some formality of construction. This incipient operatic melody contains certain significant points which become apparent in later works. Whoever wrote these solo and ensemble numbers was not composing for professional singers, even though a few of these were to be found in the cast. He was writing for amateurs, for courtiers, whose musical training and experience, to say nothing of their technique and quality of voice, were limited. Nevertheless, he contrived some interesting vocalisation and no doubt the singers were duly flattered.

The *Dialogue entre Glauque et Téthys* is the first instance of its kind in theatre music, but there is little differentiation between the male and female quality of melody.

This Dialogue is sung through five times, with a short choral interlude between the stanzas, the accompaniment to the solos being purely chordal, but the last stanza is different and forms an early example of a florid vocal line. It occupies an important position in the history of music and gives a complete picture of the contemporary approach to this kind of expression.

The *Chanson de Mercure*, not being conversational, is infinitely more suave and graceful, and has a mobile bass. Its charm, however, wears thin by the end of the sixth stanza. If the previous example illustrates the happy medium between recitative and measured melody (although far removed from the much later *recitativo stromentato expressivo*), Mercure's song illustrates an early lyricism which speaks for itself. It is the true ancestor of Luigi Rossi's *Orfeo*.

After the quasi-liturgical Entry of Jupiter, that deity sings a solo of four strophes (mainly over a pedal-point) whose melody has some breadth and dignity:

The choral writing is in four and five parts, the instrumental in twelve.

It is impossible to decide exactly which movements were written by the composers concerned. Baltazarini, while claiming full honours, was probably responsible for very few, although he may have had something to do with those which show a tendency towards florid cadenza, his Italianism making this style of writing natural to him. The *Chanson de Mercure* therefore might be ascribed to him, as it flows more evenly than the others.

Circé contains all the ingredients of spectacular *Opéra-Ballet*. It was regarded more as a phenomenon than as something to be repeated and absorbed into the normal run of entertainment. The *Fête de Cour* was slowly to be superseded by the *Ballet de Cour* which, in its turn, was to be replaced by the *Acte de Ballet* and *Opéra-Ballet*.

Baltazarini, after basking in the full glory of his triumph, faded into obscurity. He is referred to again only once, in 1687, in a description written by Bauderon de Sénecé of the arrival of Lully in the Elysian Fields. Here, by general consent, it is Baltazarini who, as the deviser of the first *nearest approach* to French Opera, heads the musicians who have assembled to welcome the great composer.

Circé cannot correctly be regarded as the first French Opera, or even as an Opera. It has elements and features which were to constitute the material of opera. Its complex structure and complicated episodes anticipated many of the characteristics of the first Italian Operas to be produced in Paris, but there is more spoken dialogue than vocal and instrumental music and this precludes consideration of it as an *Opéra-Comique*. Opera, to deserve the name, must have a preponderance of music. At the most, *Circé* may be considered as an over-elaborate secular *Mystère*, in which all the arts were associated. Nothing like it was ever seen again within the confines of four walls, but it foreshadowed, in splendour, the operas of the Romantic Era.

From the musical point of view, the most important moment was the *Dialogue entre Glauque et Téthys*. This has all the qualities (save that of contrast) of the later conversational musical duo. The choruses marked the departure of the polyphonic aesthetic. It is easy to criticise their squareness, but this was necessitated by the importance of all the singers singing the same words at the same moments. This will be found to be the principle underlying Lully's choruses, and it may be said to find its pinnacle in the broad unison lines of Meyerbeer. There is a certain dignity about choruses like the *Descente de Jupiter* and the *Chant des Satyrs*, but the harmony is elementary to a degree. There is none of the Italian warmth of Monteverdi and the curious progressions and false relations, to which reference has already been made, cannot be regarded as being authoritative, although those looking for precedents can find them here.

The use of independent orchestral bodies may be said to anticipate Gossec, Lesueur, and Berlioz. The approach was novel, if obvious, as were the small pieces of mechanical stage machinery which, hitherto, had been confined to the *Mascerades nautiques*. Considering that the performance took place in a room and not in a properly equipped theatre, the producers may be congratulated upon their resourcefulness.

Circé remained a legend, a tradition handed down probably by word of mouth and almost completely unknown until revealed by 19th century research. Yet it stands as one of the most important and authoritative dramatic works in the history of the theatre and of opera. It is a landmark and a stepping stone to the future. Given an audience of sufficient endurance, a production today would be both interesting and valuable.

CHAPTER THREE

IF THE splendour of the Valois was not reflected in the reign of
the first Bourbon (Henri IV), it was because that King had no
money, not because he was parsimonious. Essentially a humanist,
he took a sympathetic interest in his subjects and, seeing their
poverty, refused to spend what he had not got on court entertainments. He was beloved by his people; Tolerance now sat on the
throne of France and the Edict of Nantes proved that the age
of religious terror and persecution was over – at least for the
time being.

The court, however, was by no means austere. It was lively,
in a less expensive and sophisticated way, with a general trend
towards simplicity. The *Ballets de Cour* enriched routine existence,
though they were nothing more than *Mascerades* based upon
formal dances or otherwise improvised. More than seventy of
these *Ballets* were produced between 1592 and 1610. Their titles
show the difference between the scheming and suspicious tempera-
ments of the Valois and the bluff, good-humoured, sensual honesty
of the first of the Bourbons. Henri IV had little patience with
court etiquette; he had no wish to spend his life dancing the
traditional ballet. He preferred the society of a few genuine
friends to the fawning sycophants of a full court, and the entertainments were overtly vulgar and amusing rather than uplifting
and ornate. Titles such as *Ballet de Grimaceurs* (1597), *des Coqs* and
des Bouteilles (1604) would have been unthinkable under Henri III
and his predecessors.

On the other hand, in 1607, 1608, and 1609, something of
the old régime was restored when three *Ballets de la Reine* were
produced. The first of these resulted in the King's infatuation
with Mademoiselle de Montmorency, and the third in one with

Mademoiselle de Paulet; but no such result attended the second. It was indeed a change to see the *mignons* disbanded in favour of normal amours.

On October 5th, 1600, Henri married Marie de Medici by proxy, and this led to an event of considerable artistic importance in the latter part of his reign.

It so happened that Jacopo Peri (1561 – 1633)[1] and Giulio Caccini (c.1545 – 1618)[1] had just completed an opera, *Euridice*, to a libretto by Ottavio Rinuccini, a court poet who fondly imagined that Marie de Medici was madly in love with him, as he was with her. Rinuccini and Peri had produced *Dafne* in Florence in 1597; this was the 'first opera and first recorded opera on record anywhere'.[2] The first performance of *Euridice* took place (also in Florence) in 1602, in the presence of the Duc de Bellegarde, who had acted as the French King's proxy. Struck with the novelty of the work and its general idea, he and Marie de Medici decided that it should be taken to Paris. The Duke of Tuscany at first did not want to lose his two artists, particularly Caccini, who was reported to be suffering from a leg so damaged as to prevent him from making such a long journey. Caccini himself strenuously denied that there was anything wrong with his leg or with any other part of him and eventually, on September 30th, 1604, he left Florence for Paris. He was accompanied by his daughter Francesca, a beautiful singer and the composer of an opera, *La Liberazione di Ruggiero*. Rinuccini found a place in the household of Marie de Medici and became one of the Gentlemen of the Chamber to the French King.

It was in this way that real Italian Opera was heard in Paris for the first time. Contradictory theories abound as to the origin of the work. Henri Prunières[3] and Ludovic Celler[4] maintain that the work was a composite one. Parry, however, describes two operas upon the same subject, one by Peri and the other by Caccini,[5] quoting examples from each and handing the palm to Peri,

---

[1] See list of 'irrelevant recordings'.
[2] *Everyman's Dictionary of Music* – Eric Blom (Dent).
[3] *L'Opéra Italien en France avant Lulli* (p. 28).
[4] *Les origines de l'Opéra* (p. 333).
[5] *The Oxford History of Music*, Vol. III (pp. 30–36).

whose work, he states, was that performed during the wedding festivities. This performance is confirmed by René Dumesnil,[1] who maintains that Caccini wrote a setting of the same libretto.[2] Parry's evidence appears to be quite conclusive since there are two Prologues in existence; yet it is unlikely that a scholar of the calibre of Henri Prunières should not have discovered these. The difference between the works lies in the more musical approach to the Prologue shown by Peri and the absence of a complete instrumental episode in that of Caccini.

Confusion becomes worse confounded, however. The writer on Caccini in the Fuller Maitland edition of '*Grove*' ascribes part of *Dafne* to Caccini, while he on Peri makes no reference to any connection with *Euridice* on the part of Caccini.

From the evidence so far it may be deduced that there were two versions of certain scenes, and that both these versions have survived. Indeed, Dr. Percy Scholes[3] puts the matter in a nutshell: '. . . certain portions were supplied by Caccini, and this composer then immediately reset the whole text (also 1600). The *Euridice* by Peri, with parts supplied by Caccini, is nowadays generally spoken of as the first opera and can be conveniently considered as such.' This opinion is not held by Mr. Eric Blom,[4] in his section on Opera. There is no mention of *Euridice* in the few words bestowed on Caccini, and the work is ascribed, without reservation, to Peri in the paragraph devoted to him.

It is reasonable to take the view that the work was a joint creation and that this was performed at the wedding. Later, since Peri was an amateur, Caccini thought he could do better and set the whole libretto himself – but who can tell? It is a pity that the composers did not sign or initial their respective contributions to the combined operation.

Euridice commences with a Prologue in recitative, delivered by the personification of Tragédie, each of its seven verses ending with a ritornelle. The first scene opens with a chorus of shepherds,

---

[1] *Histoire illustrée de la Musique* (p. 74).
[2] *Histoire illustrée du Théâtre Lyrique* (p. 19–20).
[3] *Oxford Companion to Music* (O.U.P.).
[4] *Op. cit.*

mostly in recitative, but sometimes interrupted by ensemble passages. Euridice enters and joins in the shepherds' conversation. On her exit Orpheus comes in, while Thyrsis, another shepherd, joins them and plays on his triple flute (this is omitted by Caccini in his own version). Dafne appears and tells them that Euridice has been bitten by a snake and has since died.

The second scene takes place in the Infernal Regions and shows Orpheus pleading for the return of Euridice with Venus, Pluto, Proserpine, Charon, Rhadamanthus and others. He wins them over with his music and Euridice is at last restored to him.

In the third scene the two wanderers rejoin the shepherds, who are sitting in their original places. The scene is sung mainly in chorus after Orpheus has expressed his joy, and there are directions for a *Ballo à tre*, for which the choral music is used.

Side by side, the two versions show an interesting difference of approach. Caccini was a singer; Peri was not. Caccini uses a slightly ornate type of melody,

while Peri concentrates upon simple harmony that is both poignant and expressive.

The choral writing is mostly square in style, but occasional attempts at polyphony and imitative writing make their appearance.

Ex.15

It will be noticed that the original story was changed to restore Euridice to Orpheus instead of returning her to Hades, a suggestion of the later 'happy ending' which became so popular. This may have been dictated by the circumstances of the production which would not have welcomed sadness or unrelieved melancholy.

Henri IV was so enraptured with the singing of Francesca Caccini that he begged her father to leave her in Paris when he returned to Italy; but nothing further is known about her or about Caccini's stay in Paris. His presence, however, was felt by those French musicians curious to know what could come out of Italy, his most influential work being a singing method known as 'nuove musiche'. Its lessons directed the French composers towards recitative and ornamental Air, and away from the prevailing interest in instrumental music for dancing. They studied the art of natural declamation and became interested in vocal music for its own sake as distinct from its use in drama.

Rinucci took the idea of the French *Ballet de Cour* back to Florence with him, together with some French instrumentalists.

Caccini himself was charmed with the French Airs and, on his suggestion, the Duke of Mantua sent over his private singer, Giovanni Maria Lughars, to study French music. This early instance of musical exchange had the happiest results and was most beneficial to both cultures; each succeeded in keeping its own characteristics, the Italian *gout* adding decorative ornamentation to the French simplicity.

Henri IV was as enthusiastic about comedy as he was about music and he placed all visiting actors under his personal protection. In 1603, he persuaded the famous Italian 'Harlequin', Tristano Martinelli, to visit Paris. The Italian influence had first become operative in 1597, when the King had employed two Italian violinists in his private band. He had not the keen artistry of Henri II, Charles IX or Henri III, but he loved entertainment, and music was a source of constant pleasure to him. His natural ebullience, grown somewhat slower with age, found its outlet in amusing Italian comedies, for Henri IV, unlike his immediate predecessors, knew how to laugh.

The Italian company of Giovanni Andreini arrived in Paris in 1603 while the negotiations for Caccini were in progress. Andreini was not a consummate creative artist, but he had ideas, and his company of actors indirectly influenced the course of the future *Comédie-Opéra*. The plays were full of amusing situations; they were not quite *Mélodrames* (for the music played a secondary role), but their production presaged the future emphasis upon stage machinery. Parisian audiences, therefore, were prepared in advance by these comedies for the later style called *Drame-lyrique*.

There were no actual opera singers at this time. The parts in the lyric tragedies were given first to the 'virtuosi da camera' and then to any of the actors who happened to have singing voices. These were naturally the more useful as they had stage sense and experience. Italian actors accordingly took part in the Italian Operas. Andreini's works may justly be regarded as lyric dramas since, after 1613 (when he produced *Maddelena* and *La Centaura*), the music played a role of the highest significance; use was made of it in his religious poem *Adamo*, a work which inspired some scenes of Milton's *Paradise Lost*. It was dedicated to Marie de Medici and required stage production with scenic effects, exactly as if it had been an opera. The chorus represented the Angels, the Cherubim and the Seraphim; 'Vana Gloria' sat in a chariot drawn by a giant and sang to her own lyre accompaniment; Lucifer was portrayed by instrumental effects, while there were ballets of Nymphs and Follies.

Maddelena (1617), performed by a troupe known as the 'Fidèle', was very nearly an opera. It showed a decided advance in the Italian style of the *Pastorale*, which was destined to reappear in Paris many years later. It marks the transformation of ballet and dialogue style into Opera as understood today. The composers were Salomone de Rossi, Claudio Monteverdi, Muzio Efrem, and Alessandro Giunizzioni da Luca.

When Andreini returned home in 1622, he left a wealth of ideas behind him; but the Parisians were slow to adopt these and it was not until very much later that his influence became perceptible. In addition to those mentioned above, other works were *Amor nello spechio*, *La Sultana*, and *Li duo Leli simili*; these were comedies with incidental music. They were dedicated to the Queen and to certain prominent courtiers. The first two are particularly interesting since they contain the germs of *Opéra-Comique* and of the *Comédie-Ballet* perfected by Molière.

La Ferinda was the direct result of a number of operas, performed at Mantua, whose singers ('Cygnes fortunées') and composers ('Qui harmonieusement et d'une manière angelique composèrent') immediately fulfilled all Andreini's aesthetic ideals. He hesitated to continue his tradition of elaborate costumes, stage effects and machinery, because he feared that they were detracting from the plays themselves. Among the operas heard by Andreini must have been *Orfeo*, *Dafne*, and *Psyché*. They gave him the idea of the *Comédie-Ballet*.

By setting the scene of *La Ferinda* in Venice, he was able to include marble palaces, sea-scapes, and rich Venetian costumes; his passion for stage machinery was satisfied by gondolas, filled with people, circling the stage. Everything, therefore, was justified in the context. Mythology played its part; Thalie rose out of the waves to recite the Prologue. The music consisted of Airs and Ballets designed to break the monotony of the recitative, although Andreini had intended in the first place that the whole work

E

should be sung. If this had been the case, the work would have acquired an added importance.

La Centaura was different. The first Act was written in prose, in comedy vein. It disclosed the fact that the Centaur's wife was the daughter of the King of Rhodes. The second Act, also in prose, contained a sacrificial scene with appropriate chorus. This moved the work away from the style of the *Pastorale*. The scene was placed inside the Centaur's house. The third Act was a mixture of prose and poetry, with a preponderance of the latter. It was tragic, and terminated with the Centaur's wife claiming her rights at the foot of her father's throne.

The work itself opened with the customary Prologue, which was entirely musical. Allegorical and mythological characters announced themselves with their respective musical counterparts. The entry of Pan was accompanied by flutes and 'I Pifferari', Sagittarius by 'stridenti regali', the muse Thalie by an 'organo da legno in suon mesto', while the tragedy to come was suggested by 'trombe sorde' and 'tambuni discordi'. The Prologue itself opened and closed with trumpet fanfares. The curtain revealed the colonnades of a city and pyramids. Thalie was discovered in the middle of the stage, holding a crown in her hand. Her Air was interrupted by orchestral ritornelli.

The work as a whole laid the foundation of what was to come. It was a definite 'art form', without an ulterior motive (unlike *Circé*), and it showed exactly what Italy could offer in the way of spectacular opera as opposed to the French *Ballet de Cour*.

The French composers did not altogether welcome these Italian innovations. The far-sighted among them realised that each had much to learn from the other – the correspondence between the French Mersenne and the Italian Duni, both of whom were eminent scholars, is evidence of this – but the majority viewed the invasion with mixed feelings. A fuller appreciation of Italian art was attained by those who were able to make collections of Italian pictures, books, and musical scores, and to study the lute and guitar.

The most famous of the visitors to Paris was Ottavio Corsini; he spent two years there, from 1622 to 1624. Corsini had been instrumental in producing *L'Aretusa* of Filippo Vitali (? – after

1653) at his palace in Rome, and it is likely that he brought some Italian musicians to Paris with him.

It was during the ministry of Cardinal Richelieu that the Italian 'castrato' made his first appearance in Paris, creating a sensation both by the purity of his voice and the singularity of his physique. He became an object of derision; but, as Madame de Longueville observed: 'Mon dieu, que cet incommodé chante bien'.[1]

Louis XIII sent his favourite singer, Pierre de Nyert, to Rome in the entourage of the Maréchal de Crequy, to study what he could find there. Nyert, Benigne, de Bacilly and Michel Lambert decided to try to combine the Italian and French methods of singing, the last-named writing a number of Airs to French words, in the Italian style. Among the many reforms they effected may be mentioned clear enunciation and proper phrasing, together with the ability to ornament 'airs de couplets'. These reforms led, in due course, to the formation of a French recitative style, and the later *Pastorales* (now established as a species of *Opéra-Ballet* based on a pastoral subject and treated allegorically) showed an ever-increasing attention to musical declamation, culminating in the French recitative of Lully.

At this period France had no composers to place next to Caccini, Gesualdo, or Monteverdi. This was deplored by Mersenne in his *Harmonie Universelle*, 1686, in which he spoke his mind freely upon the timidity with which the French musicians adopted the new ideas. This conservatism was rooted merely in prejudice, stemming not from fear that the natural culture would be contaminated, but from indignation at the influx of aliens. Many years were to pass before the foreign composer was considered as an additional element to French culture rather than as a parasite upon it.

It is appropriate to close this chapter with a quotation from the *Réponse faite à un cuerieux sur le sentiment de la musique d'Italie*,[2] written, in 1639, by André Maugars. He, a member of Richelieu's

---

[1] Quoted in *L'Opéra Italien en France* by Henri Prunières (Champion, Paris, 1913) from *Historiettes* by Tallemant du Réaux (3rd edition, Vol. V, p. 140).

[2] *Bibliothèque Mazarin* (24,988). Reprinted in *Maugars célèbre joueur de viole* (Claudin, 1865).

private band, was driven to extensive travel in order to escape the Cardinal's wrath over an indiscreet remark; and, in 1620, is known to have played in the private band of James I of England. Maugars had an excessive admiration for Italian music, but did not blind himself to its faults. He expressed the opinion that 'pour nos compositeurs, s'ils vouloient un peu plus s'émanciper de leurs règles pédantesques, et faire quelques voyages pour observer les musiques étrangères, mon sentiment est qu'ils réussiroient qu'ils ne font pas'.

CHAPTER FOUR

LOUIS XIII – "LE MERLAISON" – BALLETS – CARDINAL
MAZARIN – ANNE OF AUSTRIA – LEONORE BARONI – ATTO
MELANI – "NICANDRO E FILENO" – "LA FINTA PAZZA" –
TORELLI – "AKABAR, ROI DU MOGUL" – "ORFEO" (BUTI
AND ROSSI) – SALLE DU PALAIS ROYAL – PROGRAMME
NOTES – "MAZARINADES" – "ANDROMÈDE" (CORNEILLE)
– "BALLET DE LA NUIT" – CAPR(I)OLI – FUSION OF BALLET
AND OPERA – "NOZZE DI PELEO E DI THETI" – RÉSUMÉ
OF SITUATION

THE FRENCH tradition was kept alive by Louis XIII, whose
interest hovered between the *Fête* and the *Ballet de Cour*. On the
5th, 6th and 7th of April, 1612, he revived the old spirit of France
with a *Fête* entitled *Le Camp de la Place Royale*. It was a carousel
which in every way recalled the old *Fêtes Royales* of the time of
François I. The music was taken from works already in existence.
There were Quadrilles representing the siege and defence of
Happiness, one side being dominated by Montparnasse crowned
by the Goddess of Harmony, an enormous figure made of musical
instruments . . . .

A similar display took place on March 19th, 1615, on the
departure of Madame for Spain, the work being *Le Triomphe
de Minerve*; and the spirit of *Circé* very nearly returned when,
on January 29th, 1617, the King married Anne of Austria.
This was celebrated with a performance of *La Déliverance de
Renaud*, over which the leading composers, Pierre Guedron
(1565 – 1625), Antoine Boesset (Boisset) (1587 – 1653) and
Gabriel Bataille (dates unknown), had collaborated. Louis himself took the part of the Demon of Fire and the Duc de
Luynes that of Renaud. There was a chorus of sixty-four voices
and an orchestra of twenty-eight violins and fourteen lutes. The
subject was *Armide*, the ultimate triumph of Renaud forming an
illuminated Apotheosis.

The halcyon days seemed to have come back, but economy
once more became necessary; and when *Les Aventures de Tancrêde*

dans la forêt enchantée was danced, on February 12th, 1619, being produced with the utmost regard for expense, the comparisons made were not in its favour.

The court was becoming more and more pompous and dignified. Whereas the Valois had not objected to kicking their slippers in the air, the Bourbons, from Louis XIII onwards, reduced their dance movements to a minimum. Under Louis XIII they were slow and restrained; under Louis XIV they became almost imperceptible, hardly to be distinguished from ordinary walking. Clothes became longer and wigs heavier. The cassock reached the knee, while a pair of shapely stockinged legs terminated in buckled shoes of some delicacy. High heels were affected by those deficient in inches and, since this was a failing of Louis XIV, all the sycophantic courtiers followed suit regardless of their height. Dancing in the Valois manner would have resulted in a plethora of broken Bourbon ankles.

Nevertheless, Louis XIII was a man of action. His famous remark, 'Come, gentlemen, let us be bored together', was occasioned only when the weather was so bad that it was impossible to go out of doors. Dancing, therefore, offered some relaxation in the evenings and music was one of the King's favourite indoor pastimes. Not only did he dance in the ballets but he designed décors, arranged steps, and composed music and scenarios. The ballet *Le Merlaison* was but one of his own creations.[1]

The ballets of the era appear in the *Collection Philidor*, but unfortunately Philidor, concentrating upon the original dancers, did not indicate the composers. The works bear no direct titles and are headed 'Ballet du Roy'. Two of them, however, one performed in 1621 and one in 1635, are designated 'Ballet du Roy Louis XIII'. It may be assumed that both were original compositions by the King. Prunières suggests that the latter was *Le Merlaison*,[2] quoting as its reference the *Collection Philidor*, Vol. III, page 25. Beauchamps, in his *Recherches sur les théâtres de France* (Vol. III, p.110) notes that this ballet was danced at Chantilly on March 15th, 1635, which was 'mi-carême'. Philidor remarks

---

[1] Alexandre Dumas père centres the climax of the affair of the Diamond Studs round this ballet (*The Three Musketeers*).
[2] *Le Ballet de cour en France avant Benserade et Lulli* (Laurens), p. 173, fn. 7.

that it was danced at *Gentilly* on that date; but, while there is a château at Chantilly, there has never been one at Gentilly. He also mentions the date as 'mi-carême'. Only fifteen Entrées and the Grand Ballet are quoted in the *Collection Philidor*. The last Entrée and the Grand Ballet are the most interesting; and comparison with the dance movements of *Circé* and of Lully will show the continuity and the sources from which Lully formed his conception of what French music should be.

The third and seventh Entrées – 'pour les Lorrains' and 'pour Thomas le Boucher' – reveal a certain sprightliness and humour.

The harmonies have to be guessed at, but this is not a difficult task.

Further consideration of these dance styles is outside the scope of the present context. It is a pity that this particular ballet cannot be categorised under any of the characteristic genres of the period.

These genres were: 'Ballets sérieuses', 'comyques et mixtes', 'historiques', 'fabuleux', 'poëtiques', 'fantastiques', 'nymphales', 'pastorales', and 'bacchanales'. Among these were the 'Ballets des Usuriers et des Matrones', 'des Singes', 'Chercheurs de midi à quatorze heures', 'Quodlibets', and 'Andouilles'. These were the smaller productions which took place in the ordinary course of court life, prepared in a hurry on many occasions. There was a final attempt at reviving the *Fête de Cour* in 1635, when a *Mascerade nautique* was performed. The King and Queen, seated upon a dais, received the homage in dumb show of all the aquatic divinities in mythology.

The ballets took place either in the Petit-Bourbon or in the Louvre (in the 'Salle des Caratiades'). They were invariably scenes of the utmost confusion. Conditions of entrée were haphazard, to say the least. Admission could be obtained simply by wearing a hat and a sword ('epée de ville'), and, as these articles were easily obtainable, hundreds of unauthorised and unqualified people came crowding in. On one occasion, the crush was so great that the King was unable to get near the hall; on another, the music stands were turned round the wrong way and the musicians found themselves facing the audience instead of the dancers. The populace in general thronged up to the windows and sat on the sills; these conditions indicated the popularity of the son of Henri IV, who could pass without fear of assassination among the thickest of crowds. There was, of course, no charge for admission since the entertainments were domestic; the Kings of France were thoroughly used to living in public.

The last *Ballet de Cour* of any magnitude in Louis XIII's reign took place on February 7th, 1640, in the Palais-Cardinal (Royal). This was organised by Cardinal Richelieu in order that the décors and stage properties constructed for the production of his tragedy *Mirame* (produced a few weeks earlier with indifferent success) might be used a second time. In spite of its grandiloquent title – *Ballet de la Prosperité des Armes de France* – the work left but one memory behind it, that of an Italian (Cardelin) who, representing Victory, danced on a tight-rope concealed inside property clouds.

Disillusioned by the disloyalty of his friends and tortured by his physicians,[1] the King gradually withdrew from public life. He spent his closing years composing choral pieces, which his valets de chambre sang with him. Although Richelieu was falling into a rapid decline, his political vigour was undiminished. His interest in the theatre, however, was more that of an opportunist than of an enthusiast, and, although his agent, Mazarin, sent him the newest Airs from Italy (by Rossi, Capr(i)oli, Carissimi, and Marco Sevioni), he took no real or practical interest in them. The hey-day of music in France was not to dawn until Mazarin (1602–1661) stepped into Richelieu's shoes.

Mazarin's artistic tendencies had been fostered during his youth by his experiences in the choir of Saint Philippe Neri in Rome, where he took part in several 'rappresentazioni', and in the canonisation of Saint Ignatius Loyola. As Richelieu's agent, he had become acquainted with the wealthy Cardinal Barberini, who had entrusted him with the control of the affairs of the Duchy of Mantua. Among Mazarin's most lively musical memories were the performances of Vitali's *L'Aretusa* in 1622 and of four operas produced in 1637 in Cardinal Barberini's palace. He became a naturalised Frenchman in 1639 and, before leaving Rome for Paris, took care to show the French Ambassador an opera by his friend Ottavione Castelli, whose libretto was dedicated to Richelieu and whose content sang the combined praises of the French King and his Minister.

---

[1] *Louis XIII: un grand Roi méconnu* – Romain (Hachette) p. 205.

Richelieu died in 1642 and, in the space of a few months, Mazarin had insinuated himself far enough into the King's good graces to be considered the Cardinal's successor. On the death of Louis in 1643, Mazarin became a member of the Regency set up to govern the Kingdom during Louis XIV's minority; and in this way he was able to gratify all his extravagant ideas. One of the first things he did was to instruct his Rome agent to send over a complete Italian Opera Company, together with the composer Marco Marezzoli.

Mazarin was anxious to obtain the services of the singer Leonore Baroni, but she, after accepting the invitation, then declined it for fear of losing her high position in Italy during her absence. She was also afraid of scandal, as it had been reported that she had been Mazarin's mistress during his stay in Mantua. Mazarin worked upon the interest of Anne of Austria to such an extent that, in a personal letter, the Queen Mother authorised the Marquis de Fontenay to offer Leonore 1,000 pistoles for the expenses of her journey, and an annual pension. Leonore eventually gave way.

Her reception would have flattered anyone of greater importance. Anne of Austria gave her the entrée to her private apartments at any hour, requiring her in return to sing at any time that she was asked to do so. The court viewed this intrusion with dislike and suspicion; but the Queen Mother ignored their complaints and Mazarin smoothed the matter over by letting it be known that the invitation had been sent for diplomatic reasons. Before long the court was won over by Leonore's personality, but her singing they found too emotional.[1]

News of Leonore's successes must have travelled to Italy very quickly for, by 1644, there was a distinct leaning among Italian musicians towards Paris and the fleshpots which, apparently, were available in that city. This may have been brought on by the death of Pope Urban VIII, when Cardinal Barberini fled to France, being made welcome by Mazarin. Leonore was anxious to return to Italy to resume her former eminence before anyone could displace her. The Queen Mother offered her every induce-

---

[1] Milton heard her sing in 1639 in Italy and, in a Latin sonnet, compared her with Tasso's Leonora (Appendix Nine).

ment to remain but, in 1645, she took her leave. Mazarin, however, had appointed her his chief agent at the Papal Court and had given her full authority to recruit an opera company for Paris from among the best Italian musicians.

In the meantime, Mazarin had to be content with some Italian comédies, whose performances Anne of Austria attended incognito at the Comédie-Italienne. It looked as if Italy was about to be denuded of her best actors and singers, and Pope Innocent X began to consider a project suggested to Louis XIII by Pope Urban VIII, that the King of France should establish a genuine French Opera with, of course, Italian foundations. This would have the effect of infiltrating Italian culture into the French and would halt the rapid exodus of musicians from Italy; as Louis XIV was still in his minority, the Pope kept silent, watching events with some misgiving.

The first notable Italian singer to arrive was the young castrato Atto Melani whose voice made even Leonore jealous. The French were again filled with curiosity over this physical phenomenon, and with no little disgust. A concert lasting four hours took place every evening in the Palais-Royal and, according to his own account, Melani swept the audiences down to his feet. Mazarin's ambition was fulfilled at the end of February 1645, when an Italian Opera was produced at the Palais-Royal. The audience was small, since it was confined to senior members of the court. Even the foreign ambassadors appear to have been excluded, as there is no mention of the event in any of their reports. Renaudot, in the *Gazette de Paris*, referred to the work as a 'Comédie' (Appendix Ten).

Henri Prunières suspects this work to have been *Nicandro e Fileno – Poemetto dramatico per musicca*.[1] The libretto is all that has survived. This, printed in Italian and French, was distributed to the audience, thus establishing a precedent. The story is conventional enough, even for a *Pastorale*. Nicandro and Fileno arrange marriages for their respective daughters, who both refuse. They are in love with Lidio, a young man with a particular fondness for women.

---

[1] *Op. cit.* p. 340.

After some episodes and accidents Fillis marries Lidio, and Cloris an amorous shepherd named Eurillo. The music is presumed to have been written by Marco Marezzoli. After the performance, the audience moved to the royal apartments for a concert, which proved to be a veritable orgy of music.

Anne of Austria's interest was now fully aroused. On December 14th of the same year Mazarin produced another Italian work at the Petit-Bourbon, *La Festa teatrale della finta pazza*, by Giulio Strozzi, a melodrama known generally as *La Finta Pazza*. This had been composed for, and performed at, the inauguration of the new theatre at Venice, in 1641. The libretto was an extravagant work upon the usual type of subject: Achilles, on the island of Scuros, tries to avoid marrying the Princess Deidamie, whom he has seduced, by wearing female apparel. The original work was filled with comic and unexpected effects, but, for the performance at the Petit-Bourbon, these were changed, and a ballet of bears, monkeys, and eunuchs[1] was substituted to accord with the youthful fancies of the child-king, Louis XIV. It concluded with a ballet of Indians dressed as parrots. Prunières suggests that this might have been written either by Sacrati or by Andreini, who was in Paris at the time.[2] The chief point of interest lay in the stage-machinery, which was built and controlled by Jacomo Torelli, the most noted expert of the day.

Torelli, who was born in 1608, was a many-sided genius: mathematician, mechanician, architect, painter and poet. Among other things he invented a device for changing an entire scene in one mechanical action. He had a generous notion of his own importance but, on his arrival in Paris, his pride suffered a heavy blow. He found that, instead of directly serving the Queen Mother, his work was confined to the theatre. In a letter to the Duke of Parma, he protested that 'servir les comédians est chos [*sic*] contraire à mon génie et à mes habitudes'; he would serve the Queen and nobody else, and it was insufferable for a man 'exerçant une profession aussi honorable et relévée que la mienne soit aux gages d'une troupe d'acteurs'.[3] The Duke of Parma left the letters

---

[1] Surely 'pseudo'!
[2] *Op. cit.* p. 74.
[3] Quoted by Henri Prunières (*op. cit.* p. 69).

unanswered, realising that the best thing for offended dignity was to allow it to work itself out. Torelli wrote several more letters, pointing out the extent of his damaged prestige, and waxing particularly indignant over the fact that the work in the 'Grande Salle de la Reine' was being carried out by workmen and not by himself in person. He wanted everything both ways. His threat to return to Italy disturbed nobody, and in due course he found that his best plan was to merge his positions of 'Gentleman' and 'Constructor of Machines' as closely as possible. Mazarin gave him every facility, and unlimited financial resources.

The *Gazette de Paris* reported the production factually (Appendix Eleven). Torelli's share in the work eclipsed everything else, but not even his brilliance could maintain the interest of the audience. Everyone, according to Madame de Motteville,[1] nearly died of boredom and cold. After the second performance, on December 27th, a better account was given (Appendix Twelve).

Rumours of the cost of this production rose or fell with the popular indignation. Starting at 10,000 livres, a figure of 100,000 livres was soon reached. It was reported that Mazarin was growing concerned, but the mere cost of a theatrical venture made no difference to the prodigality (in this respect, at least) of the Cardinal. He put Torelli into communication with the Duc d'Enghien, superintendent of the ballets, so that they could devise a *Ballet des Machines* for production at the Palais-Royal. At the same time Andreini completed an opera to a libretto by the Abbé Buti, which was to make further use of Torelli and his inventions. Such, indeed, was the interest aroused by these machines that Cavalli's *L'Egisto*,[2] produced in 1646, was received completely without interest; the strictest economy had been practised, and there were no stage effects for the audience to marvel at.

In the meantime, Mazarin had authorised Cardinal Biche to produce *Akabar, Roi du Mogul* at the Episcopal Palace at Carpentras; the libretto and music were by the Abbé Mailly. This was only a series of scenes with musical recitative and interludes. It was a *Tragédie-Lyrique*, but in no sense an opera. Nothing remains of it.

---

[1] *Mémoires.*
[2] *Musici della selva* – H.M.V. History of Music HLP 11.

On March 2nd, 1647, *L'Orfeo*, by the Abbé Buti and Luigi Rossi (1598 – 1653),[1] was performed for the first time. There were considerable delays, and things would have drifted indefinitely had not Anne of Austria insisted that it be ready by this date.

The rehearsals took place in what is now the Reading Room of the Bibliothèque Nationale and the performance in Richelieu's theatre. This had been altered by Mazarin to accommodate not only the vast audience and huge cast, but also the complicated pieces of stage machinery which Torelli had devised. Nevertheless, the auditorium was not large enough to hold all those who might have expected to receive invitations. Mazarin accordingly gave orders that only the most important personages should be admitted and that all questions of precedence should be set aside. This led to the utmost confusion. The Ambassadors from Brandenburg, the Palatinate and Poland refused to give way to those from Florence and Portugal, and other equally important strangers made further difficulties. The concourse, therefore, was divided into two parts, one for Sunday, March 3rd, and the other for the following Shrove Tuesday. The first performance took place before a selected audience on Saturday, March 2nd, but there was still confusion as the choice had been made by favouritism. Those who did manage to get in found themselves in the wrong seats. Anne of Austria was exceedingly angry. She wished both to see the performance and prepare for Mass on the following day, and had ordered the opera to begin at an hour which would allow her to see it to its conclusion and still leave time for her spiritual preparations.

Mazarin had leaflets printed explaining the argument of the story, but these were handed out only on entry to the theatre so that the effects of the machinery should come as a complete surprise. In addition to a résumé of the work as a whole, each scene was analysed in detail, making everything clear to those who did not understand Italian.

The mythological and allegorical complexities which, in some

---

[1] For many years it was supposed to have been Monteverdi's work of the same name. In 1868 Ludovic Celler wrote that it had also been ascribed to Zarlino (*Les Origines de l'Opéra*, p. 341 – Didier). See list of 'irrelevant recordings'.

respects, were to be typical of all early operas, made these analytical notes essential.

The Prologue glorified the French Royal Family and explained that the intention of the work was to extol the virtue of human fidelity. The scene was a besieged town under assault, through whose breached walls the French Army entered in triumph. Victory, descending from the sky, crowned the King.

The first act is set in a grove surrounding a temple. To this Endymion, the father of Euridice, comes to consult the oracle on the question of Euridice's marriage with Orpheus, the son of Apollo. Two vultures swoop down, each carrying off a tortoise, and the omens are shown to be bad. Endymion retires and Euridice and Orpheus sing a love duet. From this moment the story becomes chaotic, its broad outline cluttered up with humorous episodes designed to relieve the tragedy.

Aristeus, the son of Bacchus, who is also in love with Euridice, comes to claim her, but he is disappointed. A Satyr tries to console him with his dancing, while Venus descends from the sky and promises him every assistance. The wedding of Orpheus and Euridice is celebrated with great pomp, Momus singing some facetious verses while Nymphs dance a ballet. Venus chides Aristeus for neglecting her. The act ends with a chorus of shepherds invoking the protection of Jupiter.

The second act moves to the Temple of Proteus, and it is here that Torelli's genius for scene-changing is given full scope, as there are no fewer than four such changes.

Venus, disguised as an old woman, attempts to win over Euridice, who has gone into the Temple; she fails. The Satyr enters with Aristeus and proposes to carry him into the garden of the Sun where Apollo is offering a *fête* to Jupiter. Euridice appears in the garden and dances with the Nymphs, to the accompaniment of castanets. Suddenly, the Satyr and Aristeus appear and try to carry her off. She is bitten in the leg by a snake and dies, cursing Aristeus. Apollo and the Nymphs join in a lament, during which the Sun carries Euridice away in his chariot to his palace. The act concludes with Orpheus and the Nymphs chanting a song of despair.

(By this time, the records[1] say, the audience was nearly speech-

---

[1] *Mémoires* (Madame de Motteville), *Gazette de Paris* (Renaudot).

less with admiration. Not only had they been able to follow the plot – with the translated résumé – but they had also witnessed such marvels on the stage as to be uncertain whether they had really seen them or were merely the victims of their own disordered imaginations. There was, however, a contretemps. It was time for Anne of Austria to go to her confessor, and she left the theatre, much to the chagrin of Mazarin.)

The third act shows a desert with dark and dimly lighted caverns. Orpheus comes to consult the Fates who counsel him to plead with Pluto; Endymion laments his daughter's death. The shade of Euridice appears and, following Orpheus, sends him aid. Juno descends from the sky and, in spite of Venus' efforts, persuades Orpheus to go down to Hades. Pluto is vexed at Orpheus' approach, but Charon tells him about the wonderful music which Orpheus played on his lute while crossing the Styx. Orpheus, who has continued to play while awaiting Pluto's pleasure, overcomes him with the beauty of his music. There follows a Ballet of Monsters, who 'bow themselves' when Orpheus sings. Charon leads Euridice back to earth, but Orpheus turns round to look at her, and she disappears into the shadows.

The scene changes to a Forest where Orpheus is sitting in black despair. He calls on Bacchus and the Bacchantes, but Venus interrupts, telling Bacchus that Aristeus, his son, is dead. The Bacchantes claim Orpheus in his place. The final tableau is situated in Olympus, where Jupiter deifies Orpheus and places his lute among the constellations. The work ends with a full chorus.

This more or less straightforward plot is enlivened by several bizarre and comic characters, including an elderly, fat nurse. Morality and modesty are illustrated at their highest level when Euridice forbids Orpheus to raise her skirt in order to suck the poison from her leg. This was done as a tribute to both Anne of Austria and Mazarin, who professed an almost prudish respectability.

Torelli's scenic changes were effected by blacking out the stage while the sets were raised and lowered, a completely novel process at the time; what is commonplace today, therefore, originated in 1647. In *Orfeo* the changes were as follows:

Act Two	*First Change*	The Garden of the Sun
	Second „	The Temple of Venus
	Third „	The Temple of Love
	Fourth „	The Palace of the Sun
Act Three	*First Change*	Hades
	Second „	A Forest
	Third „	Olympus

The music is continuous: arias (many in the *da capo* style), ensemble numbers and choruses connected by recitatives of some length. The last of these are perfunctory and suggest that Rossi was not particularly interested in them. Spoken dialogue would have been preferable but it would, of course, have destroyed the essential quality making the work 'opera'. When expressive of an emotion, however, the recitative can be very beautiful.

The solos and the ensembles are exceedingly moving. Rossi composed the lament for Euridice at a poignant moment in his life for, as he reached that point in the composition, he received the news that his young wife had died in Italy. His melodies have

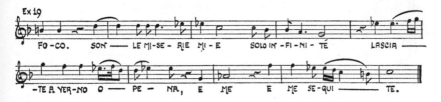

shape and distinct emotional qualities, while the ensemble numbers have a freedom and elasticity which made their style quite new to France.

They are, however, disfigured by long passages in thirds.

The ritornelli in the expressive recitatives are of a high quality (Ex. 22). Rossi's ideas seem to have flowed easily when emotion was to be expressed. The conversational passages he regarded merely as necessary evils to be accomplished as quickly as possible.

Ex. 22

The choruses, in spite of their polyphony, are dull.

The ballets were not composed by Rossi. Their occurrence is indicated in the score by the statement that dancing is to take place at that point. The music for them was provided by the French Court composers and by some others. In this manner, the Italians were repaid for what they had taught the French.

Orfeo was given several performances and was revived, in 1660, during the wedding festivities of Louis XIV. It made Mazarin more unpopular than usual. Its production in Lent was regarded as a scandal by the clergy, although much of the indignation served as a pretext for lowering the Cardinal still further in the eyes of the world. A more reasonable objection was the expense entailed at a time when poverty was rife in France; but it may be argued that the sum laid out would have done little to ameliorate the situation in general. The cost was rumoured to be between 400,000 and 500,000 crowns, though the Cardinal's apologists maintained that it was not more than 300,000 crowns. Popular indignation might not have been so strong had the venture been French in origin and execution; but the Italians had made themselves much disliked by their arrogant attitude towards their hosts, and they were accused of taking advantage of the Cardinal's original nationality to help themselves liberally from the national exchequer. It made no difference that the work was unique. Its novelty and historical values would have made little impression at that time, even if they had been realised.

Lampoons and pamphlets appeared everywhere,[1] in spite of

---

[1] *Choix de Mazarinades* (Societe de l'Histoire de France – Moreau).

Mazarin's severe measures to suppress them. *Orfeo* was parodied, and while this might be a compliment today, such parody, then, was both bitter and venomous. Advantage was taken to pillory Mazarin in other directions. He was held up to ridicule in a lampoon dated February 9th, 1649, and entitled *La Plainte du Carnival et de la Foire-Saint-Laurent*, because he had made

> icy venir de si loin,
> A force d'argent et de soin,
> de ridicules personnages
> Avec de lascives images.

The lascivious images referred to were pictures and statues which Mazarin had bought in Italy.

The castrati caused some ribald laughter, as might be expected, and everything else Italian came under censure. The singer Della Bella was saved from the violence of the mob only by a sympathetic onlooker, who pointed out that she was Florentine and not Italian, a distinction too specious for the crowd to dispute. Mazarin, however, was quite accustomed to unpopularity and was more aggrieved than angered at the refusal of the French to absorb the new culture which he had imported at such cost.

A scapegoat had to be found and, since the greater part of the expenses went in the manufacture of the machines, the unfortunate Torelli was the obvious choice. The mob threw him into prison in spite of his protests that he had, after all, only taken advantage of the *carte blanche* given him and had carried out his work to the best of his ability.

The only thing for which *Orfeo* could not be blamed was its character. This was as 'honnête' as anyone could have desired. Virtue had triumphed over vice on every possible occasion, and even Love himself, in the person of Cupid, had refused to obey his mother, Venus.

Luigi Rossi departed for Italy on the morrow of the production of *Orfeo* and was well out of the way before the trouble started. Mazarin had the wit to see from which direction the wind was blowing and forbade the creation of any other such work, although one was pressed for by Anne of Austria, who had no tact or acumen whatever.

The novel features of *Orfeo* remained in French Opera once it was formulated. The elaborate and mysterious caves and grottoes, the suspension of chariots in the air, Venus' descent with hosts of little cupids, weird and horrific animals in Hades, Bacchantes with little bells, Dryads with castanets, together with the closing moral on conjugal love – all these, except the moral, can be found in the later operas of Lulli and Rameau, and they swing back to the general conception of *Circé ou le Ballet comyque de la Royne.*

The French reply to *Orfeo* was a tragedy by Corneille, *Andromède.* Corneille did not believe in music if it in any way obscured the verse or was imposed upon the drama for its own sake. At the beginning of his career he would have none of it, but, as time went on, he modified his opinions and, in *Andromède*, he used it as an accessory to the drama (Appendix Thirteen).

Only one fragment of the music, composed by Dassouci (Charles d'Assoucy), remains. An opinion of this, though by no means a musically informed one, was given by Voltaire,[1] who erroneously ascribed the music to Boesset (Appendix Fourteen). Were it not for Voltaire's eminence in other directions, his opinion would be valueless, but it is always 'interesting to know the ideas, even the erroneous ideas, of geniuses and men of great talent'.[2]

The music makes its first appearance in the Prologue. The God of the Sun and a Muse recite a panegyric – 'ils unissent leurs voix, specifié poème, et chantent un air à la louange du roi'.

The second Act, portraying the love of Andromède for Phinée, calls for the most music. The chorus sings while Persée fights the monster and then celebrates his victory; it comments only on the action, forming a musical counterpart to the Greek chorus. Later performances used different music. From notes made on Molière's copy of the tragedy, suggesting a possible cast, it would appear that he had, at one time, hoped to produce it with music by Marc Antoine Charpentier.

Memories are short. When Mazarin returned to Paris on February 3rd, 1653, the storms had blown over and the populace

---

[1] *Commentaires (sur Corneille).*
[2] *Revue d'art dramatique* – Vincent d'Indy, February 5th 1899.

was inclined to regard life as a perpetual carnival. The national celebrations included a performance of the *Ballet de la Nuit*, with machines designed by Torelli, now released from prison. This work was on an enormous scale. From six until nine o'clock the action moved from the country to the town, then back to the country. The second part consisted of a ball held at the palace of Roger and Bardamente. The third, which began at midnight, evoked the loves of Diane and Endymion, interspersed with scenes between sorcerers and monkeys, and the fourth was devoted to Aurore, as well it might have been. There were no complaints as the production was on a national scale and was open to all.

Mazarin took advantage of this promising situation and sent the Abbé Buti to Italy to recruit another Italian Opera Company. The Abbé carried out his duties with the utmost zeal and did not hurry over them. In time he brought back the necessary singers and the libretto of a new opera, *Nozze di Peleo e di Theti*, for which he had engaged Carlo Capr(i)oli to write the music. Cardinal Barberini, now returned to Italy, gave all the assistance in his power and the work was produced on April 14th, 1654.

Far from resenting this fresh influx of Italians, the Parisians now welcomed them. They had neither heard nor seen the castrati for some time.

Caprioli was immediately appointed Maistre de la Musique du Cabinet du Roy, a position which gave him direct control and responsibility. The first performance had been announced for April 16th, and Louis XIV returned from Saint-Germain in order to attend the rehearsals. He had undertaken to dance six roles, including those of Apollo, a Dryad, a Fury, and an Indian. Anne of Austria and Mazarin hoped that the appearance of the King would make an instant appeal to his people, and they were not disappointed. Torelli surpassed himself in ingenuity, a fact not overlooked by Loret, the rhyming author of *La Muze Historique* (Appendix Fifteen).

For once, the arrangements went comparatively smoothly. There was none of the confusion which accompanied the production of *Orfeo*. The Petit-Bourbon was capable of seating thousands. The theatre in the Palais-Royal was far too small for the Cardinal's ambitious schemes and in any case had been allowed to fall into a state of disrepair. The audience was given candles so that they could follow the detailed programme notes thoughtfully provided by the Cardinal.

Mazarin was not present at the first two performances, being a victim of 'douleurs nephrêtiques'.[1] He was absent from the third for a political reason, but attended the fourth, by which time everybody had become familiar with their parts and things went almost mechanically smoothly. It is supposed that the wily Cardinal determined to see what the reaction was before putting in an appearance.

The work was described as a *Comédie Italienne en musique en-tremeslée d'un ballet sur le mesme sujet*. It was a complete fusion of Italian Opera and French *Ballet de Cour*, for the ballet, instead of being added to the opera to form an *Intermède*, was an integral part of the story.

We have thus reached the point when Opera and *Opéra-Ballet* were inaugurated in France, the former being represented by *Orfeo*, the latter by the work under discussion.

The Italians wrote and formed the operatic element, and the French, the choreographic. The minor roles were filled by French artists and by one Englishman, Thomas Stafford, who took the parts of Prometheus and one of the Nereids.[2] A large part of this music has disappeared. So much written up to this time has vanished that one must consider the possibility that it was not held in much esteem. It would be interesting to know for how many productions composers used previously written material. The libretto, however, is available, thanks to Mazarin's anxiety that his name should be perpetuated as the originator of the *Fêtes* and other entertainments.

The work was written in two distinct parts, each scene giving occasion for choreographic entries; the choreographer was the Comte de Saint-Aignan.

The Abbé Buti, it will be remembered, cluttered up the story of *Orfeo* with facetious irrelevancies. He did so again with *Nozze di Peleo e di Theti*. The story, in brief, is that Peleo, King of Thessaly, is in love with Theti, but has two dangerous rivals in Jupiter and

---

[1] *Mémoires* – Madame de Motteville.
[2] Stafford came from Rome with Luigi Rossi, whose pupil he had been.

Neptune. Peleo invokes the aid of Chiron and Prometheus, who persuade Jupiter and Neptune that they are too old for a young girl like Theti. Moved by Peleo's endeavours to rid her of her elderly suitors, Theti marries him, the wedding being solemnised before a great concourse of Gods and Goddesses.

Nothing could be more straightforward than this, but the Abbé Buti contrived to produce an entertainment lasting several hours. He opened with a Prologue in which the King of France, representing Apollo, descends from the summit of Parnassus to be greeted by Rivers and Meadows with respectful songs. The scene for the first Act is Chiron's grotto, built upon rocks, and open at each end. Peleo is telling his tale of woe to Chiron who advises him to consult Prometheus, chained to his rock in the Caucasus. Four sorcerers and four sorceresses conjure up a flying chariot for Peleo. A sea scene follows. Theti appears in a large shell drawn by a merman. She meets Neptune in his sea chariot and he declares his love for her. Refused, he strikes the waves with his trident and lets loose a terrible storm. Theti takes refuge on shore and is greeted by fishermen, who dance in order to divert her. In the next scene, Jupiter employs all his wiles to seduce Theti, but, after carrying her up to his kingdom in a cloud, he has to face an outraged Juno, who calls the Furies to her aid and, in a bizarre dance, forces Jupiter to flee on his eagle.

In Act Two, Prometheus discusses the situation with Peleo. 'J'ai ravi le feu du soleil', he says, to which Peleo replies: 'Et moi, j'ai brûlé mon âme aux flammes des yeux de Theti'. Prometheus prophesies that Jupiter will, perforce, retire from the contest, at which Peleo is much relieved. Peleo leaves during a wild dance of savages. In the second scene, Prometheus' prophecies are fulfilled. Jupiter learns from Mercury that Theti will bear a son stronger than his father. Fearing the dire results of this, Jupiter renounces his love for her and invites the Dryads to dance in celebration of his release from thraldom – the third scene consists of mime and dancing to this end. The Knights of Thessaly assist at a *Fête* in honour of Mars. The Knights, however, beginning to take the fight enacted in the ballet seriously, are separated by a small crowd of people who have come to sacrifice on the altar of Mars. The scene concludes with a chorus and dance between the Knights and the worshippers.

Act Three opens before the porchway of Theti's palace. Chiron orders Peleo to find the Goddess while the Sages, dressed as Indians, dance in honour of the return of the King to Thessaly. In Scene Two, Peleo declares his burning love for Theti, and, in spite of being changed into a lion, a monster, and a rock, he does not falter in his declarations. This convinces Theti that Peleo is sincere. They are married, amid scenes of great pomp, upon Olympus. Theti and Peleo appear seated on a high throne, while the deities of Olympus move across a large cloud. Hercules leads forward Prometheus, now released from his rock by order of Jupiter. Juno and Hymen, accompanied by a celestial choir, descend in a large machine and all unite with those liberal Arts and Sciences conjured into being by Prometheus. They reach the earth and dance a ballet, while Cupids form clusters in the sky.

Beyond this formulative combination of two genres must be mentioned the happy results of the mixture of French and Italian artists who, at long last, found themselves in pursuit of a common ideal. Mazarin had his praises sung by Renaudot in the *Gazette de Paris*, an unusual experience for him. 'La France n'est moins obligée de ses plus beaux divertissements à Son Eminence qui fait venir de si excellens hommes d'Italie que du bon succés de ses affaires'. Mazarin, in return, was not ungrateful to those who had made his position so unusually happy. The Abbé Buti was given French nationality and a pension of two thousand livres. He became almost a Minister of Fine Arts, his duties being to assemble the finest Italian musicians for the French Court and to organise all the *Fêtes*. Caprioli returned to Italy with a warm letter of congratulation which earned him a position in the household of Cardinal Barberini.

The Italians went home well-satisfied in both mind and purse. Mazarin must have kept the accounts to himself, for his popularity did not wane and there was no repetition of the trouble following *Orfeo*.

Meanwhile, a certain young Florentine was coming slowly but surely to the forefront of affairs and beginning to work out the dazzlingly brilliant destiny awaiting him. Before passing on to him, however, it may be valuable to consider what the events and activities related in this chapter have in common with those connected with *Circé*.

The subjects continue to be taken from mythology and to be treated in a meandering and complicated way. The Scenes have become Acts and have intervals between them. Use is still made of the *Intermède*, as a means of relief from continuous vocal music. Ballet has become wider in scope.

The elementary mechanical contrivances have evolved, under Torelli and Vigarini, into elaborate flying machines (the staircase to Olympus has been mentioned). Already there is a tendency towards absurdity, a point which was finally reached when ingenuity was stretched to its utmost.

The music generally is more expressive and Italian recitative has taken the place of spoken dialogue. This prevents verbosity, but not the fulsome *double entendre* of the text which, in the earlier Prologues, was directed shamelessly at the King and his Family.

Only imagination can supply the orchestral sonorities of *Circé*, which were obtained mostly with wind instruments. In the Italian operas, the orchestration was perfunctory and, except in the Ritornelli and the Symphonies, played an essentially supporting role. The portable organ has disappeared, to be replaced by the harpsichord, a step hardly calculated to reduce monotony.

The works are still very long and the French found them exceedingly tedious. The cast of *Circé* was fundamentally French. The operas were performed largely by Italians experienced in a genre previously unknown outside their own country. Money continued to be no object. No effort was ever spared either to make the performances magnificent or to reward the participants generously.

The French did not take kindly to Opera, but they responded whole-heartedly to Ballet. This, though wholly artificial, was not as markedly so as the 'new-fangle' lyrical drama which Mazarin had imported from Italy, and they consequently became accustomed to it much more quickly.

CHAPTER FIVE

LULLI ARRIVES IN FRANCE — NOTICED BY LOUIS
XIV — LULLI AS DANCER AND GUITARIST — LIFE
AT COURT — HIS STUDIES — "LA VERITA REMANGA"
— "BALLET DES BIENVENUES" — "AMOR MALATO" —
MOLIÈRE — "LES PRÉCIEUSES RIDICULES" — VIGARINI
— MAZARIN — CAVALLI — "SERSE" — "ERCOLE AMANTE" —
MALANI — ITALIANS DISBANDED — LULLI BECOMES LULLY —
COURT MUSICAL ESTABLISHMENT — VERSAILLES — "LES
PLAISIRS DE L'ILE ENCHANTÉE" — "LES FÂCHEUX"

GIOVANNI BATTISTA LULLI (Jean Baptiste Lully) was born
in Florence, on November 29th, 1632. His father was a miller.
Nothing is known about his life up to the age of fourteen except
that he taught himself to thrum a few chords on the guitar and
belonged to a band of strolling players. The well-known story of
his discovery is partly true, but has been distorted by misunderstanding. What, in fact, happened was that Mademoiselle de
Montpensier asked her brother, the Duc de Mayenne, to find a
young Italian capable of teaching her the language. The Duc
happened to notice a winsome boy playing his guitar casually
in the street and, being taken with his appearance, promptly
engaged him.

Tradition has it that Lulli, serving as a scullion, was acci-
dentally discovered playing and singing risqué songs to the kitchen
staff; and it is quite simple to see how this legend, which contained
a modicum of truth, came about.

All châteaux included a building set apart from the main
house, where those not immediately connected with the family
were quartered. This building (or wing) was known as 'Le Grand
Commun' or, alternatively, 'Le Potager' (Appendix Sixteen).
There was nothing derogatory about living there and questions
of rank, position and precedence did not arise. All the food for
the main house was cooked there and carried along a covered way.

Lulli, therefore, would have lived in 'Le Grand Commun',
where life was perfectly free. There was no etiquette of any kind.

The inmates mixed according to their personal inclinations. It is extremely likely that Lulli, even at that early age, was an exhibitionist and, being a bright-eyed boy, attracted the notice of the kitchen wenches whom he entertained with his songs and pleasantries. Had he been a regular scullion or turn-spit, the smell of cooking would have clung to his clothes and rendered him unpleasant to Mademoiselle when the Italian lessons took place; but there is no reason to think that he was averse to lending his services at the spit now and again in return for favours bestowed by a pair of flashing eyes. In any case, he was a *gamin* and would have found ample scope for his gifts among his own kind.

Lulli had obviously formed some idea of the path he proposed to pursue. His guitar-playing made him popular. He wrote some dance pieces and *chansonettes*, which gave pleasure to his associates and brought him to the notice of his employer in a second capacity. He was also a good dancer.

However, not being content with his natural gifts, he studied the violin and the theory of music with three organists, Roberday, Metru, and Gigault. The first of these was a man of vision. He held that, if music sounded satisfactory, it must necessarily be within the rules; the pedant would say that being outside the rules would make it unsatisfactory. This dangerously easy-going, but far-seeing, philosophy was well suited to the unruly temperament of Lulli.

In 1652, Mademoiselle decided to cast in her lot with the Frondeurs; and Lulli, being unwilling to bury himself in the country, resigned from her service. It is not known how he found employment at the Court, but he would have been acceptable to any *Grand Commun* and taken for granted. Many inmates had no justification for being there and no qualifications beyond a certain amount of aplomb and a plausible story, should occasion demand it. Nobody asked any questions.

With his dancing, his guitar playing, and his newly-acquired skill upon the violin (he seems to have made rapid strides with this instrument) it was not difficult for Lulli to attract attention. He was an excellent clown and mimic. The King was young and wanted amusement; Lulli was able to satisfy the want, and the world was at his feet.

The whole of Lulli's life will be seen to have consisted of waiting for favourable moments, and at this time he exercised considerable patience, knowing that a false or too sudden step would ruin his opportunities. He attended the Court Ballets, and it was these which fostered his love for splendour and splendid music. At an impressionable age, he reacted whole-heartedly to the magnificent *Ballets de Cour* which had almost superseded the equally magnificent *Fêtes de Cour* of the Valois. He was encouraged to shine as a dancer as well as a musician by Michel Lambert (c.1610 – 1696), Director of the Royal Concerts, and a composer and lutanist of some repute. Lambert introduced Lulli to the French songs popular at the period and kept him under his wing. One positive side of Lulli's nature was that, although he never forgave an enemy, he never forgot a friend.

During the ballet in *Nozze di Peleo e di Theti*, Louis XIV first noticed the young Florentine dancing beside him. He was instantly attracted by him and the skilful manner in which he danced. This was exactly what Lulli had hoped for. The event marked not only the first step in his rise to authority but also laid the foundation of the remarkable personal friendship that was to grow between the two men.

When Anne of Austria found that Italian Opera had become popular, she considered founding a permanent Italian Company; but this Mazarin forbade on account of the cost. Interest was aroused, however. The King fancied himself in the role of dancer, although his dancing was little more than posturing and gesturing. He took part in many ballets, notably *La Verita Remanga*, composed by a Fr. Sbarra, who is otherwise quite unknown.

The argument of this work is not without interest and significance, being nothing less than a commentary upon the unpopularity of Truth. In the opening scene, Time distributes notes explaining the subject. The first *Entrée* represents a Chemist and a Doctor who express their pleasure in the evil atmosphere that pervades the world. Truth, pursued by Lawyers, asks them for help, but the sincerity in her face drives them away in terror. A Knight promises to help her, but he abandons her; she appeals to a soldier, who turns out to be both blusterer and braggart. The *Entrée* ends with a Ballet of Villagers, all armed with cudgels.

In the second *Entrée*, Truth is pursued successively by a Merchant and a Banker, and her grief is increased when Womankind turns against her. Finally, she appeals to the Theatre, which welcomes her on the understanding that she disguises herself and remains as inconspicuous as possible. The work concludes with a Ballet of Buffoons.

Having made his first impression, Lulli did not allow it to tarnish. On May 10th, 1655, he played an important role in the *Ballet des Bienvenues*, performed at the marriage of Mazarin's niece to the Duke of Modena. He was again prominent in the *Ballet de Psyché*, which took place in the following year, and finally established his position both as dancer and composer in *La Galanterie du Temps*, a Mascerade.

By this time he had attracted the attention of Mazarin, who recognised in him a fellow Italian. He commissioned a comedy, whose argument should introduce dancing, and Lulli produced *Amor malato*, written in Italian.

The work opens with a comic scene, in which two Doctors, Time and Vexation, enquire tenderly after the health of Love, who is confined to bed. They prescribe a facetious ballet as the only cure.

This ballet divides itself into ten *entrées:*

1. Attendants upon the Doctors.
2. Astrologers.
3. Treasure Hunters.
4. Four *galants* in pursuit of a *coquette*.
5. Eleven Doctors.
6. Eight Huntsmen.
7. Alchemists.
8. Six male and six female Indians.
9. Gypsies.
10. A Village Wedding.

This marked the first appearance of the traditional Gypsies, or *Bohémiennes*, in Ballet. They remained an integral part of the tradition for many years.

The fourth *Entrée* was the most popular. In it Lulli, disguised as Scaramouche, presided over a conclave of Doctors, which solemnly conferred a degree upon a donkey. (This anticipates a similar scene in Molière's *Le Malade Imaginaire*.) Lulli earned the praises of all for his work, Benserade remarking:

Aux plus savans docteurs je scay faire la loye
Ma grimace vaut mieux que tout leur préambule
Scaramouche en effect n'est pas si ridicule
    Et si Scaramouche que moy.

Lulli was gradually showing his independence. As author, composer and dancer, he was in sole control. He had already decided upon his future policy, which was to substitute French actors, singers and dancers for the Italian ones; but, as Mazarin was still alive, it was impossible to put it into practice.

He was, however, able to take a preliminary step. He had an intense dislike of the castrati, whose leader, Atto Melani, plagued him by asking, several times a day, which part he was to play. Lulli kept him on tenterhooks and handed him his part only at the last moment. The part was – Love, who spent the whole time lying silently in bed. This made Melani the laughing stock of the whole court.

The music was in a slightly exaggerated Italian style, although not being in any way a parody; to have gone so far at such a moment would have been too rapid a step. However, he cleverly inserted an Air in the true French style – *Que les jaloux sont importuns* – which was sufficient to show the difference between the two goûts.

Lulli found some unexpected support among the French musicians, who were anxious to see the end of the Italians, including Lulli himself. He put them on his side at once by persuading the Duc de Guise to produce the *Ballet des Plaisirs troublés*, on February 11th, 1658; in this, only French artists took part. It was followed the next year by the *Grand Ballet d'Alcidiane et Polexandre*, which was performed before the Queen Mother of France, Queen Christina of Sweden, the 'Princesse d'Angleterre', Mazarin and the entire court. Louis XIV danced in several *Entrées*. Lulli, dressed as a Moor, played the guitar, and danced in three *Entrées*; and composed the first 'French Overture', which was designed in direct contradiction to the Italian style.

Lulli must have been very sure of his position by this time, for he dared to make a reply to the King which otherwise would have ruined his career on the charge of *lèse-majesté*. There was some delay in commencing the performance, and the King sent an imperious message that he was waiting. To this, Lulli replied: 'The King is master here and he alone is in the position of being able to wait.' This impertinence, true as it was, amused instead of angered the King.

In due course, Lulli found a splendid opportunity to demonstrate the essential differences between Italian and French music. On February 19th, 1659, he produced the *Ballet de la Raillerie*, whose argument makes the policy plain to see.

After a preliminary recital of French poetry, the curtain rises on a palace before which are seated Mockery, Wisdom and Folly. They sing a long Italian Prologue in solo, duo, and trio. The music is in the Italian style, but with certain twists and cadences not to be found in Caprioli or Rossi. There is a significant duologue between Italian and French music. 'Do you believe,' asks the latter, 'that people like your long, boring, ornamental passages? The style in which I sing expresses my feelings far better than yours.' Lulli illustrates the points, first with a mock Italian roulade, and then with a genuine French Air.

The scene concludes with an Epilogue, the music of which has vanished. Henri Prunières suggests[1] that it might have been written by Tagliviacca. This would account for its loss, as Lulli might well have destroyed it in order to claim full credit for himself.

In the next scene Criticism, Fashion, Contradiction, and Disgust sit in judgement upon Ballet. Criticism accuses Ballet of being old-fashioned and full of worn-out ideas; Fashion says that Ballet dates her ideas from the days of the Old World (*i.e.* the days of the Valois *Fêtes de Cour*). Contradiction claims that nowhere else can such bad dancing be seen to the accompaniment of such good instrumental music and instruments, while Disgust can only express the hope that matters will soon show some improvement. Ballet replies upon the principle of *tu quoque*, and they then (surprisingly enough) celebrate a Love Festival.

---

[1] *Op. cit.*, pages 209, 210.

This represented Lulli's first major triumph. That he, a Florentine by birth, should be so anxious to rid French art of all Italian influences cannot be ascribed to any idealistic motive or to any love for the French *per se*. His character was not quite like that. He considered that the easiest way to popularity and to the accomplishment of his own ideas was to encourage the national goût and the national musicians, to form natural French aesthetics. His knowledge of people showed him exactly what to do and how to do it; and it will be seen later to what extent he considered those aesthetics to be the same as his own.

The first real turning point in Lulli's career, however, came in 1659, when Molière produced *Les Précieuses ridicules* at the Petit-Bourbon, to incidental music by Lulli. Molière, a man of vision, saw the promising material latent in Lulli. He had evolved the genre of *Comédie-Ballet* and, through their collaboration, it became the theatrical counterpart of the later *Opéra-Ballet*. From this moment, the names of Molière and Lulli became closely linked, although each scored successes independently of the other. Molière had come a long way since opening his 'Illustre Théâtre' in the Rue Mazarine in 1643 (Appendix Seventeen).

In 1659, Mazarin put his scheme for building an ideal theatre into operation. For this purpose, he engaged the septuagenarian Vigarini as architect and the old man's two sons, Gasparo and Lodovico, as manufacturers of the stage machinery. Torelli was available but, as a friend of Fouquet, he was out of favour. The building was ornate in design and elaborate in execution. The machines included some large effigies of the mythological deities, and there were certain sets which could be used as standard bases for future productions. The work was completed in 1661, not an unreasonable period considering the detailed craftsmanship that was entailed.

The stage figures consisted of Juno, Venus, Hercules, the Celestial Influences and the Planets. The figure of Juno was fitted with an internal mechanism to make it mobile. The effigy of the Moon, which occupied the centre of the stage, was made to open and close; it contained a golden grotto representing the ice-bound surface of the Moon herself. The standard sets were two Sea Scenes. In one of these, the Sun rose as the Moon descended;

G

the other contained a floating barge, a chariot for Venus, the Three Graces and a Chorus. There were also a Royal Palace, Juno's grotto (which contained the goddess' mechanically-voiced peacock), the Gardens of Venus and Mercury and, finally, an elaborate mechanism for the realisation of the traditional Apotheoses.

The manufacture of these machines and sets brought trouble to Lulli. His *comédiens* could no longer use the Petit-Bourbon, as it was in the process of demolition following the construction of the colonnade at the Louvre. The King gave Vigarini permission to take anything he wanted both from the Petit-Bourbon and the Salle du Palais Royal.

The new building was enormous. The amenities included secret galleries into which the King could retire after dancing and through which the Queen could walk from the Palace without going outside. There were also large and small rooms where the King, the Princes, and courtiers taking part in the performances, could change their costumes (Appendix Eighteen).

There was only one oversight. No account had been taken of the acoustic properties of the theatre. Its vastness made clarity of diction altogether out of the question and it was impossible to hear the dialogue from the back of the auditorium, even when the actors all but shouted. After a few fruitless alterations, the theatre had to be abandoned as such; but Mazarin was not to be deterred, and he proceeded with his plan to produce an opera by the Italian composer, Pietro Francisco Cavalli (1602 – 1676), for the occasion of the King's marriage.

Cavalli was not particularly interested. He held a high position in Venice and was unwilling to prejudice it by absenting himself from that city. All the blandishments of Mazarin were necessary, especially as the Cardinal's emissary, the Abbé Buti, could only promise payment far below that made in the original offer. Eventually, after receiving a guarantee that his post in Venice would be kept open for him, Cavalli gave way and his opera *Serse*, already completed, was performed in the Gallery of the Louvre on November 22nd, 1660. The actual wedding of the King had taken place on the previous June 9th.

Serse did not make a great impression, in spite of Vigarini's mechanical wonders. Cavalli was in the process of composing another opera, *Ercole amante*, but he had been forced to put this aside for the moment and was slightly disgruntled at having to do so. Lulli was in charge of the ballet but, owing to the shortness of available time, had to use music which he had composed for earlier productions. The six ballets had no connection whatever with the opera and were included simply as *Intermèdes*, but they were remarkable for their variety.

1. Basques, half French, half Spanish.
2. Male and female peasants, singing and dancing *à l'espagnol*.
3. Scaramouche in a crowd of doctors is recognised in spite of his disguise, and is mobbed.
4. A ship-owner with slaves carrying monkeys dressed as clowns, and sailors playing on a 'trompette marin'.
5. Buffoons.
6. Bacchus and his train.

Among the numerous characters there was one named Clinton, described as 'Page de Romildo qui ne parle point – Soprano'. The silent character was not unknown, but we can find no other instance of such punctilious vocal casting.

The performance, according to the lyrical Loret, lasted eight hours; and in his report in the *Muze historique* he says that he found difficulty in sitting through it all (Appendix Nineteen).

To occupy the period between the completion of *Ercole amante* and the opening of the new theatre in the Tuileries, a *Ballet de l'Impatience* was devised by the Abbé Buti and Benserade. This was more or less upon the same lines as the *Ballet de la Raillerie*, but instead of being an argument between Italian and French music, it was one between French dancers and foreign singers. Prunières is of the opinion that the real author was Molière, as no trace of it can be found in the collected works of the Abbé Buti. The music itself suggests that Lulli was the composer, though this theory rests entirely upon texture and style and not on any written record. The work was an assemblage of all the talents, but its production was challenged by a fire which destroyed the picture gallery in the Louvre. Vigarini proved his adaptability by reconstructing the stage and sets so that they were ready by February 19th, 1661.

The ballet opened with the usual Prologue, in which Love instructs Patience and his school to combat Jealousy, Caprice and Sensuality, with the aid of Constancy, Humility, Prudence and Fidelity. Each act opens with a recitative, the most entertaining being that in Act IV, where a music master extols tobacco in a 'recit crotesque (*sic*) italien'.

Mazarin, ill at Vincennes, did not attend the performance. He died shortly before the production of *Ercole amante*, leaving behind him the foundations of a tradition which was to culminate in something rather different from that at which he had aimed. Before long, the Parisians showed again that they would have no more of the Italians or their wares.

The Cardinal's death, however, did not interfere with the production of Cavalli's opera. Once more there was considerable dismay at the expense and considerable anger at the manner in which the Italians had monopolised the whole concern. Only two of the singers were French and the foreigners behaved as if they were in a country of barbarians. Cavalli tried to overcome some of this prejudice with a pathetic attempt to meet the French on their own level by writing the directions himself in the band parts in French – 'Tou douxemains' and 'Bien fort, messieurs' being typical examples.

The cast was enormous. One name was unexpectedly absent, that of Atto Melani, whose intense conceit had made him exceedingly unpopular; he had become a bitter enemy of the Abbé Buti. The Abbé, who had the casting of the opera, deliberately ignored him, hoping that in due course he would ask what role he was to fill. Melani refrained from asking but, at last, could hold out no longer. The Abbé replied that he could be one of a great number of deities who would journey from the clouds in one machine . . . .

Prunières quotes the full cast:

PROLOGUE

Cinthia   .   .   . Giuseppe Melone (*castrato Soprano*)

DRAME

Ercole	. .	. Piccini (*basso*)
Venere	. .	. Mdlle Hylaire (*soprano*)
Giunone	. .	. Antonio Rivani (*castrato contralto*)
Hyllo, figlia d'Ercole		. Gio. Agostino Poncelli (*tenore*)
Iole, figlia del re Eutyre		. Signora Anna Bergerotti (*soprano*)
Paggio	. . .	? (*castrato soprano*)
Déjanira, moglie d'Ercole.		Signora Leonora Ballerini (*soprano*)
Liccio, suo servo .		. Chiarini (*castrato contralto*)
Pasithea, moglie des Sonno		Signora Bordoni (*soprano*)

Sonna, personnaggio muto⎤
Mercurio . . ⎦ Tagliavacca (*basso*)

Nettunno . . ⎤
Ombra del re Eutryo, ⎬ Bordigone (*basso*)
    padre d'Iole ⎦

Ombra de Bussuride . Zanetto (*castrato contralto*)
Ombra di Lamedoute re di
    Trois . . . Vulpio (*tenore*)

Ombra di Clerica Regina ⎤
La Ballezza . . ⎦ Mdlle de la Barre (*soprano*)

Coro musico delle tre Grazie Sigra. Ribera, Sig. Melone e Zanetto
Coro musico de' fiumi
  ,,   ,,   d'Aure e Ruscelli
  ,,   ,,   de' Sacrificanti al sepolcro d'Eutryo
  ,,   ,,   d'Animi infernali
  ,,   ,,   de Sacerdoti de Giunone pronuba
  ,, Armonico di' Tritoni e Sirene
  ,, Muto di Damigelle d'Iole

Cavalli, given *carte blanche* by Mazarin, acted as anyone else would have done under the circumstances. General admiration was expressed over Vigarini's machines, which were on view to the public before the performance. The final Apotheosis promised to eclipse all others. Vigarini arranged that the entire Royal Family, who were to take part in the ballet, should be swept up to the skies in a basket. It was to be decorated to represent an enormous and magnificent chariot and to be carried across the stage. This caused some apprehension, but the best Italian authorities were called in to give the necessary assurances, not only on this point but also on the special fire precautions which had been taken. The Queens sat in an iron box or *loge* placed near the door of the theatre through which they could escape quickly in an emergency. Sabotage was suspected during the rehearsals as some of the machines refused to function properly. Louis XIV showed the greatest interest in these rehearsals, and was compelled to suppress the news of the death of his father-in-law, the King of Spain, as the court would have had to go into mourning and the production be postponed. Not for the first time did the King grow impatient at delay, and he finally ordered that everything should be ready for February 7th, 1662.

The performance took place before a truly distinguished audience who extolled everything except the music, which seems to have passed unnoticed. The whole thing lasted for six hours.

Ercole amante may be classed as an *Opéra-Ballet de Cour*. Each act terminated with a ballet danced by the courtiers, the music again being composed by Lulli. The whole work was an admirable compromise between the Italian goût for singing and the French one for dancing.

As usual there is a topical Prologue which, in this case, celebrates the union of France with Spain through the marriage of Louis XIV and Marie-Thérèse. Hercules then laments his love for Iole; she is the daughter of King Eutyre, whom he has killed in a fit of anger. Venus promises him her help, but Juno interferes and, in order to ruin their plans, calls down a violent storm. This provides an admirable opportunity to present a ballet of Storm and Wind.

In Act II Hyllus, the son of Hercules, and Iole swear eternal love, but a page brings Iole a *rendez-vous* from Hercules. Hyllus is, not unnaturally, jealous; but Iole reassures him. The page, a veritable *ingenue*, asks himself what this thing called love may be. Déjanire, followed by her clownish servant Licco, asks the Page what has happened. She promptly falls into despair, as she foresees the betrayal of her husband and fears for the life of her son, Hyllus.

The scene changes and, at the Altar of Sleep, Pasithea invokes the Breezes and Streams to soothe the slumber of her husband. Juno follows, and takes Sleep into her chariot. Dreams then dance a ballet.

In Act III, Hercules awaits Iole; she enters with Hyllus. First, she repels the advances of Hercules; then seated upon a magic box, which Venus has placed there, proclaims her love for him. Hyllus, in desperation, gives chase to his father but, just as Iole is about to surrender, Juno arrives in her chariot. Sleep touches Hercules, who immediately sinks down to the ground. Juno then exhorts Iole to kill him. Iole is about to do so when Hyllus reappears and snatches the dagger from her hand. Hercules, opportunely awakened by Mercury, thinks that his son has intended to kill him. Déjanire thrusts herself between the two men, but Hercules threatens to kill them both. Iole promises to give herself to Hercules if he will relent. Hercules banishes Déjanire and imprisons Hyllus.

The Page and Licco discuss the whole affair and in order to relieve the tension, sing some gay songs. The statues become animated and dance.

In Act IV, Hyllus is in prison. A barge approaches carrying the Page with a message from Iole. She is about to intercede with Hercules for her lover. Hyllus then abandons himself to despair. A storm comes up and submerges the barge. Juno calls on Neptune, who rises from the sea and saves Hyllus. Juno comforts him and the Breezes dance to celebrate the return of the Sun. The scene quickly changes to a cemetery planted with cypress trees. Déjanire and Licco see a funeral procession approaching, led by Iole. The Priests invoke Death, and Iole asks forgiveness of her father for her sacrilegious union with Hercules. The ghost of Eutyre appears and forbids her to ask this of him, saying that resistance is preferable. Déjanire then announces the death of Hyllus. The ghost of Eutyre continues his imprecations against Hercules, and disappears.

Iole weeps for the death of Hyllus. Licco begs Déjanire to give him the cloak of the centaur, Nessus, as this will be the means of reconciling her to Hercules. Ghosts appear from the surrounding tombs.

In Act V, all the victims of Hercules cry from Hell for vengeance. With a quick change, the scene moves to the wedding of Hercules and Iole. Iole gives him the cloak of Nessus and he is immediately united with Déjanire. Hyllus appears and is married to Iole. The entire gathering sheds tears over the iniquities of Hercules. Juno then proclaims that the immortal Alcides has married Beauty on Mount Olympus. The sky opens for the Apotheosis of Hercules who sings, with Beauty, to the glory of the royal couple (Louis XIV and Marie-Thérèse). The Celestial Influences descend from the sky and dance a ballet.

The Abbé Buti may not have been a great poet, but he had the ability to extend and elaborate a straightforward story to the point of complication. Cavalli had learnt all that was necessary about recitative from Monteverdi and had succeeded in imbuing it with expressiveness and musical feeling. He allowed the orchestra to be independent and, in the Cemetery scene, showed considerable orchestral acumen. The solo movements were in the style of *canzoni* and *canzonetti*; a few bars from one of these, together with Pasithea's invocation to Sleep, will show the beautiful music Cavalli could write when inspired.

Cavalli was more mature than Rossi; and he was different. Rossi indulged in harmonic sonorities whenever they occurred to him; Cavalli applied harmonic expression to each dramatic section according to its requirements.

Vigarini's machines were more ambitious than those of Torelli, who had been content with those built to hold four or five people; Vigarini hardly recognised that there were any limitations. 'An entire palace descended from the sky, supported on clouds. It re-ascended, to give place to another which, on leaving the ground, hung suspended over the stage.' The Royal Family's aerial flight took the audience's breath away. Vigarini showed that he had perfect confidence in himself when he hoisted this distinguished gathering up to Olympus.

The French were not altogether impressed by *Ercole amante*, Cavalli, and the Italian company. It was felt that they themselves could produce something quite as good and much less expensive. The King, though disappointed at this national reaction, was not discouraged; but, in spite of repeated performances and a subsequent acknowledgement of its finer points, the work never became popular. Cavalli returned to Italy, his purse, after all, well filled, and, although the Italian company remained in Paris, interest in Italian opera rapidly waned.

Italian Opera had served its purpose. It had cost a great deal of money; it had given employment to a large number of Italians and to a smaller number of Frenchmen. It had laid the foundations of a culture by stirring patriotic sentiment to a realisation of its own potentialities, encouraging it to formulate a technique of its own. The way now became clear for real French Opera, and certain trends in this direction had already manifested themselves.

In 1661, Lulli became a naturalised Frenchman, changing the spelling of his name to Lully. He claimed noble parentage; but this deceived nobody. The musical establishment of the court required a Surintendent who was capable of more than the mere arrangement of court concerts. The holder of this appointment, at this time, was Jean Baptiste Boisset, Seigneur de Dehault, who had succeeded his father, Sieur de Villedieu, in 1644. Lully was unable to usurp this position entirely, but arrangements were conveniently made that Boisset should be responsible for duties from January to July, and Lully for the rest of the year. Under them were four 'maistres de musique', whose period of duty lasted for three months at a time: 'Le sieur Gobert' (January), 'le sieur Robert' (April), 'le sieur Spirly' (July) and 'le sieur Du Mont' (October). Lully, however, gradually pushed them all into the background. They drew their salaries and were encouraged to efface themselves as much as possible. Lully became the sole figure in court musical circles.

The musical establishment consisted of three departments, the Grande Écurie, the Chapelle and the Chambre.

The first of these included twelve violinists who were quadruple-handed, as they had to change to hautbois, sacquebotte (trombone) and cornett at a moment's notice; four hautbois de poitou; eight players of fifres, tambourins and musettes, and twelve of trumpets and drums, making thirty-six players in all. This force attended the King wherever he went (hence the necessity for quick changes-over); and its trumpets and drums supplied the music for hunts, processions, *Fêtes champêtres* and other court occasions.[1]

The Chapelle consisted of fourteen adult singers, eight children and a player of the Serpent. It formed the choir for High Mass and entertained the Court with secular vocal music in the evenings. The church music, until then unaccompanied, was written in four, five and six parts. When Lully took charge, he wrote cantatas in up to ten parts for double choir with orchestral accompaniment. This was supplied by the Grande Écurie together with the music of the Chambre, the famous 'Vingt-Quatre Violons'. Lully was the first 'Maître de Chapelle' to introduce an orchestra into Church services.[2]

The 'Vingt-Quatre Violons' played at State Balls, Dinners[3] and Concerts.

On the death of Mazarin, the King, relieved of the Cardinal's parsimony, immediately augmented his household. The final

---

[1] Lully – *Fanfares pour le Carrousel de Monseigneur; Marches pour les Mousquetaires du Roy et pour les Mousquetaires gris; Marche du Régiment de Turenne*, London International TWV 91092.

[2] Lalande – *Confitemini (Te Deum)*, Oiseau Lyre OL 50153. *De Profundis* (Psalm 129), Vox PL 9040. Lully – *Miserere*, Oiseau Lyre OL 53003. *Te Deum*, Ducretet-Thomson DTL 93143.

[3] Lalande – *Sinfonies pour les soupers du Roy*, London International TWV 91092, Oiseau Lyre OL 50152 and OL 50106.

glory, however, dates from 1661 when the King, visiting the *Fêtes* at Vaux, organised by Fouquet, the Finance Minister, found this minister, and others of the King's subjects, living in greater state than the Royal Family.[1] That Louis went to the extreme is therefore understandable. It was necessary at the time to maintain prestige, and for this reason, Versailles and its attendant splendours were called into being.

In 1664, the Château de Versailles was completed, after stupendous efforts which had cost the lives of hundreds of workmen. The building was inaugurated by a *Fête* worthy to rank with the most elaborate of the Valois *Fêtes de Cour* and which surpassed the contemporary *Ballets de Cour* in both lavishness and costliness. It was entitled *Les Plaisirs de l'Ile enchantée*.

Three days were devoted to plays by Molière, with Lully's music, and four to processions, tourneys and other elements of a State Carrousel. The importance of this work to Lully was that it suggested the possibilities latent in theatrical production and it played a large part in forming his ideas in the future.

Les Plaisirs de l'Ile enchantée consisted of plays within plays, a general scheme similar to that of Ariosto's *Orlando Furioso*. The performances took place in different parts of the grounds. The first day's *Fête* was in the moat, the spectators being ranged on the bank facing the château. The second moved to the 'Tapis vert', on an incline, where a proscenium curtain had been erected, the backcloth being the splendid vista through the proscenium. The curtain was stretched from tree to tree. The third day was set around the 'Grand Bassin', which was decorated as the Palace of Alcine.[2]

The Duc de Saint-Aignan was responsible for the main production and for the seating of the audience; the Duc de Noailles was nominated judge for the various Tourneys; and the machinery was in the charge of Gaspard Vigarini. The proceedings bore a strong resemblance to a 20th century pageant.

---

[1] For a not too highly coloured and, on the whole, authentic account of these *Fêtes*, *The Man in the Iron Mask*, by the indefatigable Alexandre Dumas, should be read. The *Fêtes* are used as subsidiary elements in a political episode which has no historical foundation, but the story affords an enlightening picture of customs of the period.

[2] Lalande – *Concert de trompettes pour les festes sur le canal de Versailles* – Oiseau Lyre OL 50152.

The procession was headed by the Chevalier d'Artagnan, confidant of the King, one of his closest friends and almost the only honourable man among them. The Grand Écurie supplied the music and was divided into separate groups, that for this first procession consisting of four trumpeters and two drummers. The Duc de Saint-Aignan followed, in the guise of Guidon le Sauvage. He carried 'une cuirasse de toile d'argent qui était ecaillé d'or et des bas de coie; son casque était orné d'un dragon'. The main body followed with more trumpets and drums. Then the King appeared in all his glory. He was mounted on a superb horse whose harness shone with gold and precious stones. He was dressed 'à la grecque comme tous ceux de *sa quadrille* et portait une cuirasse de lames d'argent couverts d'une riche broderie d'or et de diamants; son casque était orné d'une profusion de grandes plumes couleur de feul selon un témoin; jamais un air plus libre ni plus guerrier n'avait mis un mortal au-dessus des autres hommes'.

Behind the King came the Duc de Noailles, dressed as Ogier-le-Danois; the Marquis de la Vallière; the Duc de Guise as Aquilant-le-Noir; and other courtiers. Monsieur, the King's brother, representing Orlando, brought up the rear. Molière's entire troupe of players also took part. The procession advanced to the sound of choral and instrumental music, the musicians surrounding an enormous chariot upon which were seated Apollo and the Four Ages. On each side of them marched the Four Seasons, the Twenty-Four Hours of the Day, and the Twelve Signs of the Zodiac.

The Four Ages recited some verses, and then the Tourney took place. This was won by the Marquis de la Vallière, brother of Louise, the King's mistress. The Queen Mother rewarded his prowess with a gold sword bedecked with diamonds.

In the evening, the feast was illuminated by coloured torches and accompanied by music – 'on vut entrer Orphise de nos jours, vous entendez bien que je veux dire Lulli (*sic*) à la tête d'une grande troupe de concertants, qui s'approchent au petit pas et à la cadence de leurs instruments, se séparèrent en deux bandes, à droite et à gauche du haut dais'. The guests were waited upon by actors in character, headed by the god Pan, impersonated by Molière himself. The Twelve Signs of the Zodiac and the Four

Seasons danced a ballet. During supper 'trente-six violons, très bien vêtus' entertained the company with interludes and divertissements. The most important musical works played that night were *Rondeau pour les violons et flutes allant à la table du Roy* and the *Marche pour hautbois pour le dieu Pan et sa suite*, both composed by Lully.

Molière's triumph began on the second day.

'Le dessein de cette fête était que Roger et les chevaliers de sa quadrille, après avoir fait des merveilles aux courses que, par ordre de la belle magicienne, ils avaient faites en faveur de la Reine, continuaient en ce même dessein pour le divertissement suivant, et que, l'île flottante n'ayant point éloigne le rivage de la France ils donnaient à Sa Majesté le plaisir d'une comédie dont la scène était en Elide.'

This somewhat slender excuse justified a performance of Molière's *La Princesse d'Elide*. It took place on the second stage prepared for the *Fête*. Next, there was a *Mascerade nautique* on the 'Grand Bassin', during which the palace of Alcine went up in a blaze of fireworks. The music was again provided by Lully and his musicians, who occupied a rather dangerous position on an island in the middle of the basin.

Divertissements of all kinds occupied the fourth day.

On the fifth, *Les Fâcheux*, the *Comédie-Ballet* produced at Vaux was played. Most of the music had been composed originally by Beauchamp, the King's Maître de Ballet, Lully contributing only a few short dance movements. Lully was wily, knowing that Fouquet and his friends were out of favour with the King, although he was not prepared to stand aside altogether. He denied all knowledge of Fouquet's private and political life but, on the occasion of the Versailles *Fête*, there was no danger in associating himself with the play.

The sixth day was celebrated by the first performance of the first three acts (the only ones written by that time) of *Tartuffe*, and the whole *Fête* terminated on the seventh day with *Le Mariage Forcé* by Molière and Lully. The *Fête* was almost a Molière-Lully Festival.

A collaboration so brilliantly started was bound to continue. Their most successful productions were: *L'Impromptu de Versailles*

(previously produced in 1663); *Le Mariage Forcé* (already mentioned); *Ballet des Muses* (1666); *Georges Dandin* (1668), an *Intermède*
from the spectacular *Les Festes de Versailles* produced during a
second Royal *Fête*, together with *Le Grotto de Versailles* (whose
performance can only be assumed, as there is no record of the
actual date); *Monsieur de Pourcéagnac* (1668), for which Lully
wrote Italian words; *Le Bourgeois Gentilhomme* (1670) and *Psyché*
(1671). The music varied in quantity. In *Le Misanthrope* (1666)
there was a single song; while *Le Bourgeois Gentilhomme* was, in
style, almost an *Opéra-Comique*.[1]

Not all the entertainments at Versailles took place in the open
air. The 'Salon de Mars' was set aside for indoor performances,
a dais being erected on each side of the fireplace for the musicians.
It was partly for these entertainments that Lully obtained the
King's permission to form a smaller orchestra. This, known as
the 'Petits Violons', played only simple music and was therefore
both more acceptable to the musically unenlightened and more
suitable for use in the 'Salon de Mars'. As a result, Lully had a
hundred and fifty musicians to draw upon, and, by virtue of his
official position, he could use them in any way he liked. He could
transport them to Saint-Germain, Versailles, Paris or any of the
royal châteaux at a moment's notice, and he could use them as
the orchestra in the Salle du Palais Royal whenever necessary.

Unfortunately for the King, Colbert, the new Minister of
Finance, refused to sanction the grant necessary to erect a theatre
in the château, and it was not until the reign of Louis XV, in
1770, that one was finally built.

In 1663 Lully married Michel Lambert's daughter, who
brought a useful dowry with her.

One interesting effect of all this musical activity was the influence it had on Charles II of England, then in exile. When he
came to restore court life to London, it was the musical establishment of Louis XIV which set his standard. In terms of actual
music, however, the influence went very much further. (See
Appendix Forty-Two.)

---

[1] For *Le Malade Imaginaire* Molière engaged Marc Antoine Charpentier (1634 –
1704), who had studied in Italy under Carissimi and consequently was anathema to
Lully.

CHAPTER SIX

PERRIN – CAMBERT – "PASTORALE" – "LA TOISON
D'OR" – FOUNDATION OF ACADÉMIE D'OPERA – JEU
DE PAUME DE LA BOUTEILLE – "POMONE" – FIRST
"READING PANEL" – GILBERT – "LES PEINES ET LES
PLAISIRS DE L'AMOUR" – PERRIN IN PRISON – PRIVILÈGE
SOLD TO LULLY – FOUNDATION OF ACADÉMIE ROYALE
DE MUSIQUE – "LES FÊTES DE L'AMOUR ET DE BACCHUS"
– QUINAULT – "CADMUS ET HERMIONE" – DEATH OF
MOLIÈRE

WHEN POPE INNOCENT X suggested to Louis XIV that he
should institute a national French Opera, and thus establish a
culture which would be unique to the French way of thinking, the King had not yet reached a state of independence.
Further, as far as was known, there were no French composers
capable of making the initial step sufficiently significant, and
the King realised that the experiment would have to be successful from the start. If it were not, the Italian style would have
every justification for further encroachment, this time upon a
failure.

Unknown to the King, the matter was being taken in
hand by Pierre Perrin and Robert Cambert, who had composed
a *Pastorale* upon certain novel lines. As they had no means
of producing the work in Paris, they had gone to the provinces in the hope that their venture would be discussed far
and wide.

Pierre Perrin was born at Lyons in 1619 or 1620. He bestowed
the title of 'Abbé' upon himself, thinking that this would give
a certain prestige, and he kept the title in spite of being married.
The fact that his brother was a genuine Abbé helped to perpetuate
his legend. Perrin recommended himself to Gaston, Duc d'Orléans,
the King's uncle, by a mutual admiration of, and love for, the
theatre (Gaston was Molière's protector). Perrin introduced
himself to the Duke by means of his poetry, for Gaston enjoyed

taking part in the comedies and ballets, both 'comiques et souvent licencieux', which were performed in the Palais de Luxembourg.

Perrin was almost the first man of the theatre to study the question of completely fused poetry and music. He wrote a good deal of verse expressly for musical setting. This was of so little value as poetry that Boileau inveighed against it, and against its writer, in his *Satires*. Perrin sought a style which would suggest music both in its metre and in its syllabic rhythms. In the Preface to a collection of 'Paroles de musique',[1] he set out his ideals as follows:

> 'Tu trouveras un recueil de "Paroles de Musique" ou vers à chanter, mis en musique en divers temps par les plus illustres musiciens du royaume. Ces vers sont ceux que nous devrions proprement appeller lyriques, c'est à dire propres à estre chantez sur la lyre ou avec l'instrument, et demandent un génie et un art tout particulier que j'ose dire peu connu et presque ignoré jusqu'icy de tous les poètes anciens et modernes, Grecs, Latins, Italiens, Espagnols et François; entre lesquels on ne trouve que peu ou point d'Orphées, c'est-a-dire de poètes musiciens ou de musiciens poètes, qui ayant sceu marier les deux soeurs la poésie et la musique, leurs vers lyriques et leurs chansons prétendues n'estant rien moins que du lyrique et des chansons au témoignage des musiciens les plus éclairez : mais comme cette matière curieuse est trop vaste pour estre traitée dans un avant propos, je me contenteray de te donner en ces paroles de musique des exemples de la prattique de cet art amirable, me reservant, si j'ay du loysir, à t'en donner un traitté particulier . . . .'

Here is a specimen of Perrin's 'Paroles de musique'.

> Sus! Sus! pinte et fagot!
> Sans soucy de l'ecot
> Buvons à tasses pleines;

Achevons, achevons de remplir nos bedaines.
En deussions-nous crever, trinquons jusqu'à demain,
Il est beau de mourir les armes à la main.

---

[1] Paris, D. Pellé, 1667.

Du vin, du saulcisson,
Du pâté, du jambon,
Du ragouts, des saulcisses,

Du salé, du salé, du poivre, des epices,
En deussions-nous crever, trinquons jusqu'à demain.

Etc., etc., etc.

After this profound encouragement of the gastric juices, one casts an approving eye upon Boileau. Perrin, however, had his admirers. The following testimonial, for example, comes from the *Comparaison de la Musique italienne avec la Musique française*, by La Viefville de Freneuse (Lecerf de la Vieville).

'S'il avait plus limé ce qu'il faisoit, il suroit été un auteur excellent. Pour l'esprit, il l'avoit hereux et fécond. Lisez le recueil de poésies, vous y remarquerez souvent ce tour aisé et coulant qui est le fond des bonnes paroles chantantes, et des paroles latines, qu'il assemble pour le mariage de feu Monsieur avec Henriette d'Angleterre, m'ont fait juger qu'il auroit le même talent pour fournir des paroles excellentes aux compositeurs de musique d'église.'

Perrin found many composers willing to set his *airs de cour, airs à boire, dialogues, noëls, motets et chansons de toute sorte*. These included Cambert, Camefort, Lambert, Perdigal, Martin, and Molinier. Cambert set no less than thirteen, and their first lines and descriptions will give some insight into Perrin's sources of inspiration:

I	'Dans le désespoir, où je suis'	– *air de cour sur une absence*
II	'Amour et la raison Un jour eurent querelle'	– *chanson*
III	'Quand je presse ma Sylvie'	– *chansonette*
IV	'O charmante bouteille!'	– *chanson à boire*
V	'Sus! Sus! enfans, voici le jour Du grand patron de la vendange'	– *chanson pour le jour de Saint-Martin*

H

VI	'Vous qui ronflez endormis sous les couppes'	– *chanson*
VII	'Pauvre amoureux transy'	– *chanson*
VIII	'Fi, fi, fi, fi, de ce vilain ius. C'est du verjus. Que l'on m'apporte'	– *chanson*
IX	'Sus! Sus! pinte et fagot'	– *chanson*
X	'Que l'inventeur de la bouteille Fut un grand fat'	– *chanson*
XI	'Faisons bonne chère'	– *chanson, sur une sarabande du M. Cambert à deux dessus·*
XII	'Que les plaisirs attendent ses amours!'	– *épithalame, ou paroles pour un mariage en avril* 1661
XIII	'J'ayme la notre, et la blonde et la brune, Je sers Suson, Madelon, et Gogo: De tous costez je cherche ma fortune: Mais en amour je veux vivre à gogo: Et si je n'ay l'affect ou l'espérance, Je fais bien-tost la révérence'	– *paroles sur une sarabande du Sieur Cambert*

Less is known about Robert Cambert than about Perrin. According to Fétis,[1] Cambert was born about 1629. He was at one time a pupil of Jacques Champion de Chambonnières and was afterwards organist at Saint-Honoré; by 1666, he was Surintendant de la musique to Anne of Austria. He married in 1665, his daughter becoming the wife of a musician named Farinelli (who is not to be confused with the famous castrato of that name). In addition to setting Perrin's jingles, Cambert composed motets and pieces for the Queen Mother's musical evenings. His reputation stood high. It was at the court, of course, that he came into contact with Perrin. Cambert had clear-cut ideas upon the method of

---

[1] *Biographie universelle des Musiciens.*

setting words to music, and these ideas he printed in an *advis au lecteur*, the foreword to a collection of his *airs à boire:*

> 'Vous y trouverez quelques nouveautez singulières, et qui n'ont point este pratiquées par ceux qui m'ont devancé, comme des dialogues pour des dames, et des chansons à trois, dont tous les couplets ont des airs différents; vous observerez aussi que la pluspart des airs à trois peuvent chanter en basse et en dessus sans la troisième partie, et se jouer en symphonie avec la basse et le dessus de viole, ainsi que je l'ay pratiqué dans quelques concerts?'

Perrin addressed a madrigal expressly to his composer:

> Ces vers melodieux sont des chants à ta gloire,
> Qui nous obligeront à boire
> (Après que nous aurons chanté)
> Milles brindès à ta santé.

Cambert's 'response de l'autheur' ran as follows:

> Pour vous faire raison je vuideray la couppe
> Et je ferai à la trouppe
> Que j'entends à pinter
> Aussi bien qu'à chanter.

Each was ready to accept the other's point of view. They concentrated on making the music so express the sentiment of the words that there could be no separation. Perrin was uncertain how these new ideas would be received. He felt that they might well supersede the established Italian tradition, and this disturbed his peace of mind, for he aimed at an international reputation.

Perrin wrote a long letter to the Archbishop of Turin, in which he explained that, while he had a great admiration for Italian music, he felt that the style was not altogether expressive of French ideas, and, although his own style differed in many respects from the Italian, this did not mean that he found the foreign ideal wanting in any respect. The letter is irrelevant in many places, but a résumé is necessary in view of the then almost revolutionary idea it was expressing. Perrin took his own *Pastorale* as his model and put forward ten salient points:[1]

I.   Dramatic music had become too redolent of plainchant and was not fully expressive, since the poets did not write their verses specially for music. He found the result ridiculous and uninteresting. All the scenes in *Pastorale* expressed human emotions at their highest intensity and the music underlined the spirit of the words to the last letter.

II.   In the past, music had been too simple. Expert and fully-trained singers would be required for *Pastorale*.

III.   The habit of writing fifteen hundred verses and thus lengthening the performance to six or seven hours was insupportable. Two hours was the limit of human endurance. *Pastorale* was planned to take one hour and a half.

IV.   Recitatives were too long. One voice declaiming fifty or sixty verses lacked variety, however beautiful that voice might be. In *Pastorale*, the recitatives and *dialogues* were no longer than a dozen verses each except in the last scene, where there were thirty-two, many of which were sung in chorus.

V.   There were too many solos, and too many set for one type of voice. In *Pastorale* it was so arranged that each voice sang not more than two recitatives and a single duo with one of its own type. With ritornelli, this effect was 'marvellous'; so great was the variety that the hour and a half occupied in performance would seem to the listener no more than a quarter of an hour.

VI.   The language (Italian) of the libretto was usually unknown to the audience and the work, therefore, was completely incomprehensible.

VII.   The verses were not clearly expressed, for their meaning was often obscured by metaphors; these gave the impression of being clever and 'literary' but, in reality, were meaningless.

---

[1] The letter bears the heading: '*Première comédie françoise en musique*, representée en France, Pastorale mise en musique par le sieur Cambert, representée au village d'Issy, près Paris, et au chasteau de Vincennes devant leurs Maiestez en avril 1659. 30 avril 1659'.

VIII. The theatres in general were so large that neither the words nor the music could be heard by more than half the audience. At Issy (where *Pastorale* was produced) the theatre held no more than three or four hundred people; everything was distinct and there was no need to issue printed copies of the libretto.

IX. All the human emotions, particularly that of love, had become grossly exaggerated, had passed the bounds of reason, and had become completely artificial.

X. The lyrical verses of *Pastorale* were more suitable for the medium than the old alexandrines, and were more suited to the French language.

In this way, Perrin drew a clear dividing line between the Italian and French ideals.

Pastorale had all the elements of the Ronsard *Eclogue* and made itself popular by its simplicity. There were no stage effects or complicated stage machinery to divert the attention from words and music. There were only seven characters – three Shepherds, three Shepherdesses and a Satyr. The work consisted of five very short acts, the music amounting to fourteen movements, scored for eleven strings and two flutes. It was performed in a room with a great many windows, the lighting thus being natural and the changes being regulated by the drawing of blinds and curtains. The stage was decorated with real flowers and shrubs from the garden of the château. The Marquis de la Haye saw to it that the news was spread around Paris, and so fashionable did the production become that the little village of Issy was crowded with the carriages of the nobility and persons of the court.

It was performed ten times at Issy (Appendix Twenty). In due course its success was reported to the King and the Cardinal, and a performance was ordered at Vincennes for May 1st, 1659.[1] Loret rhapsodised over it in his *Muze Historique* (Appendix Twenty-one). There is little doubt that it was the performance at Vincennes which made the King come to a final decision on the Pope's suggestion.

---

[1] Perrin waited for this confirmation of success before offering the work to the Archbishop.

Other noblemen followed suit and held festivals in their provinces. The most notable of these was that organised at the Château de Neubourg in Normandy, owned by the Marquis de Sourdéac, who was later to become Perrin's evil genius. This consisted of a melodrama specially commissioned from Pierre Corneille, originally called *Les Amours de Medée* but later altered to *La Toison d'Or*. The actors were the 'Comédiens du Marais', who were enjoying an uneasy career at the Hôtel de Bourgogne in Paris. The production was in the hands of the Marquis himself who had a considerable talent for stage machinery, his ideas rivalling those of Torelli and Vigarini.

The composer of *La Toison d'Or*[1] is not known, and from the absence of any mention of it in the contemporary records, the music would appear to have played an unobtrusive and secondary part in the proceedings. The production is important for itself, and also for the fact that the word 'opera' was used in connection with it, for the first time, by French writers. In 1674, Chappizeau published his *Théâtre français* in which he wrote, of *La Toison d'Or:* 'Tout Paris luy a donné ses admirations, et ce grand opera qui n'est deu qu'à l'esprit et à la magnificence du seigneur dont j'ay parlé (*i.e.* de Sourdéac) a servi de modèle pour d'autres qui ont suivy'. Voltaire, in his *Commentaires* (*sur Corneille*), wrote with similar enthusiasm (Appendix Twenty-two).

La Toison d'Or influenced the King still further in his idea of establishing a true French Opera, but in the meantime, Perrin and Cambert had completed *Ariane*. This was rehearsed, but not produced owing to the death of Mazarin. The rehearsals must have been held in public, for all the authorities proclaimed it as Cambert's masterpiece; the words were described by Triton du Tillet, in his *Parnasse françois*, as 'plus méchantes que celles de la première Pastorale'.

Mazarin's death left Perrin without a protector, and it was at this moment that Lully began to attract attention. Cambert, however, still had a few friends and supporters. In 1666, he was invited to compose the incidental music for a comedy by Guillaume de Marcoureau, sieur de Brecourt, called *Le Jaloux invisible*. Of

---

[1] Not to be confused with *La Toison d'Or*, Opera in three acts by J. G. Vogel, produced in Paris in 1786.

this, only one movement, a *Trio italien burlesque*, remains. For many years it was attributed to Lully, until a copy of the play itself was discovered, revealing Cambert as the composer.[1] The similarity of style is not, perhaps, very close, but, in default of any other theatre composer, it would be natural for the name of Lully to be associated with it.

Meanwhile, Perrin had been petitioning the King for a Privilège, and on June 28th, 1669 the necessary letters-patent granting the monopoly were at last issued. Perrin was authorised to form an 'Académie d'Opera',[2] with branches wherever he liked to establish them. This made him a virtual dictator and anyone wishing to produce a work of this nature would be forced to ask his permission and pay a heavy fee. The date '1669' can still be seen on the proscenium curtain of the Paris Opera (Appendix Twenty-Three).

From this moment, French Opera ceased to be merely an aristocratic form of entertainment.

In addition to vesting all rights in the syndicate under Perrin's name, the Privilège contained a clause stating that henceforth 'tous Gentils-hommes, Damoiselles, et autres personnes, puissant chanter ausdits opera, sans que pour ce ils dérogent au titre de Noblesse, n'a leurs Privilèges, Charges, Droits et Immunitez'. More important still, it ordained that nobody could claim any right of free entry, not even the members of the Court. This suspension of the customary free list naturally met with violent disapproval.

The regulations applied to any 'Académie d'Opera' in France, over a period of twelve years, and heavy penalties were instituted against those who broke any of them.

His Privilège obtained, Perrin set to work at once to form his company. Cambert was appointed Musical Director, de Sourdéac was put in charge of the stage machinery and décors, while a financier, Bersac de Champeron, undertook to raise the necessary funds. Beauchamp, the King's Maître de Ballet, was the obvious choice for a similar appointment at the new Académie, and a

---

[1] 'Trio italien burlesque, composé par le sieur Cambert, maistre de la musique de la feue Reyne Mère.'

[2] It was not until 1690 that the word 'Opera' came into general use, the original term having been imported from Italy. It was never written with the acute accent or with the plural 's'. Thus it was 'L'Opera' and 'Les Opera', not 'L'Opéra' or 'Les Opéras'. The French version of the word came even later.

singer, La Grille,[1] from the Comédie-Française, was sent in search of artists.

La Grille scoured the countryside of Languedoc, pressing into service the best voices that the district could offer, and thus impoverishing the choral resources of the Cathedrals.[2]

De Sourdéac, with every opportunity for experiment, was in his element. His resources were almost unlimited.

With this galaxy of talent and enthusiasm, therefore, the situation appeared to be most promising. The only thing lacking, in fact, was a theatre.

Guichard, the 'Intendant des bâtiments du Duc d'Orléans', was given the task of finding suitable quarters. A lease was taken of the Tennis Court in the Rue Mazarine, known as the 'Jeu de Paume de la Bouteille', a building with frontages on that street (No. 42) and the Rue de Seine (No. 43). Champeron found the money, and the lease was signed by de Sourdéac. The site was owned by Maximilian de Laffemas and the sum paid was two thousand four hundred livres, the lease being a very favourable one (Appendix Twenty-four).

The alterations took five months, the chief of these being the construction of the stage and of boxes for the audience. The former, for the period, was immense. It was found necessary to encroach about twenty-five feet on a timber yard in the Rue de Seine. The machinery was elaborate and provided ample scope for the Apotheoses that were by then traditional.

The first work to be performed was an *opera ou représentation en musique*, composed by Perrin and Cambert, entitled *Pomone*. This may, with justice, be considered the first genuine French Opera. The performance was given in March, 1671, under the aegis of the 'Académie d'Opera'; why it took the place of *Ariane*, which was in an advanced stage of preparation, remains a mystery. The rehearsals for *Pomone* were held in some part of what is now the Bibliothèque Nationale, the exact room being doubtful. It may very well have been the present Reading Room.

---

[1] Henri Prunières says that it was Pierre Monnier, the singer. *La Revue Musicale*, January 1925 (Page 10).

[2] Charles II of England sent Captain Cooke round England on a similar errand with similar powers of impress when he revived the Chapels Royal.

The original title-page of *Pomone* reads as follows:

POMONE, opera ou représentation en musique, Pastorale, composée par Monsieur Perrin, conseiller du roy en ses conseils, introducteur des ambassadeurs près feu Monseigneur le duc d'Orléans, mise en musique par Mr (*sic*) Cambert, intendant de la musique de la feue reyne, et representée par l'Académie royale (*sic*) des Opera. A Paris, de l'imprimérie de Robert Ballard, seul imprimeur du roy pour la musique, rue S. Jean de Bauvais, au Mont Parnasse. 1671.

Avec Privilège de Sa Majesté (In-r)

The cast was a large one. It is quoted exactly as printed in the original copy.

MUSICIENS

Personnages Véritables

POMONE, déesse des fruicts

FLORE, soeur de Pomone, déesse des fleurs

VERTUNE, dieu des lares ou follets, amoureux de Pomone

FAUNE ou FAT, dieu des villageois, amoureux de Pomone

LE DIEU DES JARDINS, amoureux de Pomone

JUTURNE, VENILIE, nymphes de Pomone

BEROE, nourrisse de Pomone

Choeur des Jardiniers

Personnages feints et transformez

Vertune transformé
- En Bergère de Lampsac, ville de Grêce, ou naquit le dieu des Jardins
- En Pluton, dieu des tresors
- En Bacchus
- En Beroe

Follets transformez
- En Bergeres de Lampsac
- En Satyres
- En Amours, Muses et Dieux

DANSEURS
Personnages Véritables

Bouviers
Cueilleurs de fruicts   Follets transformez { En Fantômes
                                                    En Démons
                                                    En Esclaves

Personnages Muets

Troupe de Follets
Vertune transformé   En Dragon
                       { En Buisson d'epines
Follets transformez   { En Buisson d'epines
                       { En jouers d'instrumens

La scene est en Albanie, au pays Latin, dans la maison de Pomone.

There were five acts and a prologue, the book describing the 'decorations ou changemens de théâtre' like this:

La veue de Paris à l'endroit du Louvre (Prologue)
Vergers de Pomone   (1er Acte)
Parc de Chesnes   (2ème Acte)
Palais de Pluton   (3ème Acte)
Jardin et berceau de Pomone   (4ème Acte)
Palais de Vertune   (5ème Acte)

The Prologue (Appendix Twenty-five) was nothing more than a panegyric upon Louis XIV, although it was shared in this case with his City of Paris. The Dedication was equally fulsome (Appendix Twenty-Six). This operatic eulogy was in accordance with the traditions of *Circé* and the *Fêtes* and *Ballets de Cour.*[1]

---

[1] Some authorities have credited Quinault with being the first to write a theatrical eulogy of this type, but one appeared in 1650, in Pierre Corneille's *Andromède*, a work which approached the style of the later opera. A few lines from this prologue will show that under such circumstances even a great dramatist can falter:

> Cieux, écoutez; écoutez mes vers profondes; et vous autres, et bois,
> Affreux déserts, rocherz, battus des ondes,
> Redites après nous d'une commune voix:
> 'LOUIS est le plus jeune et le plus grand des rois.'

Corneille was a greater poet and dramatist than Perrin, but the latter's eulogy in *Pomone* was the superior effusion. This may be ascribed to the fact that while Corneille was trying to descend, Perrin was writing upon his own level.

Perrin's irregular metres caused some sensation, as no French composer had ever been faced with such a problem before. This was duly noted by Père Ménestrier when, in 1682, he wrote in his *Des représentations en musique anciennes et modernes :*[1]

'Les vers libres de mésures inegals, qui s'étoient depuis peu introduits en France pour les lettres enjouées, ne contribuerent pas peu à faire réussir des actions (*les actions en musiques*, autrement dit les operas) par la liberté que l'on eut les seuls qu'on récitoit sur nos théâtres. On connut que ces petits vers etoient plus propres pour la musique que les autres, parce qu'ils sont plus coupé et qu'ils ont le plus de rapport aux *versi sciolti* des Italiens qui servent à ces actions.'

Here is a specimen from an *Ariette* in which Le Dieu des Jardins avows his love for Pomone:

Soulange donc les flammes
Du grand Dieu des Jardins;

De plaisirs eternels il scait replir les âmes
Rénonce pour jamais à l'amour des blondins,
Foibles, trompeurs, inconstans et badins,
Unissons, unissons nos coeurs et nos empires:

Adjouste aux fruits de tes vergers
Les jerbes de mes potagers:
Joins mes melôns à tes poncires,
Et nesle parmy tes pignons
Mes truffes et mes champignons.[2]

Very little of the music has survived. What has done so is contained in forty printed pages bound in with a number of blanks; the original manuscript has disappeared save for two fragments, which are continuous. Cambert does not appear to

---

[1] Paris, René Guignard, 1681, pages 195 *et seq.*
[2] Much may be forgiven Perrin, however, for these lines on the castrati:
Vive à l'entrée de petites filles du ballet,
Rien n'est si mignon, rien n'est si follet,
Non pas ces grands concerts de ses veilles Laures de Signores
Et ces NON SUNT qui chantent leur LIBERA
Pour la memoire de leurs ET CAETERA.

have been altogether happy with Perrin's irregular metres. His melodic vein, although stiff and formal, is extremely chaste,

but the slight attempt at florid writing is not very convincing.

The pastoral flirtations of Pomone and Vertune are interspersed with burlesques and ballets which have little bearing on the story, but serve to enliven proceedings that are otherwise placid and commonplace. The existing musical movements are set out as follows:

> *Prologue*   Première ouverture
>> Scene dialoguée entre Vertumne (*sic*) et la Nymphe de la Seine
>
> *Premier Acte.*   Seconde ouverture
>> Introduction chantée par Pomone, Juturne, et Venilie
>> Air de Pomone
>> Duo de Venilie et de Juturne
>> Réprise de l'air
>> Trio (Flore, Pomone et Berce)
>> Air du Dieu des Jardins
>> Duo (le Dieu des Jardins, un Faune)
>> Récit de Flore.
>> Trio (les Trois Jardiniers)

(All these movements following the Prologue are sung straight through without a break.)

Symphony pour l'entrée des Bouviers
Morceau d'ensemble (le Dieu des Jardins, Faune,
　Pomone, Flore, Venilie, Juturne)
Petit récit (le Faune)
Symphonie pour la seconde entrée des Bouviers
Petit Air du Dieu des Jardins
Second Trio des Trois Jardiniers

Second Acte. Entr'acte

Air de Beroë
Air de Vertumne
Duo de Vertumne et de Beroë.

There are only two very short recitatives.

Some idea of the producer's achievements may be gleaned from these stage directions, again quoted from the original printed copy:

Second Acte – (Une Forèt de chènes)

Le ciel brille d'éclairs, le tonnerre gronde, et douze follets transformés en fantômes tombent du ciel dans un nuage enflammé. Le follets descendus de la machine environnent Beroë, et, pour l'epouvanter, dansent à ses yeux une danse terrible. Trois fantômes disparaissent, quatre autres saisissent Beroë, l'emportent en l'air, et cinq autres restent sur le théatre.

Troisième Acte – (Une scène burlesque)

Les follets placent Faune sur un gazon et mettant autour de luy trois flaçons et trois bouteilles. Lorsqu'il vient prendre une bouteille, elle s'enfuit et traverse le théatre. Il s'attaque à la séconde qui fait de même. Il veut saisir la troisième, elle s'élève en l'air ou un follet la vient prendre. Il croit s'emparer de la quatrième, elle fond en terre et la cinquième après elle; il prend la sixième et boit à même; il trouve que c'est de l'eau et crache.

Dernier Acte – (Les noces de Vertumne et de Pomone dans un palais merveilleux)

Dix-huits follets transformés paraissent en différentes
nues brillantes, six au fond du théâtre dans une grande nue,
six sur le gauche, sous les formes de Dieux, de Muses et
d'Amours, partie chantans, partie jouans des instrumens;
à la fin, les six petites nues se retirent et la grande vole au
fond du théâtre sur le centre.

French opera cannot be said to have been inaugurated silently
or uneventfully. The King had authorised the syndicate to charge
admission to everybody. Until then it had been the custom for
the court to pay nothing, the seats in all theatres being allocated
to the courtiers in order of seniority, while lackeys forced their
way in through sheer strength or weight of numbers. The new
situation was neither fully realised nor appreciated. Hordes of
people filled the vestibule, all objecting strongly to the imposition.
The public, admitted by right of purchase, was determined not
to be frustrated by the privileged aristocracy or by their servants.
The soldiers on duty were badly mauled; stones and brickbats
flew in all directions. The police were sorely bothered by the situation, and issued an ordinance which sought to deal with possible
repetitions (Appendix Twenty-Seven).

The receipts amounted to 120,000 livres.

The King did not attend a single performance. This may
seem remarkable, seeing that the production heralded the first
fruits of the Privilège, but the reasons are not difficult to find.
In the first place, Louis came rarely to Paris. In the second,
scenes like the one related above occurred every night and it
would have been derogatory to the royal dignity to expose it to
any unseemly behaviour. Further than this, the obsequious Lully
was at the King's ear. He was about to fulfil his ambitions and
had decided to do so with complete ruthlessness, regardless of
truth, open-handedness, or sincerity. He was unable to prevent
the granting of the Privilège to Perrin, but was happy to allow the
syndicate to do the spade-work while he formed some assessment
of the future. Being a courtier, he was able to criticise, silently
and in high places, with the shrug of the shoulders that is far more
devastating than any words. That he visited the 'Jeu de Paume de
la Bouteille' or, as it was now called, 'Le Théâtre de l'Académie',

cannot be doubted, and he must have duly noted the scenes of confusion which took place there.

Perrin would have been unmoved by any criticism from Lully. He was, indeed, impervious to any adverse comment. He printed a lengthy reply to his critics – in the published edition of his libretto – which indicates a light-hearted attitude towards his detractors. The salient points of his reply were that, whatever others might say, he would remain silent and apply himself to the creation of new works. He also made it clear that, if anyone else had an opera ready for performance, it could be submitted and the score studied by a panel.[1] He promised that it would be reported on in all honesty (Appendix Twenty-Eight).

History does not relate whether this invitation was ever accepted.

Quarrels soon broke out among the members of the syndicate. They were fomented by de Sourdéac, who cast a suspicious eye upon the account books and accused Perrin of taking more than his share of the receipts. When this was disproved, de Sourdéac put in a claim for repayment of the money he had advanced to Perrin at the outset of the venture. Perrin was unable to find the sum demanded and de Sourdéac had him flung into prison.

For Perrin, this was nothing new. His landlord had had him incarcerated on more than one occasion and he was, in fact, in prison when *Pomone* was produced. All the business was transacted in his debtor's cell, as nothing could be done without his signature.

De Sourdéac looked elsewhere for the writer of the next production and found him in a Protestant poet, Gabriel Gilbert. Born in Paris in 1610, he had made a reputation with the plays *Marguerite de France*, *Téléphonte* and some others, and had enjoyed the protection of Richelieu, Mazarin and Fouquet. He had one blot upon his creative escutcheon, however, although this does not appear to have done him any harm. When Corneille finished his play, *Rodegune*, his attention was drawn to another of the same name by Gilbert, then on the point of production. To his astonishment, he found that Gilbert's play contained situations identical with those in his own. It seemed that somebody in Corneille's confidence had passed his text on to Gilbert; but, in his haste,

---

[1] This is the first recorded instance of a 'reading panel' and also the first of an open invitation to composers to 'submit works' for possible performance.

Gilbert had confused certain issues. He gave, for instance, Corneille's dialogue for Rodegune to Cléopâtre, and the other way round, the result being that each spoke in the gender of the other.

The versifying Loret wrote, in the *Gazette*:

> De la plume immortelle
> De l'excellent monsieur Gilbert,
> Rare écrivain, auteur expert,
> Qu'on prise en toute compagnie,
> Et qui, par son noble génie,
> Poly, sçavant, intelligent,
> De Christine est la digne agent.

No doubt de Sourdéac thought that a poet of this kind would attract the Parisians. He therefore commissioned Gilbert to write the libretto of *Les Peines et les Plaisirs de l'Amour*, which Gilbert dedicated to Colbert, who, since the death of Mazarin, had had the close ear of the King (Appendix Twenty-Nine).

Les Peines et les Plaisirs de l'Amour was even more complex than *Pomone*, although the story was equally simple. The cast was very much bigger. The principal characters below are indicated by asterisks.

> *Apollon, amant de Climène
> *Climène, nymphe de Diane
> *Pan, amant d'Astérie
> *Astérie, nymphe, rivale de Climène
> Philis, bergère, confidente d'Astérie
> Vénus
> L'Amour
> La Renommée
> Deux petits Amours
> Mercure
> Trois Graces
> Trois Muses
> Iris
> L'Aurore
> Les Songes
> Faune et les Satyres

Six Sacrificateurs
Six Prêtresses
Spectres

Choeurs de Bergers et Bergères – Les Rois – Les Jeux – La Jeunesse.

The story tells of the love of Apollo and Climène, a nymph of Diana, who has been sacrificed to the God of Day. Apollo gives vent to his grief on her tomb, while Astérie, the cause of Climène's death, tries in vain to attract him to herself. After many episodes and subsidiary intrigues between the other characters, Climène is restored to life.

Gilbert was a superior poet to Perrin, although he did not pretend to write 'paroles de musique'. He used Perrin's irregular metres, which Cambert was now able to master. When it came to writing the panegyrical Prologue (Appendix Thirty), however, he did it no better than Corneille.

The work added to the glory of Cambert.

In his *Lettre sur les operas*[1] (addressed to the Duke of Buckingham), Saint-Evremond, the musical chronicler of the period, noted that:

> Cambert a sans doute un fort beau génie, propre à cent musiques différentes, et tout bien ménagées avec une juste économie des voix et des instrumens. Il n'y a point de récitatif mieux entendu, ni mieux varié que le sien; mais pour la nature des passions, pour la qualité des sentimens qu'il fait exprimer, il doit reçevoir des auteurs les lumières que Lulli leur fait donner, et s'assujettir à la direction, quand Lulli, par l'entendue de sa connoissance, peut être justement leur directeur.

Crowds filled the theatre, but still the King stayed away. The fact was that two rivals had appeared on the horizon: Henri Guichard, a writer, and Jean de Granouilhet, sieur de Sablières, 'intendant de la musique de Monsieur le duc d'Orléans'. These two produced a *Pastorale*, called *Les Amours de Diane et d'Endymion*, which was produced at Versailles in the presence of the King,

---

[1] *Oeuvres*, London 1711.

I

who was so pleased with it that he ordered another work from them, with a proposed production at Saint-Germain in 1672. What this was, whether it was ever performed, or whether it was even written, is not known. Guichard and de Sablières promised to be rivals not only of the Syndicate, but also of Lully. They took over a measure of control at the Jeu de Paume de la Bouteille and the situation became increasingly involved. Although Perrin had already sold his share of the business to de Sourdéac, he agreed to join Guichard and de Sablières. The Syndicate, therefore, was split into two factions, that of Cambert, de Sourdéac and Champeron, and that of Perrin, Guichard and de Sablières. Lully had to act quickly.

He persuaded the King to dismiss all the foreigners in the court bands and to replace them with Frenchmen. This proved his 'national spirit'. He then took care that the worst accounts reached Madame de Montespan, knowing that she, a tittle-tattler, would pass the information on to the King. His next step was to visit Perrin in his debtor's cell and persuade him to sell the whole Privilège, pointing out that only by doing so could he hope to have enough money to pay his debts.

Perrin was utterly tired of the instability of the Académie. He willingly agreed to Lully's proposition, without consulting anybody. No doubt he felt himself able to do what he liked with the Privilège, as it had been accorded in his name alone. He might have sold his share to de Sourdéac; he might have joined de Sabliéres with or without payment; but, incredible as it must seem, *neither had asked for the document in question.* While selling portions of it to all comers, as it were, Perrin still had written legal claim to the highest position on the board!

Lully, therefore, was able to purchase the whole monopoly and claim the actual document. The transaction reached the ears of the King, by way of Madame de Montespan; he, in high dudgeon, annulled the contract and transferred the Letters-Patent to Lully, with immediate effect. Colbert notified the police accordingly (Appendix Thirty-One). In order to distinguish between the new enterprise and the old, the King gave Lully and his heirs permission and authority to establish an 'Académie royale de Musique' (Appendix Thirty-Two).

The Syndicate, however, refused to stop production and the King ordered the police to close the theatre by force (Appendix Thirty-Three). De Sourdéac, to no avail, appealed to the Parlement de Paris on May 30th, 1672 (Appendix Thirty-Four). Guichard tried to undermine Lully's authority by scurrilous pamphlets (Appendix Thirty-Five), which Lully answered in kind.[1] Each accused the other of using poison, Lully maintaining that Guichard had introduced arsenic into his tobacco. The King's patience became exhausted. He gave Guichard a Privilège to found an 'Académie royale des Spectacles' (Appendix Thirty-Six). This enterprise failed and its founder departed for Spain where he tried, without success, to form an 'Académie des Opera'. Lully's replies to Guichard were condemned to be burnt by the common hangman which, as it was only a token punishment, disturbed Lully not at all. de Sourdéac died in 1695; nothing is known of the fate of de Sablières.

Cambert fled to England, where he lived until his death in 1677; of his life there is very little known (Appendix Thirty-Seven). There was a rumour that Lully had arranged for him to be murdered, but this seems unlikely. Cambert had been simply Director of Music and could do nothing to harm the Florentine-become-Frenchman.

Perrin died in 1675, leaving behind him a load of further debts to his landlord. His earthly possessions consisted of four unset opera libretti, which had to be forced from his stiffened fingers. The landlord petitioned the King for repayment of the debts from the funds of the new Académie, claiming that Lully, as Perrin's successor, was responsible for their redemption; but the appeal was refused (Appendix Thirty-Eight). The funeral register of Saint-Germain l'Auxerrois contains the following entry:

'Le vendredi 26 avril 1675 fut enhumé Pierre Perrin cydevant introducteur des ambassadeurs et princes étrangers de feu Monseigneur le duc d'Orléans, aagé de 55 prix rue de la Monnoye.'

---

[1] *Requeste d'inscription de faux (1676) – Requeste servant de factum* (n.d.) – *Suite de la Requeste* (n.d.) – *Reponse de sieur Guichard aux libelles deffamatoires de J. B. Lully et de Sebastion Aubry* (n.d.).

The Académie which he had formed, failure though it may have been, was not mentioned, although the credit for the initial enterprise rests with him. The theatre, of course, was anathema to the Church.

Order came out of the chaos which had been engendered by the failure of perfectly good intentions. The result was the magnificent and dignified Académie royale de Musique, directed by the only capable musician in France at the time, Jean Baptiste Lully, Musician and Businessman.

Pomone was undoubtedly the first genuine French opera, but it was a poor thing in comparison with what was to follow.

One aspect of this matter, however, reflects little credit on Lully, although he acted within his rights. The idea for a monopoly in stage musical productions came from Molière, who had confided his plan to Lully when he was his collaborator. Lully, in any case, had decided to break with Molière in order to make his own position supreme, and, without destroying Molière's enterprise entirely, he dug into his productions in such a way that any music other than Lully's own became almost an impossibility. His power under the monopoly was such that he could limit the music to two singers and two string instruments, and although the strings were increased to six, it made little difference. If Molière, or anyone else, wished to produce a work by some other composer, he had to pay Lully such a heavy indemnity that the project became impossible. The *Comédiens*[1] resorted to all kinds of expedients and tricks to overcome this difficulty, and these considerably enhanced the fun; but, even at their best, they were only makeshifts.

Lully, however, was unable to break the power of the *Confrérie de Saint-Julien-des-Ménetriers*. They, by virtue of a charter issued in 1407, still exercised a troublesome authority, even intruding into the court. One of their complaints was that foreign musicians were employed there. The 'King' of the *Confrérie* claimed that he had the right to choose the musicians himself. Lully silenced him on the first point by persuading the King to dismiss the foreigners and employ only Frenchmen; but the 'King' insisted on his right to engage and dismiss anybody in Lully's employ, and thus in

---

[1] All actors were known by this description.

that of the Court. Lully's work was, consequently, continually interfered with by the Guild, the earliest form of Musicians' Union.

Lully, otherwise complete master of the situation, now had two immediate problems to solve.

The first was to find suitable premises, as the 'Salle de Jeu de Paume de la Bouteille' was inadequate for his schemes. He also wished to sever all connection with the old régime, in order that no memory of it should remain in the mind of the public. He therefore rented the 'Jeu de Paume de Bel Air' in the Rue de Vaugirard, near the Palais de Luxembourg, stripping the old theatre of its stage machinery and everything else that he thought would be useful. The remainder he destroyed.

On September 15th, 1672, the Académie royale de Musique opened its newly prepared doors with a performance of *Les Fêtes de l'Amour et de Bacchus*, a *Pastorale* in three Acts with Prologue, the words by Molière, Benserade and Quinault, the music from scores composed by Lully for Molière's *Comédie-Ballets*. The rehearsals took place in the Salle des Tuileries.

The second problem was to find a librettist in succession to Molière, one who would understand exactly what Lully required and who would be prepared to re-write whole scenes, and even acts, until the composer was completely satisfied. Now, more than ever, did Lully submit his schemes to the King, who, being a man of taste and judgment, made constructive suggestions and gave sound advice. The choice fell upon Philippe Quinault (1635 – 1688) and, for once in his life, Lully showed a sense of loyalty, if only for his own convenience. In spite of the constant opposition to Quinault, Lully stood faithfully by him.

The first work of the new collaboration was the opera *Cadmus et Hermione*,[1] a *Tragédie-Lyrique en 5 actes et un Prologue*. This was produced on February 11th, 1673, under conditions of extreme anxiety.

The theatre had been prepared in a hurry and was already showing signs of wear. The plaster ornaments were beginning to crumble, the timbers to warp, the floor to sag. Lully took the risk and defied fate. To have closed the theatre during the run of

---

[1] *Belle Hermione* – Decca LX 3112.

Cadmus, which was filling the house at every performance, would have spelt ruin for him and would have destroyed his prestige with the King. Those who realised the dangers, and who were among those who hated Lully, openly expressed the hope that the building would collapse; but Lully trusted to luck throughout his life and it never failed him. There could be only one alternative, and a generous fate at once supplied it.

On February 17th, 1673, Molière, playing in *Le Malade Imaginaire*, had a stroke and died. Lully wasted no time. He persuaded the King that the Salle du Palais-Royal was the only theatre capable of accommodating the Académie, and moved in at once.[1] Molière's company was given the old Jeu de Paume de la Bouteille, for what it was worth; it at least had a stage and it had a roof if nothing else. This humble, if not derelict, building housed, therefore, not only the original 'Paris Opéra' but also the original 'Comédie Française'.

---

[1] 'Permission accordée au dit sieur de Lully de représenter ses ouvrages de musique dans la Salle du Palais Royal, du avril 1673.' (*Manuscript Anonyme* – Bibliothèque de l'Opéra C – 954).

CHAPTER SEVEN

THE ACADÉMIE ROYALE DE MUSIQUE was now housed in premises worthy of its name and dignity. From this moment until his death in 1687, Lully composed an opera each year, Quinault being the librettist of eleven of them. Lully had nothing to worry about. His monopoly gave him control over all the theatres in France; nothing could be performed without his consent, and he extorted a high fee for this privilege. Competition, therefore, was non-existent. Nevertheless, he did not dare to take anything for granted, for his success had increased the violence of the cabal against him. He made a point of consulting Madame de Montespan, as well as the King, on every project he had in mind, and went so far as to arrange for a performance in private of some of the movements from his second opera, *Alceste*.[1]

The King announced that he would attend the first performance in Paris, should he happen to be in the city at the time. In the meanwhile, he ordered the work to be produced in advance at Versailles on January 2nd, 1674. This performance took place in front of the château, the Cour de Marbre forming a fine, dignified setting. The stage was lighted by candles, and fireworks were let off indiscriminately all the evening. A print by Le Pautre

---

[1] *Air de Caron*, Decca LX 3112; *Les Vents*, Columbia 33cx 1277.

shows the orchestra divided into two groups, one on each side of the proscenium, to give the Royal Family an uninterrupted view. The courtiers sat at right angles to the stage and could have seen very little. A row of flunkeys stood along a dais behind the King and had the best view of anyone outside the royal circle. To enhance the lighting, the windows of the old Hunting Box, which formed the centre building of the château, and those of the flanking apartments were brilliantly illuminated.

The arrangements were far from perfect but, as this was the first venture, Lully did not argue, knowing that the difficulties and discomforts had only to be experienced to be eradicated in the future.

On January 8th, Madame de Sévigné wrote: 'On joue jeudi l'opera qui est un prodige de beauté, il y a dejâ des endroits de la musique qui ont merité des larmes; je ne suis pas seule à ne les pouvoir contenir, l'âme de Mdme de Lafayette en est alarmé.'

There were not many tears after the first performance in Paris, on January 19th. *Alceste* was coldly received, for the cabal had doubtless been active. Ten days later, Madame de Sévigné wrote: 'On va fort à l'opera nouveau on trouve pourtant que l'autre était plus agréable, Baptiste croyait l'avoir surpassé; le plus juste s'abuse. Ceux qui ayment la symphonie y trouvent des charmes nouveaux . . .' The supporters of the old régime were openly insulting:

> Dieux! le bel Opera! rien n'est plus pitoyable
> Cerbère y vient japer d'un aboy lamentable
> O quelle musique de chien!
> Chacun demon d'une joye effroyable
> Y fait aussi le musicien.

Lully's friends blamed Quinault for the failure. At a supper party they mockingly presented their swords at Lully's breast, calling out 'Renounce Quinault or die!' Lully, however, remained loyal, and after some considerable persuasion, he agreed to consider another project. Unwillingly enough, he read through a libretto, *Daphné*, by La Fontaine. He did not like it, but did not altogether refuse it, and he asked the author to re-write most of it and make it almost a new work. Lully was cunning. He knew that La Fontaine would not agree to do this, but he saved himself from having to give a definite refusal. La Fontaine took immediate offence and published a scurrilous satire upon Lully in revenge (Appendix Thirty-nine).

Lully was next offered the libretti taken from the hand of the dead Perrin. Needless to say, he refused them. There was only Quinault left, and the situation, therefore, was exactly as Lully desired it should be.

The collaboration continued with *Thésée* (1675), whose reception allayed the pain caused by that given to *Alceste*. *Atys*, produced the following year, completely restored Lully's prestige. Of this, Madame de Sévigné wrote: 'Il y a des endroits d'une extrème beauté; il y a un sommeil et des songes dont l'invention surprends. La Symphonie est toute de basses et de tons du assoupissants qu'on admire Baptiste sur de nouveaux frais.' The King ordered the work to be played as often as possible.

This success, however, did not last. In 1677, Lully received another check with *Isis*, which was pronounced to be too cold and calculating. The instrumental movements impressed the audience, but they were not moved emotionally as they were by the love *Complaintes* in *Atys*. The *Mercure* remarked that, given the resources available to Lully, anyone should be able to score a success.

Lully passed through a difficult time. Madame de Montespan recognised herself in the character of Junon, and Quinault was disgraced. Lully had to find another librettist. To add to his troubles, his secretary, Lalouette, announced that he, and not Lully, had composed the best Airs in *Isis*. Lully disproved this at once, in spite of his method of working,[1] but the worry made him ill. During his convalescence he tried to work at La Fontaine's libretto, *Narcisse*, and made little progress with it.

Fortune, however, returned at last, and from the King himself. In 1674, Louis had offered to stand as Godfather to Lully's eldest son, but the ceremony of baptism had not yet taken place. This was rectified in 1677. Lully composed a *Te Deum* for the occasion which so impressed the King that he ordered it to be performed at the wedding of the duc d'Orléans' daughter. Ob-

---

[1] Pages 147 *et seq.*

serving this, Lully's opponents kept quiet, but he was under no illusion about their silence.

Although Quinault was in disgrace, he maintained his personal relationship with Lully. He suggested that Thomas Corneille's (1625 – 1709) libretto *Psyché*,[1] which the dramatist had made out of his original play in 1671, might be useful. Lully wrote the music in three weeks and the new opera was produced, on April 19th, 1678, amid scenes of the greatest enthusiasm. The King declared that he would never tire of the music.[2]

Bellérophon, to libretto by Thomas Corneille, Fontenelle, and (it is believed) Boileau, followed on June 28th, 1679. The next year saw Quinault restored to favour and the resumption of the old collaboration. The annual operas continued with *Proserpine* (Saint-Germain, February 2nd, 1680) and *Le Triomphe de l'Amour*,[3] which appeared on January 21st, 1681, and was repeated in Paris on the following May 6th.

The last of these forms a land-mark in the history of French Opera. For the first time, dancing became an integral part of the work instead of being added to it, the ballet in question being arranged by Benserade. Hitherto, dancing had been regarded as an *Intermède*, since it was not necessarily part of the actual story. The relative positions of the two genres were reconciled by the formation of a special *corps de ballet*. From this moment, the courtiers ceased to take part in the performances. Previously, they had been purged by Royal Decree of any slur cast on their dignity by a personal stage appearance, but their services could now be dispensed with altogether. An even more important innovation was the use of female dancers instead of disguised males. This did indeed make theatrical history.

Le Triomphe de l'Amour, therefore, was the first genuine and undeniable *Opéra-Ballet*, a style of composition which the French have never allowed to fall into abeyance, and which, in the hands of Rameau, was to become peculiarly their own.

---

[1] *Marche*, Columbia 33CX 1277.

[2] Indeed, such was Louis' admiration for it, that when the ramparts of Dunquerque were completed, he ordered a performance of some of the music, the strings being augmented by flutes, oboes, military trumpets, and seven hundred drums. To round off the occasion, a battery of eighty guns fired one single round, simultaneously, on the last beat of the music. The onlookers were 'filled with joy not unmixed with terror'.

[3] *Nocturne* – Columbia 33CX 1277.

In spite of his successes and triumphs, however, Lully was not altogether satisfied with his position. Alternately snubbed and greeted at court, he determined to silence opposition and, in so doing, to spread confusion among his enemies.

When *Le Bourgeois Gentilhomme*[1] was revived at Saint-Germain in 1682, Lully played the farcical part of the Mufti and sent both friends and enemies into paroxysms of laughter. After the performance, he asked the King to make him Chargé de Secrétaire, an appointment usually restricted to the nobility. He warned the King that there would be opposition, but the King sent him to interview the various officials connected with the appointment. One of these, Louvois, hated Lully, possibly because Lully was a friend of Colbert, and he said outright that he did not see why a mere mountebank should aspire to such high office. To this Lully replied that Louvois would be the first to make others laugh, were he capable of doing so.

The rest of the story is told by Lecerf de la Viéville.[2]

> Le jour de sa [*i.e.* Lully's] reception, il donna un magnifique répas, une vraye fête, aux anciens, et aux gens importans sa compagnie; le soir, un plât de son métier: L'Opera. Ils étaient vingtcinq ou trente qui y avoient ce jour-là, comme de raison, les bonnes places; de sorte qu'on voyait la chancellerie en Corps, deux ou trois rangs de gens graves, en manteau noir et en grand chapeau de castor, aux premiers rangs de l'amphitheatre, qui écoutoient d'un serieux admirable, les menuets et les gavotes de leur confrère le Musicien. Ils faisoient une décoration rare, et qui embellissoit le spectacle; et l'Opera a prit ainsi publiquement que son Seigneur, s'étant voulé donner un nouveau titre, n'en avoit pas eu le démenti. M. de Louvois même ne crut pas devoir garder sa mauvaise humeur. Suivi d'un gros de Courtisans, il rencontre bientôt Lulli [*sic*] à Versailles. 'Bonjour', lui dit-il en passant. 'Bonjour mon confrère'; ce qui s'apella alors un bon mot de Louvois.

The opera for 1682 was *Persée*, to libretto by Quinault. Lully

---

[1] Complete recording – Decca LXT 5211–3.
[2] *La Comparison de la musique italienne et de la musique français* (1704).

did not wait for the King to name the date but produced it on his own initiative in Paris on April 18th. The work turned out to be an elaborate panegyric upon the King's Majesty. The Prologue not only enumerated all the virtues, real and imaginary, possessed by Louis, but Quinault continued in the same strain throughout the opera. Allusions to the King's achievements and successes, such as the war in Holland, were even more frequent than usual. The King was shown in his Apotheosis next to Appolon, triumphing over the python. The glories of the old *Fêtes* and *Ballets de Cour* were revived, for there were flying machines and other stage accessories to stir the audience to transports of admiration.

This exaggerated piece of flattery was succeeded by *Phaéton* (Versailles, January 6th, 1683), which made history, in a small way, for at the Paris première it scored a complete success with the masses who, for the first time, sang and whistled operatic Airs in the streets. Lully was thus able to prove to the populace at large that, although his Académie was the foremost in the world, its productions were not necessarily for the chosen few. He placed the work at the feet of the King in a Dedication which followed a new direction.

On this occasion, the King had not insisted upon hearing the music either during its composition or at its final rehearsals. The performance at Versailles, therefore, was completely new to him. The most striking feature of the opera was the number of changes of set, and it was this constant variety, as well as the easy melodies, which gave the work its popular appeal. While *Atys* was nicknamed 'The King's Opera', and *Isis* 'The Musicians' Opera', *Phaeton* became known as 'The People's Opera'. It was the first generally popular work of its kind.

Amadis de Gaule[1] was produced in Paris on January 14th, 1684, but not until March 5th of the following year at Versailles, giving fresh evidence that the King no longer felt it necessary to bless any of Lully's operas in advance. It was followed by *Roland*, whose production at Versailles on January 8th, 1685, took place actually before that of *Amadis de Gaule* in the same Palace. This occasion was marked by a break in the tradition of 'King's Weather' and, owing to a sudden storm, the performance had to be trans-

---

[1] *Air d'Arcabonne* – Oiseau Lyre OL 50117.

ferred from the Cour de Marbre to the Riding School. The building was adapted to the requirements of a spectacular opera in three hours. This is the only recorded instance of the Sun refusing to cooperate with his earthly counterpart, but he made up for this indiscretion on the occasion of Lully's last Grand Ballet, *Le Temple de la Paix* (September 12th, 1685)[1] at Fontainebleau.

Armide[2] (Paris, February 15th, 1686) saw the end of the Quinault-Lully collaboration; it also gave Lully a few anxious moments, for the King did not attend the first performance. Lully, fearing that he had lost favour, wrote an unusually humble Dedication, saying that the work gave him no pleasure because of the absence of Regal Patronage (Appendix Forty). There was a real danger that the King, with his ever-increasing devotion and acts of piety, might be tempted to forswear the theatre and all its works. It would not do, however, to ascribe Lully's fears entirely to the possible removal of royal favour, since there is no doubt that there was as strong a personal friendship between the two men as can exist between Monarch and Subject.

If consolation were possible, Lully must have found it in the generous welcome accorded to *Armide* by the public, but such feelings were mitigated by the behaviour of Quinault. For some time the clergy had been working on him. They had sown the seeds of that hatred and distrust of the theatre which they themselves professed, seeing it only as a sink of iniquity and a sure means to eternal damnation. Quinault's conscience prevailed. He retired from the theatre and settled down to compose a long poem on – *The Extinction of Heresy*. He was succeeded by Campistron.

On September 6th, 1686, Lully took his entire Académie, singers, dancers and orchestra, to the Château d'Anet where *Acis et Galathée* was produced in the presence of the Dauphin. A good time appears to have been had by all, particularly by Lully. He was assigned a special maître d'hôtel and was given a separate table, at which he held court for all those anxious to take wine with the man whom the King delighted to honour.

Campistron proving himself a worthy successor to Quinault, Lully began the composition of *Achille et Polyxène*, but no sooner

---

[1] Eight Excerpts, Oiseau Lyre OL 50136.
[2] *Air d'Armide*, Oiseau Lyre OL 50117.

had the first Act been completed than the King became seriously ill. Lully composed a *Te Deum*[1] in anticipation of the royal recovery, and it was eventually performed, by a chorus and orchestra of one hundred and fifty, at the Feuillants de la Rue de Saint-Honoré. The performance was at Lully's own expense and he was well able to afford it. The occasion ended in tragedy. Lully struck his toe with the long wand he used to mark the time. Blood poisoning set in. He refused amputation and put himself in the hands of a quack whose ministrations hastened his end.

In spite of his situation, Lully kept his sense of humour. The priest who came to confess him persuaded him to destroy what he had composed of *Achille et Polyxène*. Let Lecerf de la Viéville continue from that point:

> Lully se porta mieux, on le crut hors de danger. Un de ces jeunes Princes, qui aimoient Lully et ses Ouvrages, vint le voir. 'Et quoi, Baptiste', lui dit-il, 'tu as jetter au feu ton Opera? Morbleu, étais-fou d'un croie un Janseniste qui revoit, et de bruler de belle Musique?' 'Paix, paix, Monseigneur', lui répondit Lully à l'oreille, 'je scavois bien ce que je faisois, j'en avoie une seconde Copie.' Par malheur cette plaisanterie facheuse fut suivie d'une réchute; il rétomba dans un état pire qu' auparavant, et la gangrène monte.

We take leave to doubt the final cause and effect, for Lully was too far diseased ever to have made a recovery. He died, in an odour of repentance and sanctity, on March 22nd, 1687. Lecerf de la Viéville, however, was not so sure about his sincerity:

> 'Les Italiens sont féconds et scavans en réfinemens de penitence, comme au reste, il eut les transports d'un pénitent de son pais. Il se fit mettre sur la cendre la corde au cou, il fit amende honorable; enfin marqua sa douleur de ses fautes, avec une édification qui doit vous rendre tranquillé. Retourné dans son lit, pour corroner tout cela par une morale qui demeurat après lui, embellie à sa manière, et pour gage de ses derniers sentiments, il fit cer air: il faut mourir, pécheurs, il faut mourir, ou plutot ces tons excelens sur vers, ce vers seul ne se pouvant pas appeler un air.'

---

[1] This was the second *Te Deum* composed by Lully, but only one is in existence.

The year of Lully's death saw the production, at Nantes, of the ill-fated Cambert's *Ariane*. The actual date is unknown. What induced Lully to sanction this performance, if it took place before his death, will never be known. He had been accused of poisoning Cambert, a most unlikely charge, and it is possible that he felt some *amende honorable* to be due. On the other hand, his heirs inherited the Privilège and had every right to allow the performance – on payment of ten thousand livres.

In any assessment of Lully, one point must always be remembered. He had very few precedents. That the French operatic style was, in reality, that of Lully himself, cannot be blamed upon him. He had sufficient acumen to see the differences between the Italian and French approaches and if the latter simply denigrated the former, it was only to be expected. Lully based his ideas upon what little French music was generally known, its salient features being easily recognisable. In particular, it had a characteristic clarity. It concentrated on one thing at a time, and all elaborate decoration was absent. The music came before the performer.

It is doubtful if Lully was in any way prompted by national feelings. He was a business man and the Académie was a business project. That it turned out to be the foundation of a culture probably did not strike him as an important possibility, and there is no record of his ever having shown any concern for the future of French art. His friendship with the King was a means to his own end; its reflection of the Royal Glory was something ancillary to his main purpose which, in today's homely language, was to make his music pay. He used the King much as Wagner used the King of Bavaria, the difference being that Lully's King never made himself a nuisance. He was imitated by other composers and impresarios, and many were held up to opprobrium accordingly, notably Meyerbeer; but nobody ever reproached Lully with having mercenary or commercial motives, although they were undoubtedly there. That he made a fortune out of his music cannot be laid down as a crime, for he amassed great wealth in a perfectly legitimate manner. Taking a modest sum for his own use, he always surrendered the balance to his wife's control. He was accused alternately of being a spendthrift and a miser.

He lived well and fared sumptuously, but never extravagantly, or to excess. When he entertained, he did so generously, but did not consider that a banquet was necessary every time a friend or person of rank came to dinner.

He never concealed the fact that he was a self-made man and proud of it. This was part of his nature, and he rose far above his natural station; he could not help showing his pride in the fact that he was on more intimate terms with the King than any of the courtiers. Indeed, Lully, d'Artagnan, Colbert, and Louise de la Vallière were the only genuine friends the King ever possessed. As Lully's authority increased, so he never ceased to revenge himself upon those who had despised him in his days of struggle, though he had struggled neither very hard nor very long. He was a good 'mixer'; it was only when brought into contact with arrogance that he showed either bad form or lack of taste.

He made enemies only when faced with enmity; then he hit hard. He never, however, played the *grand seigneur* in public.

The people of Paris never forgot the 'Baladin' who had amused them so much in his earlier days. Much may be overlooked in the character of one capable of making others laugh. He was not really democratic. He was probably a snob in so far as he went out of his way to make his official superiors look small. If he courted the People, he did so by means of his own legend and because it was with them that his income lay. The Académie might give 'Command Performances' at Versailles and elsewhere and the King might give personal favours and patronage; but there was no charge for these private court performances and it was the Salle du Palais-Royal which kept the organisation breathing and filled Lully's pockets – and none of his entourage ever complained of being underpaid. No record exists to show that any regular subsidy was paid and the whole affair was a gamble. It is interesting that, until as late as the twentieth century, the Director of the Paris Opera financed the whole thing from his private fortune, taking all profits as his normal dividend and being personally responsible for all losses.

Lully may have waited until Perrin found himself in chaos before acting. He may not have seen the possibilities in opera until they had been tested by others, but the fact remains that he made a success of it. No matter how much one admires his genius and honours him for his achievements, one can never make a hero of him: his faults were too patent, his ruthlessness too cruel to be justified other than by a natural dislike of bunglers. An unpleasant person, undoubtedly, but an amusing companion and a creative genius of the first order.

Lully's Académie royale de musique was not a theatre; it was a compact and mobile entity of singers, dancers, instrumentalists, scenic designers and painters, stage machinists, stage hands, librarians, box office attendants, and all the other elements which form the establishment of an opera house.

Lully was answerable to the King because he had the royal grace and favour and the Académie itself was 'royal'. In every other respect he was his own master. The Privilège granted him neither salary (this he received as Surintendent) nor subsidy; it simply allowed him the monopoly of putting opera forward without fear of rivalry, and authorised him to claim heavy indemnities in any cases of competition. Although the home of the Académie was the Salle du Palais Royal, the unit could be taken anywhere as a unit at short notice. It was always the King's prerogative to order a 'Command Performance', but it was a public and not a Court organisation. The audiences at the royal châteaux consisted entirely of the King and his Court. The audiences at the Salle du Palais Royal consisted of courtiers, musicians, savants, litterateurs, and the general public. All came under Lully's control the moment they entered the theatre, and the King himself was wise enough to let him have his own way at any Command Performance.

The Académie, let it be admitted, was primarily dedicated to the glory of Lully and only indirectly to that of the King. For this reason, Lully required the highest standard in everything. He insisted that, from the highest to the lowest, members took a personal pride in their appearance and behaviour outside as well as inside the theatre. It became an honour to be recognised as one of Lully's company (Appendix Forty-one).

As a producer, Lully was superb. He took infinite pains with his company, teaching them deportment and drilling them all in stage action. Bad acting was not compensated for by good

K

singing. The singers had to study their parts individually under Lully's father-in-law, Lambert, who taught them to sing clearly and expressively and to subordinate themselves to the music. They were encouraged to listen carefully to La Champmeslé of the Comédie Française, whose enunciation was so perfect that Lully founded all his recitatives upon it. He insisted upon the written notes and on no others; woe betide any singer who took liberties by interpolating a roulade, or inserting a rallentando not marked in the copy.

The productions were all splendid and the Académie was fortunate in having a scenic designer, Jean Berain, whose ideas coincided so exactly with what was in Lully's mind.

It was essential that the Académie should have a *panache* of its own. This was achieved by beating the Italians at their own game, even though it appeared that Lully was going directly in the opposite way. He knew the French temperament and its goût; he made sure, therefore, that the operas were less tedious, and less cluttered with irrelevancies, than the Italian examples hitherto heard in Paris.

He engaged the best artists he could find in Europe, dismissing them only when they became unmanageable. He treated them like dirt inside the theatre and like friends outside it, but he never lost his dignity and there was always a dividing line which no one attempted to cross. He was pleased to take a glass of wine with them collectively, although he sat at a separate table, and there was no air of condescension about him. He was generous where generosity was required, and he never allowed himself to be imposed on.

Choleric by nature, he would smash a violin over the head of a defaulting player and immediately give him more than enough money to buy a new instrument. Nobody left the theatre because of these outbursts, for Lully's sincerity and passionate devotion to his ideals were respected by everyone. Sincere he certainly was when it came to the composition and production of his works. Once he had laid his plans he let nothing stand in the way of their fulfilment. Many stories were circulated about his lack of human feeling, but these were exaggerated and based only on hearsay.

Lully's influence extended to his audiences. People found

that they had either to obey the regulations or stay away. He would allow no walking about either on the stage or on the *parterre* once the curtain had risen. He tried to abolish the seating on the stage and, by removing all the boxes, succeeded; but, in 1680, courtiers forced their way into the *coulisses* and sat down on chairs which they had carried there. Lully countered by charging exorbitant prices, and here he showed his judgement to be at fault, for the higher the price, the greater did the privilege of sitting on the stage become. The position had an atmosphere of its own and, for those who sat in it, the theatre lost its mysteries. It might have been expensive, but it meant avoiding the crowds. Those in the *coulisses* saw little and heard less, but they were associated with the performers.

The regular performances took place on Tuesdays, Fridays, and Sundays, and new works were first produced on Thursdays. As the repertoire was limited to Lully's operas, the habitués often heard the same work twenty or thirty times, since only two were played in any one week. Lully instituted the system of *abonnés*. They paid a fixed sum which entitled them to go as often as they liked and to sit wherever they wished.

Another such link with the past lies in the colour of the *affiches*, which today advertise the programmes of the subventioned theatres. The double-crowns to be seen all over Paris and other French cities are as yellow now as they were when Lully instituted them.

The original posters announced only the name of the work to be performed, the names of the artists not appearing until 1791. Copies of the libretti were on sale, a practice inherited from Mazarin. It is surprising that Lully, with his insistence on clear diction, should have supposed this necessary, but it brought revenue into the coffers of the Académie and into the pockets of the authors.

The music was not published until 1679, when Ballard brought out *Bellérophon*.[1]

Lully's alterations to the Salle du Palais Royal were extensive, but lack of ground space prevented their complete realisation.

---

[1] Lully had been given permission to print his works in 1673 – 'Permission au Sieur de Lully pour faire imprimer les airs de musique qui seront par lui faits, avec planches et figures, et se pendent trente ans, accordée à Versailles le 20 septembre 1673.' (*Manuscrit Anonyme* – Bib. de l'Opera c-954).

The ramp of the auditorium rose to the first floor boxes, of which there were three tiers. The third was conveniently arranged for social intercourse, and conversation could be carried on from box to box. Intrigue found a fruitful acreage here. The Amphitheatre was in almost total darkness, but the people could see and hear everything without distraction. There were no seats on the floor of the house – hence the ordinance against walking about during the performance. The audiences were naturally unruly, and it says much for Lully's personality that he was able to instil some kind of good behaviour into them.[1]

Within the theatre, all was bustle and confusion as the audience assembled, lemonade, orange, and programme sellers doing a brisk trade. Silence was imposed gradually, firstly, by the entry of the forty musicians (or fifty, as the work required), who proceeded to tune up, and, secondly, by the tap-tap-tap of Lully's wand as he gave them 'a bar in advance'.[2] There is no record of applause on Lully's entry and it was probably unnoticed. There was no difficulty about silence at this moment, for the audience had settled down to hear one of the most remarkable features of French musical life. This was the Pride of Paris, the Byword of Europe. People came to hear it and left, so it is said, as soon as they had done so (although we may, perhaps, doubt this) – the 'premier coup d'archet'.

Exactly how or why this became so famous has never been ascertained. Lully originated it as a matter of discipline. It was a simultaneous entry by all the instruments on a single octave or chord[3] and it became almost a fetish. Any work omitting it would have met with immediate disapproval. In the theatre it had the effect of attracting attention to the music, but, after it, nobody took the Overture at all seriously. The English idea of 'First' and 'Second Music' had not reached France. The 'premier coup

---

[1] *Amusements sérieux et comiques* (Du Fresnay), *Manuscrits de l'Arsenal* (Du Trélage), *Livre commode des addresses* (Abraham du Pradel), *Mercure galant*.

[2] Its equivalent today exists in the three traditional knocks on the stage which announce the rise of the curtain. The practice in Lully's time gave the musical director the title of 'Batteur de Mesure'.

[3] The 'principal first violin' in a French orchestra is still known officially as the 'chef d'attaque'. It is only in England that he is accorded a special round of applause on entry.

d'archet', however, set a standard for unanimity which may not have been surpassed elsewhere.

No matter what the subject of the opera may have been, there were always scenes of jealousy among the deities. Humans were invariably persecuted by the magic rites and philtres of Junon or Medée. Virtue triumphed in the last Act, when humanity had succeeded in combating the wiles of the magicians. Meanwhile, the deities and their attendants floated through the clouds and descended to earth in magnificent chariots, while demons sprang up through trapdoors and monsters gambolled round enchanted lakes.

These were not, as we know, original effects, for they merely continued a tradition established with *Circé*. The staircase by which Jupiter descended from Olympus on that occasion was so popular that it remained in use until the last opera of Rameau (*Les Paladins*, 1760), when the whole principle of mythological and magical French opera received its death blow.

The genius of the stage machinists was displayed to its fullest advantage and those who cared for neither lyric poetry nor dramatic music found compensation in the marvels which were unfolded before their eyes. The liaison between music, dancing, and production was perfect, the music fitting itself to the action like a glove to the hand. There were storms, tempests, battles and *Scènes de sommeil*, during which a magic rite was enacted round some sleeping figure. Lully's music brought tears to the eyes and sobs to the throats of the susceptible, while the storms and battles excited the audiences to such a degree that everyone held his breath and leaned forward, hardly able to bear the suspense.

All this is perfectly understandable. The onlookers were witnessing something entirely novel. It meant nothing to them that the machinery creaked and groaned, or that the ropes controlling it were plainly visible. The mere fact that the deities moved in air-borne chariots was sufficient. The Académie productions were something different from the vulgar, bawdy pantomimes at the Théâtre de la Foire, and, although disparaging remarks were made about the music – which was probably far above the head of the average member of the audience – there was never anything but praise for the stage business.

The subjects lent themselves to heavy décors and costumes 'au pompier'. Nevertheless, each work could be happily adapted to the various châteaux, where natural backgrounds provided settings as suitable as the ornate sets designed by Berain. It was only in the Salle du Palais Royal that the machinery could be used. It was too heavy and cumbersome for transport and naturally the chariots of the gods could not be suspended in thin air. It was similarly impossible to fit the floors of the Riding Schools with trapdoors. Much, therefore, must have been lost by performing outside the theatre, and it says much for Lully's adaptability that his operas were satisfactory when this happened. The machinery, however, cannot be written down as superfluous, because it added greatly to the spectacle and was a means of attracting the general public, but the suggestion is inescapable that Lully's music was more compelling than might have been expected.

Lully was a difficult taskmaster. Unlike Rameau, he was not content to set whatever he was given without question, for he had no place for irrelevancies. His librettists had to re-write their texts until he was completely satisfied, and this forms a striking parallel to Meyerbeer's treatment of the prolific Eugène Scribe. Quinault's libretti may follow a certain pattern, but that pattern was ideal for its purpose.

Everything had to be as near perfection as possible. Opera was Lully's business. It had to pay good dividends and these were carefully invested in property to make Lully one of the richest men of his time. As Parry[1] aptly puts it: 'His career serves as a striking exception to the theories generally held with regard to racial aptitudes for accumulating a fortune.' Without perfection there could have been no fortune.

The texture of all Lully's productions had a superb consistency. Each element was precisely complemented by each other one – and this is perhaps the most striking point about those productions. Certain gestures did become stereotyped, but only after the lapse of time. They were of Lully's own devising and were in constant use. He drilled and drilled his forces until he got what he wanted.

---

[1] *The Music of the XVIIth Century* (Volume 3, 1st Edition *Oxford History of Music*) Page 231.

The orchestra, in the pit, was very seldom prominent, and he insisted that even the most perfunctory passages should be played with care. Everyone was made to feel that he was an essential part of a machine; if he failed, the machinery would halt.

All actions and situations were approached in the same spirit, Lully's principle being 'Thorough'. It is here that his sincerity becomes obvious. It is true that he was enjoying facilities as a composer paralleled only by those accorded to Haydn. Both were expected to produce new compositions and both were responsible for their performance. It is often held that composers are indifferent performers and producers of their own music; this was not the case with Lully or Haydn, nor can it be said of Bach or Handel. Lully was not content to let things stand, and his formulation of the *Tragédie-Lyrique* was the natural corollary to what he had already accomplished.

CHAPTER EIGHT

THE BALLETS for which Lully composed the music consisted of spoken dialogue, songs, and dance movements. Some indication has already been given of their nature, and, from this small beginning, it is quite simple to see how the *Comédie-Ballet* came into being.

Comédie-Ballet may be described as a play with incidental music, often no more than a single dance movement or song, and purely accessory to the stage action. The term was somewhat elastic; Molière described only one of his plays, *Le Bourgeois Gentilhomme*, as such. *Psyché* he called a *Tragédie-Ballet* and *La Princesse d'Elide*, a *Comédie melée de danse et de musique*. *Melicerte* became a *Pastorale-Historique; Pastorale-Comique* explains itself. The last of these is interesting since, on its own, the text is meaningless. Nothing exists of the spoken dialogue and it is believed that the actors extemporised — surely one of the earliest instances of 'gagging'. From these various forms sprang the *Opéra-Ballet*, a perfect counterpart to the *Comédie-Ballet* in that singing took the place of spoken dialogue.

The musical moments were still intended to afford relief from the constant spoken dialogue, and were known as *Intermèdes*. They usually had nothing to do with the play itself other than to cast an allegorical reflection upon it. The dancers and singers were gods, goddesses, shepherds and shepherdesses, with gypsies ('Egyptiens' or 'Bohémiennes'), who were by now traditional, 'Suisses' and 'Pasteurs'. The dance sections were referred to as Entrées.

The vocal and choreographic interpolations formed complete entities in themselves and the conception was thus of two plays within a play. The *Intermèdes* in *Psyché*, for example, form a splendid opera libretto on their own.

Molière, elsewhere, wove the music into the story so that the two are indivisible. The standard example is *Le Bourgeois gentilhomme*, generally regarded as his masterpiece. Here it is impossible to separate the two elements and the work remains a model of its kind. It has always been popular because it deals with a subject which is real and not imaginary; snobbery is no new invention, and the wealthy *parvenu* is no twentieth century creation. This work must be considered in some detail since its importance cannot be over-estimated.

The first stage direction is: 'L'Overture se fait en grand assemblage d'instruments, et dans le milieu du Théâtre on voit un élève du Maître de Musique qui compose sur une table un air que le Bourgeois gentilhomme a demandé pour une sérénade.' The pupil writes a few bars, interrupts the work with an interjection, hums a phrase, strums it, and gradually builds up the whole song. Monsieur Jourdain is not impressed. He declares it to be 'un peu lugubre'; 'elle endort'. He knows a better one – 'il y a du mouton dédans' – and sings it clumsily and in an awful voice. In the original version of the play this was sung without accompaniment, but Lully added one later, and, in accordance with the custom, he made the 'cellos double the voice part.[1]

Comparison between the two songs will show how Lully differentiated between the serious and the amateur singer. The rhythm of the second song should be noted as it played an important role in Lully's melodic technique.

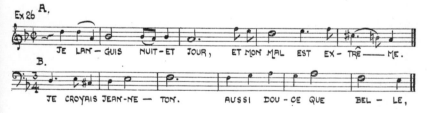

Ex 26 A.

JE LAN – GUIS NUIT-ET JOUR, ET MON MAL EST EX – TRÊ —— ME.

B.

JE CROYAIS JEAN-NE — TON. AUSSI DOU-CE QUE BEL — LE,

Two musicians, a man and a woman, sing a 'Dialogue an Musique', a real musical conversation piece, with introductory

---

[1] Henri Prunières states that the tune was composed by de Sablières, the words being by Perrin (*Lully* – Editions Laurens, p. 26). This may indeed have been the case, and Lully would have rejoiced to renew his scorn of de Sablières and Perrin. The subtle cynicism, if this were the case, would not have passed unnoticed at the time. The words, at least, are typical of Perrin's idea of poetry.

symphony and interludes. The two singers are joined by a third. At the conclusion, four dancers execute a ballet at the verbal direction of the Dancing Master in order that Monsieur Jourdain may learn the various steps. They open with a slow introduction;

then: 'Allons, messieurs, plus vite ceci!'

They break into a 'Gravement mouvement de Sarabande', but

after nine-bars-and-repeat, they relapse into the opening state of lethargy.

A Gaillarde follows 'La, entrez bien cette gailliarde', and the

Ballet concludes with an *Air de Canaries* 'Messieurs, dancez de l'accent à cet air de Canaries'.

The Dancing Master takes Monsieur Jourdain in hand and tells him that he would look superb in the Menuet. Here follows the tune by which Lully is familiar to-day, and what Menuet could be more charming? The Dancing Master demonstrates the steps, singing the tune to 'la' and interrupting it with directions. Monsieur Jourdain proves to be a very inept pupil – 'En cadence, s'il vous plaît'.

> 'La, La, La, La,
> La jambe froite.'

The second section, in binary form, is mainly instructional.

In Scene V there appear the 'Quatre Garçons Tailleurs', described as the 'Deuxième Entrée de Ballet'. They clothe Monsieur Jourdain in his new garments to music stately and dignified.

The act ends with the tailors 'se rejouissant en dansent, de la liberalité de M. Jourdain'.

The only music in Act III is the final entry of the 'cuiseniers, apportent les mets du festin, en dansent'. After the pompous introduction, the music becomes seductive and insinuating. It is in Simple Rondo Form ('en rondeau'), the episodes being solos.[1]

---

[1] Lully had already used this music in *L'Impromptu de Versailles*, set to the same words. As this had been very much an 'oeuvre de circonstance,' there could be no objection to his, or Molière's, using the material again if they considered it too good to be lost. This is the only repetition which I can find in Molière; it was, however, quite a habit of Lully's, who utilised a number of tunes from discarded Ballets for similar moments in his operas.

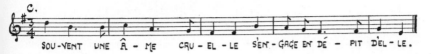

In Act IV, Scene I, there are two drinking songs for two and three voices.

In Scene III, Monsieur Jourdain is told that a mission from Turkey has called to see him. This idea originated with the visit to the French Court at Chambord of a real mission from the Sultan of Turkey. Their behaviour and mode of life so amused the King that he told Molière to introduce a Turkish episode into his play.[1] The suggestion came like manna to Molière, who was at some loss to continue the foolery upon which he had engaged. What could be more flattering to Monsieur Jourdain than the arrival of a Turkish envoy, sent over specially to decorate him with a high Turkish order?

The envoy is introduced in a dignified manner, his entourage being Monsieur Jourdain's own servants in disguise.

Ex. 38.

The ceremony is monotoned.

---

[1] The mission brought coffee to France for the first time. Saint-Simon considered the whole thing to have been a hoax (*Mémoires*).

Molière devised some gibberish which might well pass for Turkish if that language were unknown to the listener. The episode is interspersed with spoken dialogue and closes with four 'Entrées de Ballet', danced and sung.

A man enters and distributes the programme of the ballet.[1] His solemn entry is interrupted by the demands of the audience in the play for copies of the libretto.

'La comédie finit par un petit ballet qui avoit été preparé.' According to the musical score, an old chatterer sings two charming 'couplets', in ternary form.

---

[1] It is at this moment that *Ariadne auf Naxos* is performed in Strauss' Germanised approach to Molière's *Comédie-Ballet*.

Then follows the 'Entrée des Scaramouches, Trivelins et Arlequins' representing 'ung nuit à la manière des Comédiens Italiens'. Once more there is dignified music, commencing in alla breve time and concluding in triple. One of Lully's famous *Chaconnes*[1] in the style of the Menuet allows a general dance. This is succeeded by a ravishing Arioso and Duetto sung by male and female Italian musicians.

An instrumental 'Scène des Poitevins', again in Menuet style, leads straight into a duo between a contralto and a tenor, consisting of the same music as that played by the instruments. The same idea is applied to the next movement, 'Menuet pour les Hautbois Poitevins', but, unlike the preceding Duo, this is very square. The 'Choeur Final' is bold and determined, square as to vocal writing and strictly harmonic save for the ritornelli where some flowing quaver movement relieves the pomposity of the choruses. It brings the work to a fine finish.

All this naturally protracts the performance and is very much cut today at the Comédie-Française. The connection with *Opéra-Comique* is easy to see.

Psyché, the *Tragédie-Ballet*, displays no such cohesion between music and dancing, mainly because it was the work of more than

---

[1] This was a dance 'en Rondeau' and bore no relationship to the Spanish dance on an *ostinato*.

one author. The Preface explains that Quinault wrote the French verses to be set to music, those in Italian being written by Lully. Molière drew up the scenario and prepared the production, but owing to the fact that the *Fêtes* for which the work was intended were not far off, he had to call in Corneille to help with the text. The King decided that several performances should take place before Lent.

Lully used much of the music composed for the other *Psyché*, given in 1656, and it is remarkable that the work turned out to be as homogeneous as it did. It was constructed as two plays within a play. Much the same principle governed *Le Mariage forcé*, which consists of a ballet within a play. The former is detachable from the latter as a separate entity. The idea reached its most elaborate application in two *Comédies-Ballets*, *Monsieur de Pourcéagnac* and *Les Amants magnifiques*, and there is a distinct connection between them and *Circé*.

CHAPTER NINE

METHOD OF COMPOSITION – RECITATIVES – RECITATIVO
STROMENTATO ESPRESSIVO – OVERTURES – VOCAL WRITING
– CHORAL WRITING – DANCE MOVEMENTS – INSTRUMENTAL
WRITING – RÉSUMÉ OF LULLY'S ACHIEVEMENT – FORM-
ULATION OF "FRENCH OPERA" – SITUATION AFTER
LULLY'S DEATH – FOREIGN PERFORMANCES – VINCENT
D'INDY'S ASSESSMENT

LULLY's method of work never varied. He observed a strict
routine in his choice of subject, dictated partly by policy and
partly by the certain knowledge that the King was a man of
both sense and judgement. He was aware, too, that the King of
France was also King of the Académie Royale, and that it was
entirely through his instrumentality that that concern had ever
come into being. The King, therefore, had to be consulted, but
the royal taste was, no doubt, adroitly steered in the required
direction.

As soon as Lully and Quinault had assembled a number of
subjects, they submitted the list to the King. He chose whichever
appealed to him at that particular moment. Quinault then worked
out a scenario, which he handed to Lully. The composer decided
at what points in the story the divertissements, dances, chansonettes, choruses, etc., should appear, and Quinault then wrote
the book in full. When it was finished, it was handed to the
Académie Française for approval, Quinault himself giving a dramatic reading of the entire text to the assembled Academicians. The
fact that the book was approved did not prevent Lully from making
alterations during the course of composition; Quinault, in fact,
had to alter one scene in *Phaeton* twenty times before Lully was
satisfied. No matter how exasperating this may have been,
Quinault soon found out that Lully's judgement was sound,
but it is not surprising that, before long, he petitioned the King
for a pension of four thousand livres per annum in return for his
services. Vigarini and Beauchamp followed suit, and there is
every reason to think that these petitions were granted.

L

Each opera took Lully three months to compose. He wrote down the essentials himself, his assistants filling in the harmonies and doing the ordinary technical writing. In some cases this was done by the copyist. It may be said, therefore, and his enemies frequently did say, that Lully hardly composed his operas himself; but harmony was not advanced in those days and the 'right' chords were always the obvious ones. This practice, however, undoubtedly accounts for the lack of harmonic interest.[1] Lully's harmony was never enterprising.[2] He did not think in terms of expressive progressions, insisting that expression lay only in the melody. His imitative polyphony may be seen at its best in the beautiful *Scènes de sommeil*, particularly that in *Renard*, from Act II, Scene III of *Armide*. The ritornello is obviously all his own work.

Ex.43   Il faut jouer cecy avec des sourdines

When the voice enters, another hand takes up the pen. While Lully must have written the bass and the voice part, Colasse and perhaps his other helpers certainly supplied the rest.

---

[1] It also accounts for the existence of more than one version of a work.

[2] Rameau's versions of the recitatives are no more 'Lully' than are Mahler's re-orchestrations of Schumann's Symphonies, 'Schumann'. Rameau's modulations completely altered the colour of Lully's recitatives, and in some cases the melodic line was changed in the process of 'improvement'.

Ex. 44

PUIS JOB - SER - VE CES LIEUX, ET PLUS JE LES AD -MI - RE; CE PLEU —

Had they filled in the whole movement, they would have had the genius of Lully himself, but the angularities of the uninteresting top part, and the general dullness of those underneath, suggest that this was the kind of passage usually left to others.

It was in the recitatives that Lully showed a particular insistence upon correct vocal inflection. He had suffered the longevities of Italian *recitativo secco* in the work of Rossi and others, and had found it insufficiently musical. He may or may not have studied the musical *Dialogue entre Glauque et Téthys*, in *Le Ballet comyque de la Royne*, when he wrote the music for *Le Bourgeois gentilhomme*, but he knew how to steer conversational moments away from the perfunctory Italian manner of dealing with them.

To the achievement of this ideal Lully devoted many hours of careful thought. Melody may have come readily to him, but recitative required more than mere flashes of inspiration. He would first learn the text by heart, declaiming it over and over again until he had noted down the verbal climaxes and the points at which the spoken voice would rise and fall. He would then fit a musical rhythm to the words. The melodic line came next, closely following the graph of his experiments.[1] In place of the

---

[1] Sir Charles Stanford advocated the same process for the composition of songs.

punctuating chords of *recitativo secco*, Lully contrived a primitive form of *recitativo stromentato espressivo* in which the vocal style approximated to that of the Air; but, as will be seen from the examples, he accomplished only the first step in this direction. All this work he did while sitting at the clavecin. The other music was written at his table.

All consideration of Lully's recitative must be governed by the realisation that the audiences of the time knew of nothing different. This type of writing was recognised as constituting 'opera' and, consequently, they accepted what today would be regarded as monotonous and uninteresting. Lully himself gradually evolved a more melodic and measured style of recitative. This evolution was so gradual, born not of sudden enlightenment but of a desire to add interest to what was tending to become a formula, that its consummation was achieved almost unwittingly, and realised by the audience only sub-consciously.

For the immediate moment, Lully was concerned entirely with aligning spoken and sung declamation. For this purpose, he listened carefully to La Champmeslé, an actress of the Comédie-Française. This involved not only accent, and the rise and fall of the voice itself, but speed of diction. Lully's recitative, consequently, would have moved fast, the 'snap' of French dialogue being faithfully copied.

La Champmeslé was coached by Racine. Racine's approach to accent was somewhat stilted and regular, unlike his approach to inflection which, in its search for truth, became exaggerated while remaining genuinely theatrical. This, in the first place, led to intense monotony; when allied to music it is still unbearable to sophisticated ears. At its time it made everything perfectly clear to the audiences, who found the union congruous and were not disturbed by the musical setting.

The salient point is Lully's adherence to the one-note-one-syllable principle. Comparison with Ex. 17 and 18 by Caccini and Peri will show why Lully's listeners were not bored to distraction. Monsieur Bronislaw Horowicz[1] draws attention to the *Antigone* of Pasquale Anfossi (1727 – 1797), where one hundred and fifty-two notes are devoted to the second syllable of the word

---

[1] *Le Théâtre d'Opéra*, Editions de Flore (fn. p. 28).

'Amato'; they are followed immediately by a reprise. He also quotes Stefano Artega's comment in *Le Rivoluzioni del Teatro musicale italiano dalla sue origine*:[1] 'Heavens! three hundred and four inflexions on a single vowel! And that is what they call dramatic music!' Musicologists[2] may rave over the historical importance of Italian recitative, but antiquity does not always spell 'beauty', nor even 'sensibility'.

Lully, however, sought for a more lyrical solution to musical declamation. It is, in fact, unlikely that he had ever heard of *Circé*, where he might have discovered his answer; but, in his own way, he approached a type of *recitativo stromentato espressivo*, which added a lyrical flow to the musical dialogue and allowed considerable freedom of rhythm. He never, however, merged the recitative into the ensuing Air or Duo, and the former usually terminated in a typical piece of ornamentation clearly indicating the dividing line.

He did not hesitate to change the time-values, when the text demanded it, to obtain elasticity and flexibility:

The scuffle in the final measure is equalled by the following, which is more convincing because the pace is slower:

---

[1] Venezia, 1785. [2] Horowicz, *op. cit.* (fn. p. 182).

VU   MA VA-LEUR   TRI-OM - PHAN - TE.

The next example reveals a tentative approach to musical expressiveness:

Ex. 47   PROSERPINE

CET-TE FIE - RE BEAU-TÉ SIBS - TI - NE À FUIR LES A-MANTS ET L'A - MOUR.

Recitativo stromentato espressivo was not to reach its apogee until some years later, in France with Jean Philippe Rameau, and in England, rather sooner, with Michael Wise, Pelham Humfrey,[1] John Blow[2] and Henry Purcell;[3] in Germany it reached a state of perfection with Johann Sebastian Bach. Lully was the first composer to use this form of recitative and, tentative though his attempts were, it can be taken seriously for what it was meant to be.

Lully's Overtures had no thematic or synthetic connection with what followed and an interchange would have caused no comment. They were either in three sections or two, those to *Proserpine*, *Armide*, *Atys*, *Alceste* and *Les Saisons* being in the former category. They opened with dignity, the emphatic rhythm commanding immediate attention; conversation did not start again until the *allegro*, quasi-fugal section commenced. The Lully (or

---

[1] *Hear, O Heavens* – H.M.V. History of Music HLP 12.
[2] *Venus and Adonis* – Oiseau Lyre OL 50004.
[3] *O Sing unto the Lord* – Archive Production APM 14059.

French) type of Overture had a marked influence upon composers all over Europe, for it was completely effective and fulfilled its purpose to perfection. Its brevity was a commendation, although Rameau, Bach and Handel were able to expand its scope and, in the case of Rameau, to relate it thematically to the opera. In only one instance in Lully's works – Act III of *Armide* – is the Overture connected in this way to the opening Air. The wonder is that Lully was able to obtain so much variety within so small a compass.

PSYCHÉ

PERSÉE

The Prologue followed the Overture without break or pause for applause. These Prologues were all to a pattern. The décors were pastoral and the singers appeared as the gods and heroes of mythology, Apollo and Mars, for instance, or Hercules. They were dressed 'au pompier' and dilated on the glories of the King, each Prologue being founded on his latest conquest, on his courage, his military genius, or on his wisdom in bringing some treaty to a successful conclusion. The Prologue ended. Incense had been offered to the royal nostrils. The *Tragédie-Lyrique* could start.

Lully, as we know, considered musical expression to lie in melody alone. His Airs are square-cut and well defined. The words were never made to fit the music and there are, consequently, many instances of irregular rhythm. The emotional range is considerable and the rhythms are very vital. The accents upon the second beat in the triple measures became a characteristic of more than one composer (Lully's impact upon the English composers of the Restoration period is extremely marked [Appendix Forty-Two]). Let it suffice, at this point, to mark the similarity of thought between the ritournelles in *Belle Hermione*, from Act V of *Cadmus et Hermione*, which was performed in London in 1686; and those in the *Air de Mars* from *Psyché*, and the *Chaconne* from Purcell's *King Arthur*.

EX. 49 A.

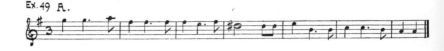

This semitonal progression was public property, so to speak. It was used by Cavalli in the *Lamento de Climene* (*Egisto*) and by Purcell in *Dido's Lament* (*Dido and Aeneas*).

In another sense, the following example from *Alceste* has a breezy *Come, if you dare* spirit about it which immediately aligns it with the chorus of that name in *King Arthur*.

For sheer beauty of melodic line, the well-known Air *Bois épais*, from *Armide*, is fully representative of a host of beautiful tunes illustrating the truth of Lully's principle that emotion lies solely in melody.

It is impossible to regard the *Dialogue de la Musique italienne et de la Musique française* in the *Ballet de la Raillerie* at all seriously, as much of it is parody, but even the parody of the Italian manner is not without an unintentional charm,

MIEUX TES LONGS FRE———————————————————DONS-EN-NU

-YEUX TES LONGS FRE———————————————DONS-EN-NU-YEUX.

while Lully seems to have taken particular care to present the French Air as ingratiatingly as possible.

LE MANIÈRE DONT JE CHAN-TÉ—— EX-PRI-ME MI-EUX

MA-LANGUEUR EX-PRI-ME MI-EUX MA—LAN-GUEUR.

This spirit pervades the *Air de sommeil* in *Armide*, part of which has already been quoted.[1]

At the same time he was graphic. The following quotation from *Roland* anticipates Rameau's descent to hell.[2]

AH! JE SUIS DE-SCEN-DU DANS LA NUIT DU TOM-BEAU.

In many respects Lully's declamatory Airs foreshadow those of Gluck; comparison, indeed, shows that the latter was a natural disciple of the former, with wider resources.

The clop-clop of the coins into Caron's bag, as he collects the fares across the Styx in *Alceste*, and the ring of the forge in *Psyché*, look forward to the wave of expressionism which was to break in the twentieth century.

---

[1] Examples 43 and 44, pages 148 and 149.
[2] Example 99, page 200.

In choral writing Lully was equally graphic. He did not hesitate to indulge in word-painting, as this extract from *Jupiter, lancez le tonnere (Proserpine)*, shows:

His immediate followers imitated him and the thunder rolled in much the same fashion.

Lully used the Chorus effectively, although he was usually content to let it remain static in a supplementary role. The writing is generally on the square harmonic side. With his passion for clarity, he was aware of the absurdity of different people singing different words at the same time. Consequently, the Choruses often consist simply of harmonic progressions.

AMADIS

Nevertheless, there is a certain feeling of exultation about the tenor and bass lines in the Victory Chorus from *Phaeton.*

When it came to setting a chorus on a single word, he allowed his thought freer rein, but even then he was careful not to confuse the syllables of the particular word between the voices.

The progression between contraltos and basses in bar five should be noted. It occurred frequently and was not the result of carelessness.[1]

However, in the *Ballet de l'Impatience*, where the scholars extol the value of tobacco, Lully achieved a certain amount of freedom

---

[1] It appears all through Purcell (in the anthem *Remember not, Lord, our offences,* for example,) and in the other Restoration composers.

between the parts, using the convenient 'fa la la' the moment
confusion seemed likely to appear.

Later, in the same chorus, he parodies the Italian style and mixes
the syllables freely.

Taking the crisp rhythm of the words 'Bacco [there is a pun
here], sacco, stacco, spacco, 'a, a, co, tabacca [*sic*]', he contrived

a patter song which anticipated the distribution of the programmes in *Le Bourgeois gentilhomme*.

This, of course, is not in the least degree seriously intended, and the chorus proceeds in a most interesting manner. Rests are inserted in the middle of words, allowing the singers to take puffs at their pipes.[1]

It was this syllabic style which caused Cambert's *Trio italien burlesque*, from the music written for Brecourt's *Le Jaloux Invisible*, to be ascribed to Lully until a printed copy of that play was found; it included the trio in full.[2] No other music by Cambert now in existence reveals him in such a flippant light.

---

[1] The oft-quoted *Smoking Catch* by Dr Henry Aldrich (1647 – 1710) was not original after all. One doubts, however, if the worthy Dean had ever heard of Lully or his ballets.

[2] See next page.

The choral writing in the operas is completely different from that in Lully's magnificent *Miserere* and *Te Deum*, where it is often polyphonic in style, there being no necessity for the listener to follow a narrative since the words were familiar to him.

The charge of squareness has naturally been applied to Lully's dance movements. It was here that he showed himself most 'French' and, as a dancer, did not attempt to alter anything which he knew from experience to be perfectly suitable. He invariably composed these movements in the Italian operas imported by Mazarin. As a dancer, he knew exactly what was wanted and, as a composer, how to get it. The tautness of the Menuets is justified by the nature of the dance itself,

PSYCHÉ

PHAETON

and he could throw fresh light upon this dance by means of crisp harmonies.

ARMIDE

LES SAISONS

His application of formal titles to some of the movements indicates the nature of the steps without any adherence to the fundamental rhythmic characteristics.

PROSERPINE

LIST OF ILLUSTRATIONS

II. Music at the Court of René II, Duke of Lorraine.

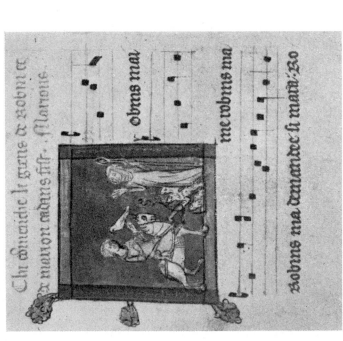

I. *Le Jeu de Robin et Marion*. An illumination from the manuscript in the Bibliothèque Nationale, Paris. (Ms. 25566)

III. Staging of a 16th century Morality play, *La Tempérance*. Engraving by Breughel the Elder. An organist, musician and singers may be seen in the domed tent.

IV. The Fair of Saint-Germain and the Theatre Nicollet in the 17th century. (Paris, Musée Carnavalet-Estampes.)

Madame de Guife à monfieur de Geneuois

ARION.

Mad. de Neuers à monfieur de Guife

LE CHEVAL MARIN.

Populi superat prudentia fluctus.

Aduerfus femper in hoftem.

R.iij.

V. The presentation of gifts (see p. 37). A page opening of *Circé, ou le Ballet Comyque de la Royne*, printed by le Roy, Ballard and Patisson in Paris, 1582.

VI. Performance of *Circé* at the Petit Bourbon. A plate from the edition of 1582.
(See p. 29.)

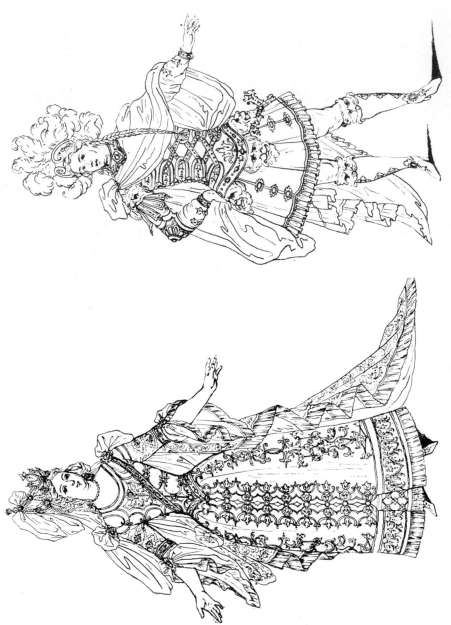

VII. Costume design by Berain, possibly for *Le Triomphe de l'Amour*. (Bibliothèque de l'Opéra.)

VIII. A performance of *Le Triomphe de l'Amour* in the Salle des Cariatides. (From a pen and wash drawing in the British Museum.)

Jean Baptiste de Lully
Secretaire du Roy et Surjntendant
de la Musique de Sa Majesté. né a florence et mort a Paris le 22. mars 1687.
agé de 54 ans.

Gravé par E. Defrochers et se vend chez lui a Paris rue St Iacques au Mecenas.

J'ay fait chanter les Dieux, ainsy que les heros,
Mes airs ont exprimé le murmure des flots,
Le Someil, les Zéphirs, la pluye et le tonnere,
J'ay même fait oüir les ombres des enfers;
Et pour vn Roy fameux, dans la paix dans la guerre
D'immortelles chanfons l'ai rempli l'vnivers.

IX. Jean Baptiste 'de' Lully. Engraving by E. Defrochers. (Print Room,
British Museum.)

X. Louis XIV in 1663, at the age of twenty-five. An
engraving by R. Nanteuil. The book of music, instruments, palette and architectural plans at lower left allude
to his patronage of the arts.

XI. The *mascerade nautique* presented on the third day of *Les Plaisirs de l'Isle Enchantée* (see p. 95).

XII. Performance of Lully's *Alceste* by torchlight in the Cour de Marbre at Versailles, 1674. Engraving by le Pautre from *Les Divertissemens de Versailles*. (Paris, Imprimerie Royale, 1676.)

XXIII B. f. [illegible] Les Fêtes de l'Amour et de Bacchus in the Petit Parc at Versailles. Engraving by le Pautre

XIV. Ball at the Petit Parc. Engraving by le Pautre from *Les Plaisirs de l'Isle Enchantée*. (Paris, Imprimerie Royale, 1676.)

THETIS ET PELÉE

XV. Engraving by Berain of a performance of *Le Nozze di Peleo e di Theti.*
(Paris, Bibliothèque de l'Opéra.)

ACTE CINQUIÊME.

Le Théâtre Repréſente le Palais Enchanté D'Apollidon,
Où l'on voit l'Arc des loyaux Amants, et la Chambre
deffenduë dont la porte eſt fermée.

Scene Premiere.

XVI. A page from the edition of 1710 of Lully's *Amadis*, published at Paris by
J.-B.-C. Ballard.

XVII. Bust of Rameau, by Caffieri.
(Bibliothèque Ste.-Geneviève.)

XVIII. Sketch of Mlle.
St. Huberty, by le Moine.
(Print Room, British
Museum.)

XIX. Jean-Jacques Rousseau, by Gar-
nerey. (Print Room, British Museum.)

PROSERPINE

The grace and dignified charm of some of the meditative dances are worthy of Gluck.

ARMIDE

In the formal Entrées, Lully echoed the slow introductions to the Overtures; indeed, some of them could easily have served in either capacity.

PROSERPINE

PROSERPINE

M

His Gigues were pointedly rhythmic.

PERSÉE

PSYCHÉ

He formulated his own March style and there is sometimes a distinct connection between that of the dignified Entrée and the formal March.

CADMUS ET HERMIONE

THESÉE

Ex. 70 A.

All these Marches are brilliant. They may sound slight in modern ears, but they are more than mere 'trumpetings' and 'pip-squeak music'.[1] Handel learnt something from them.[2] Unfortunately, Lully has never found a Hamilton Harty to score his music for a twentieth-century orchestra, and, in any case, the Marches were not intended to be extracted from their contexts. Not all of them are in quadruple time. Lully often wrote what may be called 'March Styles' in triple time, and these have both pomp and grandeur without actually being Marches.

Lully's *Chaconnes*, like those of Couperin, are movements in Old Rondo Form ('en rondeau'). He concluded nearly every Act with one of these for chorus and orchestra, the orchestra usually doubling the voices. This formed a brilliant conclusion, but the practice became a convention and, after Lully's death, was dropped.

Lully treated the instruments of the orchestra expressively, but only in a general sense; there are no subtleties of orchestration. Flutes sounded the amorous moments of the gods and goddesses, and they created the atmosphere for the *Scènes de sommeil* and nocturnes, during which magic rites took place. Oboes were used for the peasant dances, trumpets supplied the martial and warlike music, while violins underlined the slumbers of the heroes and added excitement (*tremolando*) to the battles, 'furies', and storms.

He took the greatest care over minute details, never leaving anything to chance, indicating precisely where it would be necessary 'prendre garde de n'ôter les sourdines avant qu'on ne le voie margué', while the players on occasions were exhorted to

---

[1] These epithets are surely the nadir of musical criticism coming, as they do, from two eminent critics. I refrain from mentioning their names.
[2] The March in the Overture to *The Occasional Oratorio*, for example – Columbia 33cx 1045.

play 'sans presque toucher les cordes'. The pizzicato effects, marked 'pincé', were enhanced by guitars. The percussion included castanets. It would be extremely interesting to hear this original orchestration to-day.

While Lully avoided choral polyphony as much as possible, he found instrumental counterpoint in every way suitable. There are many places where polyphony expresses situations of extreme tenderness, and the emotion itself is underlined by plain melodic lines of exquisite charm and elegance. He never hesitated to cross the parts in his polyphonic writing, and was careful to avoid any suggestion of complexity.

Lully's formulation of the French operatic style may have been *his* idea of what that style should be. This has already been suggested, but he maintained the French *esprit* and all future developments show a logical widening of his theories and practice. He deliberately avoided ornate vocalism in contradistinction to the Italian manner, and it is in this respect only that the continuity of descent is broken; yet even the coloratura operas of Ambroise Thomas (1811 – 1896), based as they were on the Italian tradition, are fundamentally French in quality.

Lully's operas set a standard initially so elaborate that development was bound to lead to bursting point. The spectacular productions and advanced technique of Rameau carried the Lully tradition very much further, and established what the latter had formulated. The stage machinery also became a little less inexpert; yet, if one may believe Jean Jacques Rousseau's accounts of the situation in Rameau's time, it was still inept and elementary. Lully's experiments succeeded even though they were primitive; it was perhaps fortunate that there were neither precedents nor competitors to provoke odious comparisons.

The audiences understood that they were witnessing genuine *Tragédie-Lyrique*. They appreciated the inner references to their King. If they found some languors now and then, they assumed them to be part of the new genre. It was some time before Lully was universally applauded, but this idea, in general, was accepted.

It is as well to remember that this great culture was founded with the sympathetic support of Colbert, the Finance Minister. Louis XIV could have initiated the idea; Colbert, who was responsible for finding the money for the lavish performances at Versailles and elsewhere, could have refused to do so. He was capable of this, as is proved by his veto on the building of a theatre at Versailles.

He has been much abused by historians, who have regarded him as a pinch-necked upstart economist with no artistic inclinations whatever, and as a man devoid of spiritual and physical feeling. Nevertheless it was Colbert who founded the 'Prix de Rome', the 'Académie de France à Rome', and various other Académies where learning and research could be cultivated. He made only one mistake – his misplaced faith in Perrin, but he was thinking in the dark, for the venture was quite novel in conception. The wily manner in which Perrin presented his plan for the association of France's poets and musicians – to the greater glory of Louis XIV and of France – may have confused Colbert, for on paper the idea was perfectly sound.

Colbert was efficient, and he liked others to be equally so. Lully gave him proofs of his efficiency and never betrayed the trust reposed in him. It should be remembered that the Académie Royale de Musique was a self-supporting concern without a subsidy, and that it proved a paying proposition. Had Lully taken one false step in his earlier days, however, the Académie might never have existed; but he had persistence, self-confidence and a prodigious amount of good luck.

There are some who maintain that, since the whole concern rapidly fell to pieces after the death of its founder, it had no real roots. This attitude is reasonable, but unjust. Whenever an outstanding genius has towered above the heads of his contemporaries there is a gap when he dies. Where an entire structure depends on the work of that genius, a reaction is inevitable when the master mind and hand have disappeared. This, indeed, set in on the day Lully was lowered into his grave. His pupil and assistant, Pascal Colasse (1649 – 1709),[1] completed the unfinished opera, *Achille et Polyxene*, and produced it on November 7th, 1687, but the public was not interested.

The public had, in fact, been saturated with Lully. He had

---

[1] Prologue (*Enie et Lavinie*) – Oiseau Lyre OL 50117.

written himself out and might have said of himself, with truth: 'Achievèd is the glorious work'. The Académie without him was unthinkable, but the mere name was not enough. Lully's sons produced their *Opéra-Ballet*, *Zéphire et Flore*, on March 22nd, 1688. This was received with scarcely-veiled hostility and only the presence of a strong body of police on the *parterre*[1] prevented it being whistled off the stage. This was not entirely an expression of loyalty to the departed *Maître*, for the work showed that the mantle of Elijah had by no means fallen on Elisha.

Lully, indeed, had become a convention and had provided the only workable model for other composers. Consequently, everything sounded like inferior Lully. It was not until 1693, when *Medée ou Jason*,[2] by Marc Antoine Charpentier (1634 – 1704) was produced, on December 4th, that anything significant seemed likely to appear. This work was a curious paradox. Charpentier had been a pupil of Carissimi, which was something Lully could not tolerate, and, up to a point, he had succeeded in blocking Charpentier's progress. Nevertheless, in spite of this Italian training, *Medée ou Jason* was written on the Lully model, and, although the style of lyricism was distinctly Italianate, the difference was not as marked as might have been expected. The libretto by Thomas Corneille was no improvement on those by Quinault. It failed in exactly that point where Quinault's succeeded; namely, in the Prologue, which is more than usually fatuous.

Broadly speaking, the work is only a little more than a pale reflection of its model, although the approach in general is less stiff and formal, and there is slightly more dramatic intensity. It owes its importance to the quality of the lyricism, but it is more French than Italian and bears few signs of its composer's Italian training. Charpentier is one of the earliest instances of the French goût being swayed by close contact with any other. This will be found to be characteristic of French Opera right down the ages. The Dance Movements are, in some cases, superior to some of those by Lully, but the Marches, Fanfares, and all the paraphernalia of pomp and circumstance, are distinctly inferior.

---

[1] The equivalent of our stalls.
[2] Excerpts – Brunswick AXTL 1049.

When it was 'discovered' by a musicologist on the staff of the B.B.C., and played in that Corporation's Third Programme, it was extremely difficult to remember that its composer was not Lully, so closely did it follow that composer's style.

Of the other composers bridging the gap between Lully and his true successor, the most distinguished were André Campra (1660 – 1744),[1] Henri Desmarets (1662 – 1741),[2] Michel Monteclair (1666 – 1737), and André Destouches (1673 – 1749),[3] each of whom showed certain signs of individuality. The same may be said of Colin de Blamont (1690 – 1760) and Madame de la Guerre (1659 – 1728), whose *Céphale et Procris*,[4] produced on March 15th, 1694, created some stir. Lully's 'man-of-all-work', Colasse, showed himself to be quite incapable of rising above the prevailing influence, so deeply had Lully's aesthetics and technique taken root in him. Mention should also be made of the duc d'Orléans and the Marquis de Brassac, who were not necessarily worse musicians and composers because of their rank.[5]

Of these composers, the most notable was Campra, whose *L'Europe galante*, produced on October 24th, 1697, presaged the twentieth century spectacular ballet. Campra's *Tancrède*, however, a *Tragédie-Lyrique* in five Acts with Prologue, made history on November 7th, 1702, as it was the first opera whose leading role was written for a contralto. This was Mademoiselle de Maupin, of whose exploits Théophile Gautier wrote such an entertaining account.

More important was Monteclair's introduction of the Double-Bass into the Académie orchestra in 1710. The instrument was used only on Fridays, this being then, as now, the fashionable evening for opera-going. On that day only the best singers appeared, and no one would have dreamed of allowing a deputy to take his place.

It was on January 29th, 1711, that the French version of the Italian generic 'Opera' was used for the first time. *Manto la fée*,

---

[1] *Air de Florise (Les Anges), Air de Menalie (Alcine), Air de Hesione (Hesione).*
[2] *Air de Circé (Circé).*
[3] *Monologue de Callirhoe (Callirhoe).*
[4] *Air de Procris.*
All these Oiseau Lyre OL 50117.
[5] Alexis de Castillon (1838 – 1879) and Vincent d'Indy (1851 – 1931) were Vicomtes.

by Batistin Stuck, was described as an 'Opéra'. The use of this word remained isolated for many years, composers remaining faithful to the more explicit nomenclature of *Tragédie, Comédie-Lyrique, Opéra-Ballet, Pastorale (Héroique)*, and so forth.

The walls of the Bibliothèque de l'Opéra bear witness to the enormous total of French operatic endeavour. Much of it is admirable in its way, but it required another genius (and nothing less) to take matters further.

Thanks to his numerous foreign pupils, Lully's works were performed in many European capitals as well as in other French cities, with corresponding financial benefits to their composer. These performances increased in number immediately after his death, the most interested countries being Germany, Belgium, Holland and Sweden. Did Johann Sebastian Bach hear any of them? It is extremely likely that he did, and he, like Handel, adopted the French Overture. Musicians such as Matheson, Telemann, Harpurg, Fischer, Erlebach, and Muffat all stayed in Paris at one time or another, some being Lully's pupils and working their apprenticeship as his copyists. It is not beyond the bounds of possibility that they may have assisted Colasse and others in filling-in the missing harmonies. This would have been excellent practice for them and, under Colasse's guidance, they could not have gone wrong.

Such a successful venture as the Académie royale de Musique could not have passed unnoticed outside France any more than did the activities at Salzburg and Mannheim at a later date outside Austria. Travellers tell tales and news flies quickly. The lyric repertoire was not so extensive that impresarios could afford to overlook anything from any country.

We can do no better than to close this section with the words of Vincent d'Indy,[1] by no means a purblind venerator of the past:

> Lully fut un homme de génie en ce sens que, malgré les succès de l'école vénitienne, il sut résister à l'entraînement trop facile, et comprit que la musique italienne n'avait pas d' avenir en France. Il saisit assez l'esprit français pour

---

[1] Vincent d'Indy:– *Cours de Composition musicale (Troisième Livre)*, pp. 43 and 46.

sentir la nécessité de faire du texte le principal facteur, tout en portant aussi son attention sur les éléments extérieurs au drame; danses, décors, etc. Et il composa en conséquence, retrouvant les principes des Académies florentines dans ce qu'ils avaient de juste. Il abolit donc la profusion d'ornements les passages de virtuosité vocale, roulades, etc., pour adopter une forme de récitation fondée uniquement sur *l'accent*. Il créa ainsi le véritable style de l'ancien opéra français, un peu solennel peut-être, mais clair d'expression et juste d'accent. Dans les airs comme dans les récits, l'accent de la parole resta la seule raison d'être de la mélodie vocale; et il ne fut ainsi jusqu'au XIX siècle, ou les faux triomphes de la 'troisième renaissance italienne' et le dévergondage qui s'en suivit vinrent en peu d'années l'oeuvre progressive et féconde de deux siècles. Toutefois, si la France pendant ces deux siècles, a réussi à se protéger de l' influence envahissante de la musique italienne et à se créer une musique dramatique propre, c'est à Lully qu'elle le doit, et à sa compréhension fine et subtile du génie français . . . . .

Lully a donc emprunté aux Napolitaines le coups de l'aria lied, mais s'en sert concurremment avec l'alerte air français tout en observant pour la déclamation les principes de l'école florentine. De plus, il emploie des combinations de rhythmes variés, qu'on ne trouvers plus guère après lui: par là, et par le souci de l'expression, il se rattache à l'art de Monteverde . . . . .

CHAPTER TEN

RACINE – MOREAU – RAMEAU – LA PO(U)PLINIÈRE –
"SAMSON" (VOLTAIRE) – "HIPPOLYTE ET ARICIE" –
ABBÉ PELLÉGRIN – OPINION OF CAMPRA – LULLYISTES
VERSUS RAMONEURS – "LES INDES GALANTES" – RAMEAU'S
INNOVATIONS – "CASTOR ET POLLUX" – "LES FÊTES
D'HÉBÉ" – LES NUITS DE SCEAUX – "DARDANUS" – "LA
PRINCESSE DE NAVARRE" – RAMEAU REWARDED – ITALIAN
LIGHT OPERA COMPANY – PERGOLESI – ROUSSEAU
– ENCYCLOPÉDISTES – ARTICLES WRITTEN FOR
ENCYCLOPÉDIE – RAMEAU'S CORRECTIONS – "LA SERVA
PADRONA" – GUERRE DES BUFFONS – ENCYCLOPÉDISTES'
PHILOSOPHY – LULLY AND RAMEAU COMPARED – BASIC
DIFFERENCES – ACADÉMIE ORCHESTRA – INTRODUCTION
OF CLARINETS – USE OF INSTRUMENTS – OVERTURES –
DRAMATIC SYMPHONIES – RITORNELLES – PRELUDES –
INTRODUCTIONS – VOCAL WRITING – AIRS – ARIETTES –
DANCE MOVEMENTS – OPÉRA-BALLET – CHORAL WRITING –
ESTABLISHMENT OF FRENCH OPERA

THE OUTLOOK, therefore, was gloomy, but Lully's monopoly had not affected the Colleges where ballet and drama had flourished for a great many years. Their activities, naturally, were restricted and enclosed, but the situation was not quite the same at the Maison de Saint-Cyr, founded by Louis XIV in 1685, at the request of Madame de Maintenon. This institution provided the daughters of impoverished nobles and army officers with an education surprisingly liberal for the period. Madame de Maintenon may have been a religious bigot and a blue-stocking, but at that time she believed, in her own words, that preparation for the Hereafter did not preclude a reasonable enjoyment of the Present.

Racine was persuaded to write two dramas, *Esther* (1688) and *Athalie* (1691), for the girls of Saint-Cyr to perform. They may be described as tragedies with music, both choral and instrumental, and ample scope was afforded for each. As Lully was approaching his end, the composer chosen was Jean Baptiste Moreau (1656 – 1733). His music (more interesting than impressive) shows how Lully's influence had begun to be felt during his lifetime. Since there is no dancing, the music is inseparable from the texts. It has sufficient character to warrant performance to-day at the Comédie-Française, in spite of attempts by other composers to write more convincing scores.[1] Lully's connection with the school was limited to a kind of 'Welcome Song', not without interest, but irrelevant here.

A certain amount of enterprise soon became evident in the theatres, and composers showed signs of advancing and widening the various genres, in spite of very limited actual musical invention and individuality. One of the earliest of these manifestations came on October 24th, 1697, when Campra's *L'Europe galante*, a ballet in four *Entrées* and Prologue, showed a trend away from mythology. This date also heralded the institution of the 'Droits des Pauvres'. Hitherto, authors and composers had received one hundred livres for each performance up to the tenth, and fifty livres from the eleventh to the twentieth, or to the thirtieth in the case of a *Tragédie-Lyrique*. The 'Droits des Pauvres' added one sixth to the price of a ticket in certain parts of the house, but this amount was deducted by the management in others. These deductions reduced the 'Droits des Auteurs' and 'Compositeurs', who were, presumably, not considered 'poor'.

The drift from mythology placed the 'locales' in European countries, chiefly Italy and Spain. Campra's *Le Carnival de Venise* (January 20th, 1698) went so far as to contain a short Italian Opera as its third Act, thus transposing the incipient *Opéra-Ballet* into *Ballet-Opéra*. Nothing further of any value or interest transpired until February 28th, 1732, when a Biblical *Tragédie-Lyrique*, *Jephté*, the first of its kind, by the Abbé Pellégrin and Monteclair, somehow or other evaded official church stricture.[2]

---

[1] A Musical Backwater (Norman Demuth), *Musical Quarterly*, Vol. XL No. 4, 1954, pp. 533–547.
[2] During a performance of this work on March 10th, 1735, in the presence of the Minister, Maurepas, Mademoiselle Catherine Le Maure suddenly decided during an

Voltaire, Rameau, and, over a century later, Camille Saint-Saens, were not to be so successful.

Salvation came in 1733, when the first full-scale work by Rameau was performed.

Jean-Philippe Rameau was born in Dijon, on September 5th, 1683. His father was the local organist. Although living in straitened circumstances, the father was determined that his son should enjoy as good a musical training as could be found anywhere. By saving and scraping, the young man was enabled to travel to Italy, where he heard a great deal of music. From Italy he journeyed to Paris, living in the utmost poverty. He was fortunate, however, in being appointed organist at a Jesuit convent, and he expended a lot of thought on musical technique and aesthetics, writing some treatises which, at that time, were revolutionary. He mixed with Paris musicians of all kinds and, before long, found that the French music he heard was more to his taste than Italian.

Rameau, therefore, had no background to help him, found no really influential friends, and held no court appointment. His way was harder than that travelled by Lully. His ambition was to shine as an operatic composer, but admission to the boards of the Académie was obtained only through reputation and past successes. On February 29th, 1726, he produced a one-act opera, *L'Enrôlement d'Arlequin*, at the Théâtre de la Foire and, later in the same year, a two-act work, *Le Faux Prodigue*. He was then forty-two years old and still without influence. Further, light works could not help a composer to the Académie, which was apparently opposed to humour of any kind.

However, one of his pupils was the wife of the Fermier-Générale, La Po(u)plinière. He, a man of wealth, maintained a private theatre, an orchestra, and a chapel in his house. Through the agency of Madame La Pouplinière, Rameau was appointed

---

entr'acte that she would take no further part in the proceedings, and expressed her intention of going off to sup with the intendant, Louis-Achille du Harlay. As she refused to return, she was arrested and taken to For l'Évêque in the full stage costume she had not troubled to take off. She announced that she would retire from the stage and enter the convent of the 'Précieux Sang' in the rue de Vaugirard. On her release, she changed her mind and returned to the Académie. Such conduct would have been impossible under Lully. (*Gibets, Piloris et Cachots du Vieux Paris* – Hillairet – p. 146. Les Editions de Minuit.)

musical director of the establishment. In due course, he was introduced to Voltaire, the result of this meeting being a *Tragédie-Lyrique, Samson*. This was accepted by the Académie, mainly because of its distinguished librettist, and was put into rehearsal. On the eve of production, some officious busybody with obvious malice aforethought, pointed out that it was on a biblical subject, and its performance, therefore, came under veto.

However, Rameau was at least known to the Académie, and half the battle had been won. The Abbé Pellégrin grudgingly gave him a libretto based on Racine's *Phèdre*, to which he gave the name *Hippolyte et Aricie*.[1] Rameau, who was now fifty years old, was at last able to put some of his theories into practice. The work was performed in La Pouplinière's theatre in 1733. The Abbé had his doubts about the venture, considering Rameau to be too inexperienced in operatic composition. He forced him to sign an agreement, undertaking to pay five hundred livres as indemnification in the event of failure; but, at the conclusion of the first act, the Abbé tore up the contract and publicly embraced the composer.

Hippolyte et Aricie was produced by the Académie on October 1st of that year, but on this occasion it was not an overwhelming success. Memories of Lully were still alive and, although Lullyistes were decreasing in number, they saw a potential danger to their idol. The new mythology was more interestingly expressed, perhaps, than the old, and was certainly more varied and contrasted, but Rameau was a completely unknown composer. However, there were many who admired the work. Campra, when asked his opinion by the Prince de Conti, replied that there was enough music in it 'for ten operas'[2] and that its composer would eclipse everybody else. Rameau himself was disappointed at the signs of disapproval, and threatened to compose no more. Such a threat is often heard from composers unable to stand up to criticism, and it represents nothing more than momentary frustration. Rameau, indeed, proved that his words were idle,

---

[1] Excerpts, Oiseau Lyre OL 50034. Overture and Fanfare; Ballet figure; *Rossignols amoureux*, Brunswick AXTL 1053.

[2] Campra was not implying that the work itself contained *too much* music but that, judged by the standards of the time, there was more music than usual.

for on August 23rd, 1735, the Académie produced *Les Indes galantes*,[1] an *Opéra-Ballet* which scored an immediate success and established that essentially French genre. The climax came on August 24th, 1737, when Rameau produced *Castor et Pollux*,[2] his first all-round complete masterpiece. Its performance by the Académie resulted in the formation of two factions, the Lullyistes and Ramoneurs.[3]

Rameau's innovations led to the obvious complaint that the works were more difficult than their value warranted. It has already been remarked that one of Lully's chief endeavours was the avoidance of all complexities. The Lullyistes, therefore, found fault with the number of semiquavers which Rameau sometimes wrote over a succession of bars. Lully's chief champion, Lecerf de Viéville, complained that he found it frightening to be confronted with thirty notes in a single measure. This was an exaggeration, the impression intended being that Rameau wrote mostly in these short notes. Such writing, however, appeared only in those situations which required special delineation. Rameau could not understand the opposition, insisting that he aimed only at a natural art and was thus emulating Lully. However, in spite of, or perhaps because of, such captious criticism and high-pitched feeling, *Castor et Pollux* attracted large audiences. Some came to cheer; others, coming to jeer, remained to join in the applause.

Emboldened by this success and no longer abashed by the hostility, Rameau started his own school of composition and drew many adherents to the 'new music'.

On May 21st, 1739, he continued his successful career with the ballet *Les Fêtes d'Hébé ou Les Talents Lyriques*,[4] which he composed for the Duchesse du Maine and which was initially produced at the Château de Sceaux.[5] The Opera *Dardanus*[6] followed on November 19th, 1740, and immediately all musical Paris

---

[1] *Clair flambeau*, Brunswick AXTL 1053. *Invocation au soleil*, Decca LXT 5269.

[2] *Nature, amour;* Minuet from Prologue, Decca LX 3112.

[3] *Ramoneur* – *Chimney sweep*, the allusion being to the semi-quavers which Rameau was accused of using so lavishly that the pages looked as if they had been smeared with soot.

[4] *Suite* – Ducretet-Thomson DTL 93070. *Volons sur les bordes de la Seien* – Brunswick AXTL 1053.

[5] The musical performances were known as *Les Nuits de Sceaux.*

[6] *O jour affreux* – Brunswick AXTL 1053.

went mad. The house was sold out a week before the production and the work fanned the flames of feeling. The two factions waged war in cafés and salons with an ever-increasing intensity. Pamphlets and free fights were the order of the day. A person rising from a café chair would find a leaflet in his pocket, or sticking to his trousers – unless he had taken the precaution of looking at the seat of the chair before sitting down. Strangers would accost strangers and, finding themselves at opposite poles of agreement, would instantly set about each other. The aggressors were the Lullyistes, but the Ramoneurs were not hesitant or passive in their support of Rameau.[1] Meanwhile, the Académie found that, popular or unpopular, Rameau was good box office and continued to hold its doors open to him.

A second collaboration with Voltaire resulted in *La Princesse de Navarre*, which was composed in 1745 for the wedding of the Dauphin (father of Louis XVI) and Marie Thérèse. It was produced in the Riding School at Versailles. Louis XV was as magnanimous to Rameau as Louis XIV had been to Lully, and Rameau did not have to seek honours or position. He was awarded a pension of two thousand livres, was named Composer to His Majesty, was decorated with the Order of Saint-Michel, and was granted letters of nobility. These he refused by declining to pay the usual fees, stating that *Castor et Pollux* and *Dardanus* were a sufficient payment in themselves, and that he could spend the money more advantageously. Since to deny him both Order and Rank of Nobility might have raised a scandal, he was given the former without payment, while the latter was held in a convenient abeyance.

Rameau reached the zenith of his career with *Dardanus*. He was never to experience triumph on such a scale again. For the rest of his life he produced works of consistent excellence, but in an unchanging style which became conventional. It was the case of Lully all over again. Other opposition arose in the shape of an Italian Light Opera Company, which arrived in Paris in 1752,

---

[1] Some misunderstanding exists as to the scope of such fracas. The turmoil was restricted to those cafés and haunts frequented by the opera-goers and the greater part of Paris was probably quite unaware of what was happening. Naturally, if one was not an opera-goer or music lover, it did not matter whether Lully was 'better' than Rameau, or *vice versa*.

with a repertoire of charming little tuneful works by Pergolesi and others, requiring a minimum of stage production and absolutely no concentrated listening.

Further, Jean-Jacques Rousseau (1712 – 1778), a prodigious talker, writer, and politician, but an uncultured musician with ideas and theories far in advance of his powers of achievement, had arrived from Switzerland. He had taken a stand with the *Encyclopédistes* who, in the persons of Grimm, Diderot, and d'Alembert (originally one of Rameau's strongest supporters), were compiling a great work, casting up the total of human knowledge and experience and laying down certain advanced philosophical and political principles. This was originally to be simply a free translation of the *Encyclopaedia Britannica*, which had appeared for the first time a few years earlier. Rousseau contributed the articles on music, and these Rameau proceeded to amend and correct. He never received the proof sheets, so published his corrections on his own account. Rousseau issued all his articles in book form, calling it the *Dictionnaire de Musique*.

The Lullyistes, therefore, were replaced by the *Encyclopédistes* – who took Pergolesi's *La Serva Padrona*[1] as their point of departure – and the *Guerre des Buffons*[2] broke out in real earnest. The battles were fought with pen and ink and, although the fight was long and bitter, there were no bruises, the pen being found to be far mightier than the sword – or fist.

The avowed policy of the *Encyclopédistes* was to break with tradition and establish a completely new *modus vivendi* based upon the principle of utmost simplicity. Their slogan 'Back to nature' did not imply a return to woad but to 'naturalness', and it involved the repression of everything savouring of artificiality. Music was to be comprehensible to everybody at a single hearing (how history does repeat itself!). Rameau's stand-bys of mythology and magic became taboo. It may be said with perfect truth that these had reached their zenith and were about to touch absurdity. A glance at Rameau's catalogue will show what the reformers were determined to eradicate for ever.

---

[1] Complete work – Archive Production APM 14064.
[2] The word 'Buffons' originated in the term 'Opera buffon' (or 'bouffe'). The Italian 'comédiens' were known as 'buffons'.

The difference between Lully and Rameau has been admirably explained by René Dumesnil:[1] 'Rameau's style seems to us to be much nearer that of Lully than it must have appeared at the time, with the difference that Rameau was much more original. Lully actually 'invented' very little, but, instead, utilised everything he knew in a routine manner. Rameau, on the contrary, was a genuine creator who proved to have a strong personality of his own through both the boldness of his harmonic writing and his melodic experiments. His dance music is full of symphonic qualities and shows signs of having been written with as much care as a symphony demands.' As we have seen, the mythological apparatus had now reached its limit. As far as the music was concerned, there was too much of it for audiences accustomed to Lully's one-syllable-one-note principle. Instead of listening to what was, more often than not, a tune with accompaniment, they found that the orchestra, if not actually obtruding itself, was impinging upon their musical conciousness. The difference between the two aesthetics was too great and the change had come too suddenly.

In defence of both composers, it may be said that each used the resources at his command to their fullest extent. Rameau had more at his disposal than Lully, and in addition, he did not believe that expressiveness lay only in the melody, but considered that expressive melody required the backing of expressive harmony.

Here we may see the mind of Rameau the theoretician. Essentially creative, he was able to translate his theories into actual composition. He heads the very short list of composer-theoreticians that can be mustered against that of theoretician-composers.

Lully was the more fortunate of the two composers in that he found a first-rate librettist in Quinault. Rameau was willing to set anything which appeared to resemble an opera libretto. His librettists were many: Pellégrin, Fuzelier, Bernard (three), Voltaire (two), Cahusac (seven), Marmontel (four), Colle, Monticourt, Autreau and Le Valois d'Orville, Le Clerc de la Bruyère; while in one instance (*Les Fêtes d'Hébé*), he called in Montgorge,

---

[1] *Historie Illustrée du Théâtre Lyrique* (1953), Plon, p. 64.

Bernard, and La Pouplinière. When Quinault retired, Lully had sufficient knowledge of what he wanted to be able to bend Quinault's successors to his will. Rameau was too amenable a composer to be really selective.

The two composers differed in another respect. Once Lully had completed an opera, he let it remain in that state and never made any revisions. When he learned from experience, he used that learning in his next work, but, as has been pointed out, the formula remained the same throughout his career. Rameau, on the other hand, made a second version of certain works, radically altering them in several respects. Thus, *Castor et Pollux* lost its Prologue in 1754, while *Zoroastre* had a completely new first Act written for it in 1756. The original first and second Acts became second and third, and the third and fourth were telescoped into the fourth, in two tableaux. The fifth underwent some fundamental changes.

This cannot be considered a weakness. Rameau was expanding the Lully tradition and, in the course of his experiments, was not afraid to submit to the test of trial and error. Lully deliberately went counter to the Italian tradition. Rameau, while remaining essentially French, was not unwilling to learn from the early Italians. It is not derogatory to Lully's genius to describe his choral and dance writing as stilted; to his formal dryness, Rameau added richness.

Rameau was not in the position of having to flatter a Monarch. Consequently he could dispense with the Prologue on occasion, or at least make it less effusively obsequious. The most obvious are those to the Opéras-Ballet *Les Fêtes de Polymnie* (1745) and *Les Surprises de l'Amour* (1748). Here the references are more direct; but neither forms a complete entity, as those of Lully unquestionably do.

The fairy element appeared, with Rameau, only in works on an oriental basis: *Zoroastre*, *Zaïs*, *Acanthe et Céphise*, and *Les Paladins*.[1] In the third of these, Marmontel admitted that he had united the mythological and fairy elements. Otherwise, fairies, magicians, genii, etc., find no place in Rameau's stage works.

---

[1] *Ballet Suites* I and II, Oiseau Lyre OL 50104.

The costumes remained 'au pompier', 'à la grecque', with massive helmets and waving plumes, the females being clad correspondingly, but more simply.

The stage machinery was much improved. Hitherto, too many ropes had been visible. This was not carelessness on the part of Lully, for the glories of his productions were primitive ones. If the clouds did not always obscure the mechanism, his audiences were quite happy to see how they worked. The chariots had creaked and groaned their way through space; superior knowledge and stage technique enabled them to move less audibly under Rameau's directorship. From the actor's point of view, the machines were more reliable, and here we may remark again that Jupiter's winding staircase, from *Circé*, must be accounted the most successful of all stage appliances since it was never either altered or improved. A 'Rameau Production', therefore, was neither more nor less splendid than a Lully one; it was more convincing, reliable and secure. If Lully's audiences opened their mouths wide in amazement at the marvels shown them, Rameau's opened theirs more widely still, but the improvements were those of experience rather than of progress.

Singers were just as subservient to the written music as in Lully's time, but they had much more freedom as the music, as written, gave more occasion for interpretation within its context. Rameau, like Lully, would not tolerate liberties or interpolated impertinences. The singers were no longer simply 'accompanied'. They were part of the texture and took their places as 'vocal instruments'. Rameau brought the orchestra up to the level of the stage, thus anticipating Meyerbeer. His orchestral writing was full of character and he was not afraid of sensational effects where they underlined the stage action.

In 1713, the permanent establishment of the Académie orchestra consisted of forty-six players;[1] in 1760, it was increased to forty-seven. Extra players were engaged *ad hoc;* when *Zoroastre* was revived in 1756, Rameau required:

> Two Flutes,
> Four Oboes,

---

[1] Plus the Double Bass engaged for Fridays (see p. 169).

Five Bassoons,

One Trumpet,

Sixteen Violins (one player doubling 'pour battre des timbales'),

Six Quintes – Violas (one player doubling the Musette),

Four Basses du petit choeur (one doubling Musette and Tambourin),

Eight Basses du grand choeur,

One Clavecin,

making forty-seven players in all, if those who doubled are reckoned as single entities. He was thus in a position to dictate his wishes.

Horns were employed when required, being hired for the occasion. After the extravagant addition of 1760, two *cors de chasse* were put on the establishment for *Les Paladins*. The clavecin was used chiefly to strengthen the bass, while punctuating the harmony in the right hand, but Rameau did not use it consistently throughout a work. He added a new orchestral colour by omitting a stereotyped instrument. This had not been Lully's practice, for his clavecin was played continuously (*i.e.* 'continuo').

Rameau's most important innovation was his introduction of two clarinets to the then normal force of the Académie orchestra. In 1748, La Pouplinière had employed them in his private band and it was thus easy for Rameau to use them in an *ad hoc* manner elsewhere. This he did in the Pastorale-Héroïque *Acanthe et Céphise ou La Sympathie* (November 19th, 1751), where they completed the four-part harmony with the two horns. There is a charming entr'acte between Acts Two and Three for these four instruments. He used them as an afterthought for the revised version of *Zoroastre* in 1756, but they have no parts in the score. It was not until later that they became permanent on the Académie establishment. Their introduction had to be insidious, but there seems to have been a certain amount of elasticity over the 'extras', and Rameau at any rate had no difficulty in hiring two or three of these.

Rameau certainly did not invent the *pizzicato*, for Lully and Campra (*Les Fêtes Venitiennes* from *Les Sérénades*, June 17th, 1710) had used it; but he established it as a special effect. It punctuates the rhythms of the dances in *Hippolyte et Aricie*; in *Les Paladins*

(February 12th, 1760) it represents the noise of the gaoler's keys; in *Abaris ou Les Boréades* (never performed) it reproduces the ticking of a clock during the *Gavotte pour les Heures et les Zephyrs*. Rameau often divided the strings into two groups playing *arco* and *pizzicato* separately or simultaneously.

The bassoons he brought up from being the bass of the orchestra to a position of melodic importance. In the final *Chaconne* in *Dardanus* the two instruments 'have the tune' as it is said.

Generally speaking, the instruments were used in accordance with the spirit of the text and situation. They made a perfect counterpart to the stage business and added to the general expressiveness. In *Platée*, the flutes accompany the chorus in the *coulisses* to imitate the cuckoo, while the oboe and second violin (in fourths) imitate the croaking of frogs.

It cannot be said that Rameau was essentially a colourist, but, whereas Lully and his successors *scored* their works for orchestra, Rameau *composed* his for it. Such an approach was not to receive fulfilment until Hector Berlioz, but, if Rameau may be said to have been one of the earliest 'composers for orchestra', he was by no means the 'founder of modern orchestration'.

Rameau was able to reproduce anything from quiet pastoral scenes to storms and battles. He could heighten the effect of the stage machinery – flying ballets, trapdoors, chariots floating through the air (if underwater scenes had been invented he would undoubtedly have risen to the occasion), and could lend significance to the deities dressed elaborately 'au pompier', to say nothing of doubling the antics of magicians. His weighty music added to the heavy décors of the *Tragédie-Lyrique* as well as of the *Comédie-Lyrique* and *Opéra-Ballet*.

The operas themselves are musical throughout and consist of choruses, airs and duos, instrumental dance movements, and 'symphonies' incidental to the stage action. Although each act moves without a break, there is nothing really symphonic about the thought, and continuity is maintained through recitatives, which lead into and follow the various measured elements.

The *Tragédies-Lyriques* are in five acts, with the exception of *Zoroastre* and *Abaris ou les Boréades* which both dispense with the fifth. The *Opéras-Ballets* have Prologues and shape themselves into three, four, or five Acts. *Les Surprises de l'Amour* (November 27th, 1748) was originally in two Acts, but the second version of *Anacréon* was added as an extra *Entrée* on May 31st, 1757, when the Prologue was omitted. *Zaïs* (February 29th, 1748), a *Pastorale-Heroique*, was in four Acts with Prologue. These Prologues were not mere glorifications of the King and the Royal Family; they served to set the scene, and led straight into the first Act, allowing the audience to see cause and effect from the moment the curtain rose. This was in the tradition of the mediaeval Liturgical Drama.

One of the most remarkable features of French Opera is its anticipation of much of what followed from other composers in other countries. Gluck's manifesto on the reforms of opera and his theories regarding the Overture, for example, will be found to be exactly those which Rameau put into practice twenty years earlier. Rameau had already declared that the Overture should form a musical Preface, so that Gluck has been credited with what was already a recognised theory and practice in France. This does not lessen the value of Gluck's philosophy and it must be admitted that Rameau was not consistent.

When Rameau's Overtures are compared with those of Lully, it becomes at once obvious that the later composer did not regard the composition of this movement as a mere routine necessity.

HIPPOLYTE ET ARICIE

The fugato themes are not dissimilar in style, but Rameau's adagios have a great deal of human intensity achieved mainly

DARDANUS

PYGMALION

by rich harmony. In this respect he again anticipated Gluck. Several of the Overtures have some thematic bearing upon what follows, but this would appear to have been more fortuitous than deliberate. It looks as if Rameau simply took some stray strand which appealed to him for instrumental purposes; otherwise there is little reason behind his selection. In the Overture to *Castor et Pollux*, the opening theme is closely related to that of the closing Divertissement.

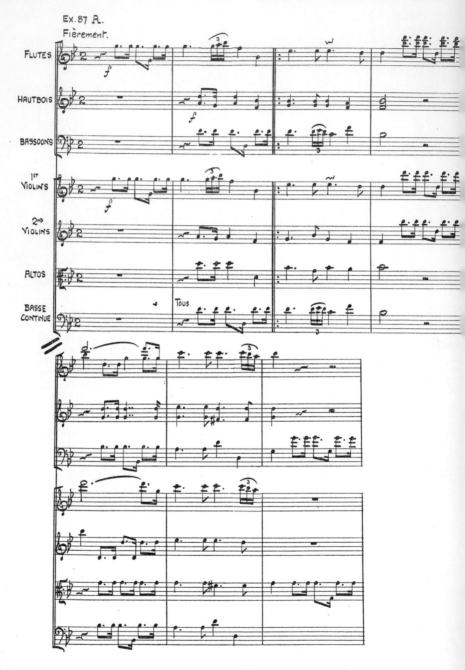

All the first part of the Overture to *Platée*[1] is an anticipation of the Symphony heralding the arrival of La Floie in Act Two. The Overtures to *Zaïs* and *Naïs* are résumés in miniature of the works they precede, that to *Zaïs* including a graphic musical description of the chaos caused by the separation of the Elements. The material is exactly the same as that of the first two scenes of the Prologue. The Overture is binary; that to *Naïs*, according to the text itself, is 'un bruit de guerre qui pient les vris et les mouvements tumulteux des Titans et des Géants'. The movement leads straight into the chorus of Titans which opens the Prologue. This foreshadowed Gluck, as was pointed out in *Le Journal des beaux-arts et des sciences* for June, 1774.

The Overture to *Zoroastre* is written on an interesting programme which, Paul-Marie Masson suggests, anticipates Lesueur or Berlioz.[2] Its divisions are explained in a note appended to the score: 'La première partie est un tableau fort et pathétique du pouvoir barbare d'Abramane et des gemissments dans les peuples qu'il opprime. Un doux calme succéde: l'espoir rénait. La seconde partie est une image vive et riante de la puissance bienfaisante de Zoroastre, et du bonheur des peuples qu'il a delivré de l'oppression.'

The Overture to *Acanthe et Céphise* is divided into three parts: I *Voeux de la Nation*, constituting a seventeen-bar Prelude; II *Feu d'Artifice*, in binary form; and III *Fanfare*, in which the different instruments play the rhythm *Vive le roi*. This caused a sensation.

The Overture to *Naïs* follows the Prologue, and is described as 'Entracte en place d'Ouverture'. The term 'Overture', however, was used rather loosely and was applied to those *Entr'actes* whose function was more than just to fill a period of inactivity and silence on the stage and, consequently, of conversation in the audience.

Fugato technique was carried very much further than in the case of Lully. Rameau sometimes omitted the introductory Adagio, and this negative innovation caused some dissatisfaction. Rameau's constant variety astonished everyone. 'Voila la sixième qu'il donne, et toutes sont aussi différentes entre elles que la

---

[1] M. René Dumesnil suggests that in this work Rameau anticipated a genre which was not to reveal itself until more than a century later – the 'Operette'. (*Histoire illustrée du Théâtre Lyrique*, Plon, p. 65.) *Chantons Bacchus*, Brunswick AXTL 1053. *Suite*, Telefunken LGM 65002.

[2] *L'Opera de Rameau*, Editions Laurens, p. 320.

Ex. 88

VOEUX DE LA NATION. (Lent.)

FEUX D'ARTIFICE

Ex. 89

189

FANFARE

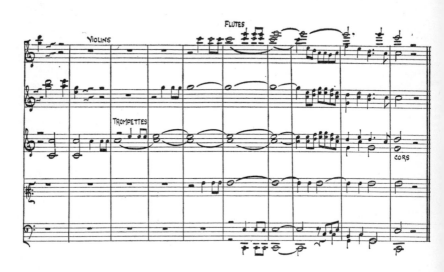

première parut différente de toutes celles qui avaient precédé' – so wrote the *Mercure* in October 1745. Diderot remarked that Rameau's invention was superior to Lully's, commenting that, although Lully was 'belle à la vérité', the Overtures of Rameau 'toutes passent pour les chefs-d'oeuvres'. This indicates that the Overture was no longer the unheeded instrumental opening number.

The Overture to *Castor et Pollux* was the first one with any significant features, although that to *Dardanus* is notable for the two-bar interludes in thirds which interrupt the repetition of the main subject. *Castor et Pollux* contains the germ of what became known as the symphonic middle-section, and its three themes are opposed and contrasted with remarkable skill. This Overture shows that Rameau was inclined to break away from the Lully tradition at an early stage in his operatic career. It must not be forgotten that he was fifty years old when he embarked on this particular career and so had had plenty of time to formulate new designs and ideas. He could therefore approach them with the touch of a practised thinker.

In *La Princesse de Navarre* (a *Comédie-Ballet*), Rameau departed from the traditional format of the Overture. This one is in three sections – lively, graceful, quick (in 3/8 time). Rameau realised the difference in atmosphere between the theatre set for Opera and that set for Ballet. Whether the audiences differed in type and quality as they do today is unknown. In any case, the demands of *Comédie-Ballet* and the *Acte de Ballet* were nothing like as opulent as those of *Opéra-Ballet* or *Tragédie-Lyrique*. Consequently, these Overtures approached the Italian Style very closely. That for *Daphnis et Eglé* (a *Pastorale-Héroique*) – produced on October 30th, 1753 – consists of a dance movement, a slow Interlude, and two Menuets; while that of *La Naissance d'Osiris* (an *Acte de Ballet*) – produced on August 12th, 1754 – shapes itself into Rondeau: Andante: Allegro. However, Rameau was not consistent in this respect where his *Actes de Ballet* were concerned.

The orchestral dramatic symphonies included music for conflagrations, battles, and storms, which the improved technique and resources of both composer and stage manager made more realistic than Lully's, graphic though these had been. The storm in *Hippolyte et Aricie* foreshadows those in Beethoven's 'Pastoral' Symphony and Berlioz' *Symphonie fantastique* and *Chasse royale et Orage*. Storms may be easy to delineate and there is a curious similarity of approach throughout the panorama of music, this including the Overture to *Guillaume Tell*, whose storm is among the most successful.

Rameau's dramatic symphonies contain many natural effects –

dawn, streams, sleep, birds, enchanted gardens, deserts – each obtained by the simplest of means and convincing by this simplicity.

Actions incidental to the text – war, the appearance of monsters from the mighty deep, riots, rejoicings, mournings – are equally explicit and, in the more serious places, exceedingly moving. However, a passage such as the following indicates the essential role of the actual orchestral sounds in making the music convincing; one is hardly reminded of monsters when it is played on the piano.

There are also descriptive Symphonies attending the arrival and departures of gods and goddesses, priests and priestesses. Rameau draws a clear dividing line between the movements of mythological deities and human beings.

One of Rameau's widest extensions of what had, by then, become a convention, may be found in the ritornelles. The ordinary four-bar preludial matter either simply set the style of the accompaniment and established the tonality in an athematic manner or, by introducing the opening bars of the Air itself, formed the little entity known as the Introduction. With Rameau the Prelude extends itself on its own axis and impulse and the ensuing vocal or instrumental theme appears as a line added to the texture. The opening of the vocal line in question springs from the opening idea of the instrumental music, thus turning it into a veritable Introduction. A fine example of this can be found in the Air

Temple sacré from *Hippolyte et Aricie*. The vocal line is derived from the instrumental ideas, the accompaniment becoming slightly varied, an inner figure being inverted with what was originally the 'top line'.

The Prelude to *Cesse, cruel amour*, from *Dardanus*, anticipates the first four bars of the vocal line (to be varied on the vocal entry) and then continues on its own for a further fifteen bars, merging into the vocal theme at the sixteenth. In *Fatal amour, cruel vainqueur*, from *Pygmalion*, the thematic connection between the Air and the nine-bar Prelude is rhythmically indirect. The theme of the Air is there but it does not reveal itself until the voice enters.

Ex.93

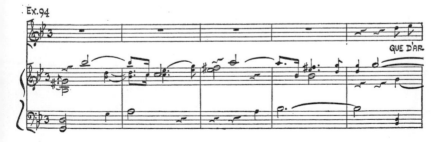

This Air opens Scene I. Much the same music is used for Scene III (Scene II being mainly recitative of both kinds). The Air – *Que d'appas! Que d'attraits!* – is superimposed upon the instrumental part after four bars and forms an added part to the texture. This is a perfect ensemble movement.

Ex.94

Opera was ceasing to be a succession of independent formal entities and was setting out to be continuous, although not by any means 'symphonic'. It was forming the foundation and authority for much of the Wagnerian philosophy which was to seem so novel so many years later. The gulf between French and Italian Opera had already widened considerably.

These Preludes are often characteristic of a dance style and create some kind of atmosphere. It is impossible to find a single instance of mere conventional note-spinning or preluding for its own sake. The voices enter at the requirements of the Prelude, and Rameau continues to keep the orchestral part significant instead of making it disappear into the background as an impersonal and obligatory accompaniment. The one is complementary to the other and it is usually possible to remove the vocal line and find a perfectly musical remainder; the voice part is, of course, always satisfactory by itself. The vocal line is directed by the spirit and declamatory exigencies of the text, and the emotional state of the various situations is supported in the orchestral harmonies. Rameau discovered the emotional evocations of the dominant ninth. Some of the harmony must have been considered crude by contemporary purists. It is certainly daring, but it is both intentional and considered. Before Rameau, only Purcell could have thought of this progression (from *Dardanus*):

and he would certainly have discovered the grace of the following, from the same work.

These two instances are taken at random. There are hundreds more.

The term 'Air' now became applicable to instrumental passages, usually in some dance style, as well as to vocal movements.

The primitive and tentative form of *recitativo stromentato espressivo* had developed since Lully. Taking it as he found it, Rameau brought it into line with the vocal Air and so measured it that it is sometimes difficult to differentiate between the two. Lully was content simply to measure it without troubling about the expressive qualities of the harmony. Rameau also found exact musical parallels to the spoken inflection, but clothed the declamation with measure and expression. To such an extent – both in this respect and in the case of the Prelude-and-Air – did Rameau pave the way for that style of opera known as 'symphonic', because it is continuous, that it is not until the final cadence, or the mergence of the music into a definite and clear-cut Air, that realisation of the passage as recitative is beyond doubt. The following example is certainly not lyrical, but it might very well be a somewhat squarely contrived Air.

On occasion, Rameau employed a form of *recitativo secco*, and in most cases it appears to have been used to induce a mood of tranquillity. If Lully's recitative is more interesting than that of his Italian predecessors and contemporaries, that of Rameau is infinitely more musical.

Rameau expected more from his singers than Lully, and he went further than merely suggesting the spirit of the words. A descent into hell, for example, is represented in this manner.

CASTOR ET POLLUX

At the same time it must be admitted that this was not altogether original, as reference to Example 54 will show.

The attempts of one character to assuage the anger of another are underlined thus:

ZOROASTRE

This indicates indignation as well as protest.

Violence and terror are depicted in disjunct rhythmic movement, *Acanthe et Céphise* being full of such instances.

Ex. 100

Vocal tremolo is used to indicate urgency.

LES PALADINS

Ex. 101

Rameau shows how the genuine French lyrical style differs
from the Italian. There are no long recitatives or Airs of a virtuoso
character.[1] Rameau's Airs are brief and to the point. He keeps
them within the framework of the dialogue and slides in and out
of his own individual recitative when conversation demands it.

One thing leads straight into another, and it is impossible
for a singer to interrupt the flow of the work to acknowledge
applause, or even for the audience to offer it. This approach
finds its authority in Perrin's declaration.[2]

The Airs are divided into various categories: *Airs de mouvement, Airs de dialogue (Airs mesurés*, as they were called), *Airs tendres*
and *gracieux.*

In general, the longer vocal Airs are devoted to moralising
and the preaching of maxims. Rameau may be said to have

Ex. 102   DARDANUS

A. AIR GRACIEUX

---

[1] But see the examples of *Ariettes* which have nothing in common with the Air (page
203).
[2] Page 102.

DARDANUS

B. AIR TENDRE

HIPPOLYTE ET ARICIE

C AIR INFERNAL

founded that lyrical type of French Opera which was to culminate in the operas of d'Indy, Dukas, Charpentier, and Roussel, while his style of *recitativo stromentato espressivo* reached a culmination in *Pelléas et Mélisande* and, to a certain extent, in *L'Heure espagnole*. Since the music moved smoothly, singers found less opportunity for mere vocal prowess *per se* in Rameau than in the Italian *bel canto* operas. In France, audiences went to hear the music; in Italy, they went to hear the singers. However, in spite of his insistence upon the musical progress of the work, Rameau wrote, from time to time, what he called *Ariettes*. These, while maintaining close contact with the matter in hand, allowed a certain licence for vocal display slightly in the Italian manner, and thus temporarily relieved the concentration on stage business.

Such an *Ariette* is *Rossignols amoureux* in *Hippolyte et Aricie*. It serves as a romantic meditation, a final anticlimactic ornament which does not interfere in any way with the continuity. Some *Ariettes* from *Pygmalion* and from *Dardanus* will show to what extent Rameau was prepared to temporise with the singers' demands, provided that nothing interfered with the progress of the drama.

In the dance movements, Rameau continued the Lully trad-

PYGMALION

Ex. 103 ARIETTE VIVE ET GRACIEUSE

JEUX ET RIS — QUE SUI-VEZ — MES TRA — CES - VO -LEZ ———————— EM-PRES-SEZ-VOUS.

B. ARIETTE GAI

RÉ ———————————————————————————————— A - MOUR

C.

FAIS BRIL-LER ——————————— TES FLAM — MES, LAN ——

CE.

D.

LA ——

CE.

DARDANUS

E. AIRIETTE GRACIEUSE

POUR LA FÊTE OÙ L'ON VOUS AP.-PEL ——

ition and established the French goût in an unmistakable manner. These dance movements appear in the *Tragédies-Lyriques* as well as in the *Opéras-Ballets* and *Actes de Ballet*. Rameau did not adhere to any of the formalised processes and, like Lully with his 'March Styles', wrote many movements whose formal descriptions were used in default of anything better, indicating only the type of movement required from the dancers.[1] The variety he displayed is quite astounding.

Rameau was blamed because his works contained such a numerous array of dance movements. Some indeed considered that opera had become merely an excuse for ballet.

The dance types were similar to those used in the *Fêtes* and *Ballets de Cour*, although the steps were by now a little more sophisticated. Rameau's music was naturally more complex and detailed than that of the earlier period. The dances include the Gavotte, Bourrée, Rigaudon, Tambourin, and Contre-Danse, all in duple time. Those in compound time include the Loure, Forlane, and Gigue, while the triple-rhythmed styles are the Sarabande, Menuet, and Chaconne, the last named being in the Lully tradition. Rameau sometimes dispensed with it. Other movements were the Passepied, Musette, and Marche, and again, as in the case of Lully, Rameau did not restrict himself to the usual quadruple or duple measure march, and it was used to emphasise dignity and to delineate battles and triumphs. Lully sometimes wrote his 'March Styles' in triple time, particularly for processions. They thus became a species of extra-stately Menuet with march-like qualities.

Comparison of Rameau's dance movements with those of Lully reveals an ever-increasing looseness of texture and ornamentation of melodic line. The two aesthetics were completely different, for while Lully disliked ornamentation, Rameau enjoyed it. Elaborate though Lully's productions were, he did not attempt

---

[1] He was fortunate in having Gaston Vestris and Mademoiselle Camargo as his principal dancers, but the arrogance and conceit of the former often drove Rameau to tears of vexation. On one occasion he told the dancer, in the hearing of all concerned, that his brains were in his toes. He was known as the 'Dieu de la Danse'. His natural son was imprisoned in For l'évêque in 1779, together with the dancer Marie Allard, for refusing to dance on one occasion. (*Gibets, Piloris, et Cachots de Vieux Paris*, Hillairet, Les Editions de Minuit, p. 148.)

to carry the elaboration into the music. Lully's dance movements were neat and compact. Rameau's were equally compact, but more charming and graceful.

Apart from the actual dance movements, there are many places which call for mime rather than dancing. These became 'Dance Figures'. Thus, in *Castor et Pollux*, there is a direction 'Entrée et combat figure d'athlètes', and in *Les Fêtes d'Hebé*, 'Oracle figure en pas de cinq'. And nothing could be more poetically suggestive, in music, than this direction: 'Endymion paraît, endormi, au fond de théâtre, sur un lit de gazon. Diane descend dans son char avec un Amour à ses pieds; elle contemple le berger, dont elle devient amoureuse. Danse de Diane et de l'Amour qui éveille Endymion: surprise, enchantement du Berger. Action pantomime représentant les amours de Diane et d'Endymion, que la Déesse enlève dans son char'. This forms a complete scene in itself and traces its origin to the Lullian *Sommeil*. Rameau wrote several of these movements.

Rameau's librettists knew what was expected of them, but they were not very gifted. He set what was handed to him without question, although his lack of judgement and critical faculty in this direction reacted unfavourably upon his works. He himself boasted, with some justification, that he could set anything to music, and that in his eyes a libretto was merely something apt for his music.

Reference has already been made to Rameau's harmonic enterprise. When he wrote semitonally, he did so with some particular expressive effect in view, and he gave the lead, both to his contemporaries and his immediate followers, in his dramatic and poignant use of the diminished seventh and the dominant ninth. This is not the place to discuss his theories, but anyone anxious to pursue the matter further will find that his treatises are still readable.

Rameau gave life to the Chorus. Instead of keeping it idle and static, with nothing to do but underline situations, he brought it forward, in an active role. His writing for vocal ensemble is masterly and he excelled in its use *en masse*.

He employed no assistants when he composed. Nobody, indeed, could have filled in his harmonies as they were by no means merely perfunctory. Harmony, in fact, had advanced a long way in a spectacularly short space of time. No one but Rameau himself could have written either this dramatic progression, as expressive as anything thought of by Gluck, or this

DARDANUS

chromaticism, an entirely new departure:

CASTOR ET POLLUX

With Rameau, Opera became its real self and acquired what is often called its 'stuff'. It required musicianly playing as well as singing, good instrumentalists as well as fine singers. Unfortunately, it quickly became both too solid and too opulent and its conventions soon passed from the sublime to the ridiculous.

CHAPTER ELEVEN

ROUSSEAU – WRITES AGAINST RAMEAU – CRITICISES FRENCH
OPERA – REVISES "LA PRINCESSE DE NAVARRE" –
"LETTRE (XXIII) SUR LA MUSIQUE FRANÇAISE" ("JULIE
OU LA NOUVELLE HÉLOÏSE") – KING'S PARTY – QUEEN'S
PARTY – "LE DEVIN DU VILLAGE" – COMPARISON WITH
"LA SERVA PADRONA" – "PYGMALION"

ALL THIS the *Encyclopédistes* proposed to alter, but, like so many
iconoclasts, they went too far and, in the end, nearly defeated
their own object. Tuneful and gay though the little Italian operas
were, they were superficial. The *Encyclopédistes* resorted to the
abuse of French music. They proclaimed far and wide that French
Opera had no *raison d'être*, as it had nothing to do with reality.
The French, proclaimed Rousseau, never had, and never would
have, any music, and if they ever did have any, it would be the
worse for them – for which pronouncement he was hanged and
burnt in effigy. He had forgotten that, in 1750, he had complained
in a letter to Baron Grimm that the Italian opera-books were
'trop réalistes et trop tragiques, et il leur préfère de beaucoup
l'opéra merveilleux, décoratif et néanmoins parfois dramatique
selon la formule de Quinault'.[1] He called for a major prophet
and, in company with Diderot, pleaded for a genius who would
put realist tragedy and comedy on to the lyric stage. On the other
hand, d'Alembert felt perfectly certain that French music could
give the world something great if the composers would consent
to alter their whole attitude.[2] Finding no answer in Rameau,
he joined the opposition.

The Baron Grimm, a German emigré who had arrived in
Paris in 1750, complained that 'the characters in an opera never
say what they mean . . . the actors speak in maxims and pro-
verbs, and sing endless madrigals, and when each has sung but

---

[1] Quoted from a translation of Jansen's *J. J. Rousseau als Musick*.
[2] *Réflexions sur la Théorie de la Musique* (1777).

two or three of these, the scene ends and the dancing recommences; if it did not do so, everyone would be bored to death'.

However, in spite of his letter to Grimm – he entered into a deadly quarrel with the Baron later – Rousseau was far from happy in his mind over the way things were going. He began his violent onslaught upon Rameau, the Académie, and French music in general. Thus, at the hands of a Swiss and a German, French music was to be completely pulverised and forced to undergo a total re-orientation of its aesthetic values. Unfortunately, the opposition became extremely influential, and, while there is no doubt that the situation required some radical change, neither Rousseau nor Grimm had enough musical qualifications for his opinion to take practical form. For the cause of this exaggerated outburst of spleen on the part of a Swiss philosopher and a German Baron, it is necessary to view the former's situation immediately after his arrival in Paris.

In order to attract attention, and to give the impression that he was of considerable repute in his own country, Rousseau had lectured to the Académie des Sciences on a new kind of musical notation based on a system of numerology. Like all endeavours to clarify what is by no means obscure, the system merely mystified the members of the Académie. It appeared to simplify nothing, but, with true Gallic courtesy, they had issued Rousseau with a certificate of thanks and duly acknowledged his erudition.

This set-back was not the full cause of Rousseau's discontent, although in due course he realised the shortcomings of his system. The matter went much deeper.

Rousseau was earning a precarious living as a music copyist. He was convinced at that time that he would be accepted in Paris as a composer of the first rank, and, in 1743, he completed an opera, *Les Muses galantes*. Rousseau managed to persuade the Duc de Richelieu (who knew nothing at all about music) that the work was a masterpiece, and, through the Duc's influence, production was arranged in La Pouplinière's house, under the direction of Rameau.

Rameau was utterly sincere. His integrity as an artist was never questioned, and with the best will in the world, he could be nothing but appalled by the inanity and incompetence of certain passages. Let Rousseau relate the episode from his own *Confessions*: 'From the start of the Overture Rameau made it perfectly clear, from certain comments, that he was out of sympathy with me. He allowed no movement to proceed without showing signs of impatience; but during an Air for counter-tenor, of which the melody was strong and sonorous and the accompaniment very brilliant, he could contain himself no longer; he addressed me with a brutality that shocked everybody, maintaining that what he had just heard was the work of a man accomplished in his art, and that the rest was written by one who did not even know anything about music; it is true that my work, written to no rule, was as sublime as it was dull, as would be the case with anything created with flashes of genius and owing nothing to science.' Rousseau had no illusions about his own gifts.

When he was penning these lines, however, he forgot that, earlier in the *Confessions*, he had admitted to the employment of a 'young man at the outset of his career' for 'some accompaniments'. This young man was none other than François André Danican Philidor (1726 – 1795), who was afterwards to make some stir in the world of composition – and the world of chess. Rameau, therefore, had no difficulty in separating the genuine from the spurious, or in detecting the hand of the amateur, which was all that Rousseau could really claim to be.

Rousseau had made the mistake of taking himself at his own valuation, but a greater error lay in the fact that he had regarded Paris as a happy hunting-ground for musicians from all over Europe. He had imagined that the ignorant French would receive him with open arms, an expectation formed because he had confused with reality what was no more than a world of egocentric fantasy. Others have made the same mistake, both in France and out of it. From that moment Rousseau spared no pains to damage the reputation of Rameau. The great French composer was not slow in taking up the cudgels in his own defence, in order to expose the enemy's ignorance and incompetence. Whatever was written by one was immediately contradicted by the other. It is possible that a 'woman scorned is a vessel of wrath', but her fury cannot exceed that of a scorned artistic amateur who finds himself unable to deceive a genuine artist.

The duc de Richelieu, however, did not waver in his allegiance to Rousseau. It was decided to revive and revise Rameau's *La Princesse de Navarre*, the text of which had been written by Voltaire. As Voltaire and Rameau were not available, the Duc asked Rousseau to undertake the work. Rousseau said that two months would be the shortest possible time in which Rameau's music could be brought to a degree of respectability, and recommended that it be renamed *Les Fêtes de Ramire*. Rousseau commenced operations by revising Voltaire's libretto. 'My work on the music was longer', he wrote in his *Confessions*, 'and more troublesome. In addition to writing extra numbers, among others the Overture, all the recitative which I had undertaken was extremely difficult, as it often became necessary to add verses and effect very quick modulations to unrelated keys in the symphonies and choruses.' Truly, Rameau hardly knew his job!

For many years, the score of *Les Fêtes de Ramire* lay hidden. It was discovered by the distinguished French musicologist, Charles Malherbe (1853 – 1911), and the fraud was immediately exposed. The Overture was found to be that originally composed by Rameau. Rousseau's additions amounted to no more than eighty-seven bars, and the modulations were all to very closely related keys. Bearing this in mind, the impact which Rousseau effected on French music is all the more astonishing.

It was now war to the knife between the two composers. The amateur surpassed himself in his daily abuse of the professional; the professional became more and more exasperated by the pin-pricks of the amateur. Perhaps if Rameau had swallowed his initial disgust and put on a different façade, Rousseau would never have fought against him in the way he did, and might have approached his reforms from an impersonal angle. This, however, would be to expect too much from an experienced musician, and the trouble really lay in the fact that Rousseau's theories held more than a grain of truth.

It is, of course, perfectly easy to poke fun and to hold any extravagance, no matter how justifiable, up to ridicule. Rousseau was a past master at this particular art. He wrote his famous *Lettre sur la Musique Française*:[1]

---

[1] *Lettre XXIII, Deuxième Partie, (Julie ou La Nouvelle Héloise).*

'The Opera in Paris is regarded, in Paris, as being the most pompous, the most voluptuous, the most admirable spectacle that human art has ever invented. They say that it is the finest monument to the magnificence of Louis XIV. It is not as easy as you might think to speak one's mind on this great matter. One is at liberty to criticise anything except the music and the Opera, and it is dangerous not to dissimulate on this point. French music is maintained by a very harsh inquisition, and the first thing that is instilled into all foreign visitors as a kind of lesson is that all other foreigners agree that there is nothing so beautiful in the whole world as the Paris Opera. Indeed, the truth is that the most tactful keep quiet and do not dare to laugh save among themselves'.

One would suggest that the first thing to be instilled into all foreign visitors might have been a measure of politeness. Rousseau refers, of course, to the attitude of the Parisians themselves, not to any politically inspired veto.

He went on: 'It must be agreed that not only are all the wonders of nature represented there at great cost, but many other wonders greater than have ever been seen, and Pope certainly referred to this bizarre theatre when he said that one could see gods, imps, monsters, kings, shepherds, fairies, anger, joy, fires, jigs, battles, and balls, all mixed up together . . . . . .

'This magnificent and well-organised assemblage is regarded as if it actually contained everything represented therein. When a temple appears, the audience is seized with a healthy respect, and provided the goddess is pretty, the pit becomes almost pagan. It is not as difficult here as it is at the Comédie-Française . . . . .

'The Opera is not here as elsewhere a troupe of people paid to give public performances; there are, it is true, some who are paid by the public and who give performances; but all that is foreign to its nature, seeing that it is an "Académie royale de musique", a kind of sovereign court making its own laws against which there is no appeal, and which does not pride itself on either justice or fidelity . . . . .'

This merely goes to prove that Rousseau had not the slightest knowledge or appreciation of the position. One might almost suppose that some of his work had been rejected by the Académie.

P

'The members of this noble Academy stoop to nobody; by way of retaliation, they are excommunicated, which is precisely contrary to the custom in other countries. [We can find no authority for this accusation in the records of the Académie.] . . . . . They never spoke in Rome with such respect of the majesty of the Roman people as they speak in Paris of the majesty of the Opéra.'

Rousseau's description of the interior of the theatre and of the stage properties is the funnier for containing more than a modicum of truth.

'Imagine a granary fifteen feet wide[1] and proportionately as long; this granary is the theatre.[2] At each side screens are placed at intervals on which are painted the objects that the scene should represent. At the back there is a large painted curtain, nearly always pierced or torn, representing either craters in the ground or clouds in the heavens, according to circumstances. Everyone passing behind the theatre [stage] and touching the curtain causes a kind of earthquake, pleasant enough to see. The sky is represented by strips of painted canvas, hung upon batons or ropes like a laundry-line. The sun, for it *does* become visible on occasions, is a lighted candle in a lantern. The chariots of the gods and goddesses consist of four laths tied together and hung from a thick rope, like a swing; between these laths there is a plank on which the god sits, and on the front there hangs a strip of thickly painted canvas which conceals this magnificent chariot. Near the bottom of the machine there is a light from two or three stinking and badly-trimmed candles, which, while the god moves and sings in his swing, smoke without hindrance – incense worthy of the divinity.

'As these chariots form the most considerable part of the machinery of the Opera, you can judge the others for yourself. The sea, always in a state of agitation, is composed of long strips of canvas or blue card which are laid out in parallel lines and are shaken by ragamuffins. The thunder is made with a heavy cart which is wheeled round in a circle, and this is not the least attractive instrument in this agreeable music. The lightning is

---

[1] This is an obvious distortion; no stage could be so small.
[2] Rousseau uses the word 'théâtre' to mean 'stage' (*i.e.* 'scène')

made by throwing pinches of wax-resin on to a flame; the thunder-bolts are crackers on the end of rockets.

'The theatre is decorated with trapdoors which, opening at will, announce that demons wish to come out of the cellar. When they have to jump into the air, they substitute, with some adroitness, demons of straw draped in brown tulle, or some-times real chimney-sweeps; these hang in the air suspended by ropes until they disappear majestically into the clouds which I have already described; but the real tragedy takes place when the ropes are badly handled or break, for then the infernal spirits and the immortal gods fall on top of each other and sometimes are killed. Add to all this the monsters which contribute to the pathetic aspect of certain scenes, the dragons, lizards, tortoises, crocodiles, and fat toads, which walk about the stage with a menacing air and make the opera seem like the temptations of Saint Anthony. Each of these figures is animated by a blockhead of a Savoyard who himself has not enough spirit to pretend to be a beast . . . . . They assured me that a prodigious amount of machinery was required to set all this in motion and several times offered to show it me; but I have never been curious to see how little things are accomplished with big efforts'.

Having thus disposed of the scenic effects, Rousseau proceeds to demolish the personnel.

'The number of people employed in the service of the Opera is inconceivable. The orchestra and chorus together number nearly a hundred persons. There are multitudes of dancers as well. All the roles are doubled and trebled, that is to say, there are always one or two substitutes ready to replace the principal actor, and paid for doing nothing until it pleases that principal actor to do nothing in turn, and that is never long in coming. After a few performances the principal actors, who are important people, do not honour the public by their presence any more; they hand over their roles to their substitutes[1] and to the sub-stitutes of their substitutes. The same money is always taken at the door, but they do not necessarily give the advertised opera.

---

[1] This was quite true, and the custom lasted for many years. When Meyerbeer wished to ensure that the tenor Nourrit would sing in each performance of one of his operas, he wagered the singer 10,000 francs that he would not do so – but Meyerbeer could afford to lose!

Each person takes his ticket as in a lottery, without knowing what work he will see. When he finds out, he will not dare to complain, for, as you know, the noble members of this Academy owe no respect to the public – it is the public which owes it to them.'

Rousseau's gall increases in bitterness as his pen moves.

'I will not speak to you about this music, for you know about it already. [He cannot, however, resist the temptation to do so.] You have no idea of the terrifying cries, the loud bellowings which fill the theatre during the performance. The actresses, almost in convulsions, burst their lungs with their screaming, with hands clenched against their chests, head thrown back, face inflamed, veins protruding, stomach panting. One does not know which is the more disagreeably affected, the eye or the ear. Their efforts make those who look at them suffer as much as those who hear their songs, and what is the most extraordinary of all, is that these shrieks are the only things that the audience applauds. From the hand-clapping one would take them for deaf-mutes delighted to have caught a few piercing noises and wishing the actors would redouble their efforts. For myself, I am persuaded that they applaud the cries of an actress at the Opera as they would the achievements of a tumbler at a Fair. The sensation is unpleasant and painful while it lasts, but one is so relieved when it finishes without an accident that one can hardly restrain one's joy. Imagine this manner of singing used to express sentiments which Quinault never expressed so gallantly or tenderly. Imagine the Muses, the Graces, the Cupids, Venus even, expressing themselves with this delicacy, and judge the effect. For the devils it is more suitable, as this music has something devilish about it. Add to this, the magicians, the evocations, and all the excitements of the Witches' Sabbath, and you have everything that is most admired in French Opera.'

From the stage he moves on to the orchestral pit, and he spares nobody.

'These beautiful sounds, as strict as they are sweet, mingle well with those of the orchestra. Imagine an endless nightmare of instruments with no melody, a perpetual rumbling in the bass – this is the most lugubrious, the most wearisome thing I have ever heard in my life and which I cannot tolerate for half-an-hour without getting a headache. It all forms a kind of psalmody with neither melody nor rhythm. When by chance some air with a lilt is discovered, there is a general stamping of feet; the entire pit follows with care, and a great deal of noise, the instrumentalist in question. Delighted at long last to hear what they hear so rarely, they use their ears, voices, arms, feet, and all their bodies in order to chase the measure which is always ready to elude them.'[1]

All this, of course, is very easy. It is a gross exaggeration and, were it not for its ultimate effect, would be passed over as the ravings of a disgruntled idiot. As it is, the matter demands attention – and Rousseau continues with a castigation of the Ballet.

'The ballets . . . are the most brilliant part of the Opera and considered separately, make an agreeable spectacle, magnificent, and truly theatrical; but they serve as a constituent part of the whole work, and it is in this capacity that it is necessary to judge them. You know the operas of Quinault; you know how the Divertissements are used there. It is the same thing, and even worse, with his successors. In each act the action is usually stopped at its most interesting point by a fête which they give the actors (who are seated) and which the Pit watches, standing up. It then happens that the characters in the work are completely forgotten, unless the audience look at the actors who are themselves looking at something else. The principle governing these Fêtes is simple; if the prince is happy, they share his happiness, and they dance; if he is sad, they try to cheer him up, and they dance accordingly. I do not know if it is the fashion at the court to give a ball to a king when he is in a bad temper. What I do know by report is that one cannot admire too strongly their stoicism at watching gavottes or listening to songs whilst their fate is discussed behind the theatre. However, there are many other subjects for dancing. The priests dance, the soldiers dance, the gods dance, the devils dance; everyone dances at their funerals, and everyone dances at the slightest provocation.

'The dance is thus the fourth of the fine arts employed on the lyric stage; but the three others try to imitate it – and what does

---

[1] In a footnote Rousseau compares the French Air with a galloping cow, or a goose that is too fat to fly.

it imitate itself? Nothing. It is thus a kind of "hors d'oeuvre" when it is employed only as dancing, for what have menuets, rigadoons, chaconnes, to do with Tragedy? I say further: it would not be in place if it did imitate something, because of all the entities, it is no more indispensible than language, and an opera where the action is half sung and half danced would be more ridiculous than one sung half in French and half in Italian.

'Not content with introducing the dance as an essential part of the lyric stage, they sometimes go so far as to make it the principal subject, and there are some operas under the name of ballets which so badly justify their description that the dance is less out of place there than in the others. The greater number of these Ballets are in the form of subjects separate from the acts, and these subjects are connected by certain metaphysical relations of which the spectator would never be aware if the author did not care to explain himself in a prologue. The Seasons, the Ages, the Senses, the Elements – what connection have these with dancing . . . . ?'

And so forth and so on.

All this arouses suspicion. Rousseau himself was capable of thinking only in terms of tunes with accompaniment. Realising this limitation, he turned the weakness into a principle. Incapable of contriving even a suggestion of continuity or development, he made it a bone of contention and slandered those more musicianly than himself, endeavouring to show that they were wrong and he was right. All this was, of course, directed principally at Rameau who had refused to recognise Rousseau as the great composer he felt himself to be.

One may ask what business it was of German and Swiss émigrés to interfere with the artistic policies of the country in which they had taken up residence. Amateurs, in the worst sense of that word, have always tried to convince experienced musicians that salvation lies only with them and that professionals know nothing. What are known as 'musical circles' remained unimpressed with Rousseau; Paris, which had not laid down the red carpet, was later to feel his political impact in no uncertain manner.

Unable to absorb more than one musical idea at a time, Rousseau ascribed a similar lack of ability to everyone else.

He found Pergolesi's *La Serva padrona* well within his compass, however, and its production, on August 1st, 1752, greatly enhanced his musical perception. Other Italian *Opéra-Bouffes* were *Il Giocetare* (August 22nd) and *Il Maestro di Musico* (September 9th), while *Tracollo medico ignorante* appeared on May 1st, 1753. Paris was indeed a happy hunting-ground for Pergolesi, especially now that he had found a champion there.

The repertoire in general consisted of *La Finta Cameriera*, by Latilla (November 30th, 1752); *La Donna superba*, by Rinaldo di Capua (December 19th, 1752); *La Scaltra governatrice*, by Cocchi (January 25th, 1753); and *Il Cinese rimpatriato*, by Sellitti (June 19th, 1753) – this last sharing the bill with *La Zingara*, by Capua. *Gli Artigiani arrichiti*, by Latilla, and *Il Paratajo*, by Jommelli, were both produced on September 23rd, and *Bertoldo in cortel*, by Ciampi, on November 22nd. *I Viaggiatori*, by Leonardo Leo, was the last work to be performed – on February 12th, 1754. No new work by Rameau was produced until February 12th, 1760, when the three-act *Comédie-Lyrique*, *Les Paladins*, made its first appearance. This work is sometimes referred to as being a Ballet.

The pamphleteering did not stop the Académie producing new French works in the traditional style, but it resulted in the formation of two operatic factions. The King (Louis XV) and Madame de Pompadour favoured the French school, the Ramoneurs; the Queen, the Italian, the Buffons. The 'King's Party' (the Nationalists) sat in one corner of the theatre, and the 'Queen's Party' (the Anti-Nationalists) sat in the other.[1] According to Rousseau himself, he and the *Encyclopédists* ranged themselves under the Queen's box. Riots constantly broke out in the theatre, benefitting no-one, and the question of what was to become of Louis XIV's essentially French culture, and Lully's dignified Académie royale de musique, became one of some delicacy and importance.

The Italian season came to an end on March 7th, 1754. The French composers, therefore, remained sole occupants of

---

[1] It is to be doubted, however, if the Queen was influenced by personal motives, for she was never hostile to Madame de Pompadour and had long since become reconciled to the King's neglect of herself. The Favourite was a true patron of the arts and her *chambre* at Versailles was the scene of many musical performances.

the Parisian lyric stage. The answer, however, had already been supplied when – on March 1st, 1753 – Rousseau produced his model opera, the opera which, he claimed, would set the standard for the future and pulverise all previously maintained philosophies: *Le Devin du Village*.[1] It had been performed privately in 1752, at Fontainebleau, the actors including the Dauphin and the courtiers. It was just the right work for amateurs.

Rousseau was none too pleased, however, at the reception of his model opera. On his own admission, he made himself as difficult as possible and betrayed all the instincts of class-consciousness to an audience which tried to set him at his ease and afford him due respect as the composer.[2] Always on the look-out for something at which to quibble, no matter how small, he complained that the King sang Collet's Air[3] in a voice more false than his royalty. Some say, however, that it was the Dauphin, afterwards Louis XVI, who made this fatal mistake. Rousseau conveniently forgot that the casual humming of a tune by one with no ear for music at all was a striking tribute to the fulfilment of his ideal – that music should be comprehensible to all and sundry at a single hearing.

Remembering what has been said about French Opera, one can see how and why these little Italian works made their immediate appeal. They were simple and humorous; they presented familiar types and situations in the daily lives of ordinary people. No concentrated listening was needed, for the music moved along pleasantly enough, the tunes were singable, and the stage business provided an amusing evening's entertainment. While the French school desired to uplift the audience by moral attitudes, spectacle, and great music, the Italian was satisfied with pure entertainment, no matter of how superficial a kind.

---

[1] Gustav Choquet, in *Grove's Dictionary*, puts forward the theory that Rousseau stole this work from a Lyons musician named Granet. It remained in the repertoire until 1829, when a wag threw a wig dating from its period on to the stage, signifying that its day was over. Revivals in the present century have revealed nothing more than a period interest. The work remains simply a unit in the history of opera, and confirms Rousseau as an amateur. (Complete work, Columbia 33cx 1503).

[2] Alexandre Dumas (père) gives an enlightening account of this Royal Performance in his *Memoirs of a Physician* which tallies exactly with Rousseau's own description of the event.

[3] See Example 108.

La Serva padrona has simple requirements – three characters (one of them mute!) and an orchestra of strings and cembalo. Published by Royal Privilège in 1782, the score bears the following notice:

> L'Editeur de cet ouvrage le donne au Public, non dans l'état de mutilation ou l'on a été contraint de la mettre à l'opéra de Paris pour satisfaire l'impatience des spectateurs, mais entier, et tel qu'il fait depuis trente ans l'admiration publique sur tous les Théâtres de l'Europe.

There is no Overture, but the orchestra must undoubtedly have played one belonging to some other opera. There is a certain similarity between the Arias, these being deft and simple, consisting of straightforward tunes with accompaniment. There are only two ensemble numbers, the various Arias being held together by *recitativo secco*. One of the two spirited Arias opens in this way:

LA SERVA PADRONA

and the only expressive one like this:

The orchestra underlines very little.

The French counterpart is equally simple but somewhat less sophisticated:

-TERUX, GRAN-DEURS, RI-CHES-SE VOTRE É-CLAT NE ME TEN-TE PLUS.

Far more potent and anticipatory of the future was Rousseau's *Pygmalion*. His firm opinion that French was an impossible language to set to music (a theory which he himself denied in *Le Devin du Village*), led him to experiment in an elaborate species of *Mélodrame*. This was quite original. The work was arranged so that each spoken line was preceded and announced by a musical phrase. This artifice saved Rousseau the trouble of dealing with the accentuations of an 'impossible' language and succeeded in making a principle out of a weakness. In this respect, he was a major prophet in a small way, and although he did not finally alter the course of lyric drama, he at least postulated a genre.

Enough has been said and written about Rousseau's musical theories. Some authorities claim him as a musical genius, others relegate him to the ranks of the inefficient, cock-sure amateurs who have always abounded in artistic circles. At the most he may be said to have caused a stir in musical affairs, but nothing more. The later history of French Opera proves this.

CHAPTER TWELVE

SALLE DU PALAIS ROYAL DESTROYED − ACADÉMIE MOVES
TO COMÉDIE-FRANÇAISE − SALLE DES MACHINES DES
TUILERIES − CRITICISM OF BUILDING − PHILIDOR −
DEUXIÈME SALLE DU PALAIS ROYAL OPENED − "ZOROASTRE"
− PERSONNEL OF ACADÉMIE − QUEUE SYSTEM INTRODUCED
BY DECREE − BOX OFFICE AGENCY − BALLET-PANTOMIME −
GOSSEC − DROITS DU COMPOSITEURS − GLUCK − "IPHIGÉNIE
EN AULIDE" − "ORFEO ED EURIDICE" − PICCINNI −
GLUCKISTES VERSUS PICCINNISTES − "ALCESTE" −
"ARMIDE" − "ROLAND" (PICCINNI) − "IPHIGÉNIE EN
TAURIDE" (GLUCK AND PICCINNI) − REVIVAL OF "THÉSÉE"
− MÉHUL − "ECHO ET NARCISSUS" (GLUCK) − "ATYS"
(PICCINNI) − DEATH OF GLUCK − HIS MAXIMS − OVERTURES −
VOCAL WRITING − COMPARISON WITH PICCINNI

THE LAST opera to be performed in the original Salle du Palais
Royal was Dauvergne's *Polyzène*. On April 6th, 1763, there occurred
an event which was to become a commonplace of Paris theatrical
life; the theatre was burnt to the ground.

This tragedy could not have happened at a more disastrous
time, for it was Easter week and the building was locked up.
The flames quickly took control, and the theatre was gutted.
A large crowd gathered and witnessed the paradoxical sight of
the Capucines of the Rue-Saint-Honoré, the Cordeliers, and the
Recollets, all pledged to consign the theatre in general to perdition
as a source of evil, trying to extinguish the conflagration with
buckets. It was reported that fifteen people perished, but Favart
says that this was an exaggeration − 'Nous somme quittés pour
un Recollet et un Capucin'.[1] Voltaire ascribed it to an Act of
God, for the performances were so bad that Divine Vengeance
was to be expected sooner or later. Some said that it was
caused by a caretaker who had left an exposed candle burning

---

[1] *Mémoires.* Quoted in *Les Treize Salles de l'Opéra* − Lasalle (Paris, Librairie Sartorius
1875, p. 59).

too near the proscenium curtain and had tried to put the fire out himself rather than face the consequences of sounding the alarm.

The fire was first noticed at eight in the morning, and it spread rapidly. Responsibility was placed upon the Duc d'Orléans and the Provost of the Merchants. Each tried to put the blame on to the other, and eventually it settled on the latter. The City Fathers decided to defray the cost of re-building, but claimed the right to house the Académie on any site they might choose. This did not satisfy the Duc d'Orléans, who suggested a compromise, and this was accepted. It was decided to re-build on the old site (at the end of the right aisle of the Palais-Royal) and to make the new building larger than the old. This necessitated the demolition of seven houses and, after some discussion, the City Fathers agreed to indemnify by purchase, four, and the Duc, three, of these buildings.

The next step was to find a temporary home for the Académie. The Comédie-Française immediately offered to lend its premises in the Faubourg Saint-Germain three times a week, for nothing. It was finally decided, however, to use the Salle des Tuileries, and the work required to adapt this awkward building to operatic needs was put in hand at once. Meanwhile, the Opera section of the Académie gave a series of performances in Rouen, while the Ballet gave its services to the Comédie-Française, producing a ballet added to Favart's *L'Anglais à Bordeaux*. After the twelfth performance of Favart's play (by which time the Parisians had realised the extra entertainment offered them) the receipts at the Comédie-Française went up by leaps and bounds. The dancers refused to take any share of the profits as a return for the hospitality given them and, instead, they were entertained to a magnificent banquet by the actors. Such an atmosphere of mutual co-operation formed a bright side to a gloomy affair.

The Salle des Machines, as the Salle des Tuileries had been called after the earlier abortive attempt to use it for Opera, had been re-opened in 1738, for the production of a *Pantomime* which displayed the marvels of Vigarini's and Ratabon's machines. The Directors of the Académie decided to divide the building[1]

---

[1] It stood on the site of the present Arc de Carrousel, erected by Perrier and Fontaine in 1806.

into two sections, constructing a hall and a theatre under one roof. The work took but eight months to complete.

The original plan had been to rebuild the Salle du Palais Royal on exactly the same model as the old theatre. This was sensible, since the sets would naturally not fit a larger stage, and the singers would be at an initial disadvantage in a larger building. The possibilities for improvement, however, seemed so vast that extra seats were put in – to the advantage of the Box Office. The cost far exceeded the estimate, and the architect, Soufflot, passed the blame on to Moreau, the Master of the Works, who duly passed it back again – to the exasperation of the populace, who were indifferent as to the responsibility and were anxious only to have the theatre available once more.

On January 24th, 1764, the newly-completed Salle des Machines des Tuileries opened its doors with Rameau's *Castor et Pollux*, by now well-known to the public. The performance had a mixed reception. The singers were ill at ease in the vast theatre – for it was still vast in spite of the alterations – and, although the production, with its startling machines and stage effects, was a magnificent one, the performance did not come up to expectations. Bachaumont, in his *Mémoires*, complained of practically everything, particularly the seating. The first boxes were too far forward and the gallery so high and detached that nothing could be seen or heard from it (Appendix Forty-three).

On the second night, he found the theatre almost empty and the performance execrable (Appendix Forty-four).

In 1768, the King of Denmark visited Paris and a Gala Night was prepared in his honour by the Académie. For the first time in history, the *affiches* bore the words 'Par ordre', signifying that royalty would be present. This custom remained in force throughout all the monarchical periods in France. No expense was spared. The costumes were opulent, the décors extravagant. The work was – Rousseau's *Le Devin du Village*, originally written to show that lavishness and extravagance were the ruin of opera! The simple-minded music must have consorted badly with décors used for *Tragédie-Lyrique* and *Opéra-Ballet*.

The records mention two composers later to become eminent in *Opéra-Comique*, Philidor, and Pierre Alexandre Monsigny

(1726 – 1798), the substance of whose operas was far too slight for such a large theatre. The most important work was Philidor's *Ernelinde, Princesse de Norvège* (November 24th, 1767), which was renamed *Sandomir, Prince du Danemark*, when it was revived on January 14th, 1769. On its second appearance a little more history was made, for the performance was announced 'au benefice de l'auteur', the first time a composer had been so honoured.

One curious relic of the Salle des Machines des Tuileries remains to this day. On the stage-sets at the Opera the words 'Cour' and 'Jardin' may be read. They were first put on the sets during the occupation of the Salle des Machines, when the right-hand side of the stage was known as 'Cour' and the left as 'Jardin', the courtyard and garden of the Tuileries being respectively to the right and left of the Salle des Machines.

The new Salle du Palais Royal opened its doors on January 20th, 1770, with Rameau's *Zoroastre*. The building contained many novel features, several of which have remained in use ever since. The erection was directed by Moreau to the plans of Soufflot. A full and detailed description may be found in the *Dictionnaire historique de la Ville de Paris*, by Hurtault and Magny, from which the following facts have been gleaned.

The new theatre was three times as large as the original, for Moreau extended it as far as the Rue des Bons-Enfans, which ran parallel to the site, at a distance. It was the first French theatre to be built on an oval plan. The earlier buildings, which had often started life as tennis-courts, were rectangular. The Salle des Machines des Tuileries was intended more for circus performances than for opera or vaudeville. One feature of the new design was the *baignoire*; in this, four people sit in the utmost discomfort in a space made for two, on hard wooden chairs, with a diagonal view of the stage. Moreau ordered three reservoirs containing two hundred *muids* (hogsheads) of water in case of fire, and for the first time the stage was fitted with a fireproof curtain.

The seating capacity was 2,500, and the four rows of boxes were constructed of wood and iron. The decoration was lavish, if not to say garish, with marble and plush. The foyer contained busts of Quinault, Lully, and Rameau, while four empty niches stood ready to receive the effigies of any future great men (Appendix Forty-five).

The personnel numbered 278, the official tally reading as follows:

ADMINISTRATION

General Administrator, appointed by the King .	I
Directors	3
Permanent Secretary	I

SINGERS

'Maîtres de Chant' and Accompanists . .	5
Basses	6
Tenors	4
Sopranos and Contraltos . . .	8
Male Choristers	34
Female Choristers	16

DANCERS

'Maître de Ballet'	I
Male Dancers	8
Female Dancers	11
'Corps de Ballet'—*male*	33
—*female*	39

ORCHESTRA

Conductor	I
Claveciniste	I
Violins	25
Violas ('Quintes')	5
Basses	15
Flutes and Oboes	7
Clarinets	2
Bassoons	8
Trumpet	I
'Cors de Chasse'	2
Drums and Drummers	2
Stage-hands, Machinists, Scenic Designers, Concierges, Inspectors, Attendants, etc.	39

A Royal Decree instituted the queue system for admission, again insisting that everyone, without exception, should pay for his seat. Each had to take his chance at the Box Office, regardless of rank. Nobody was to wear a hat during the *entr'actes* (Appendix Forty-six).

The prices of seats were:

First Balcony	.	.	.	10 livres
Amphitheatre	.	.	.	10 livres
Second Balcony	.	.	.	7 livres 10 sous
First-Row Boxes	.	.	.	7 livres 10 sous
Second-Row Boxes	.	.	.	4 livres 10 sous
Third-Row Boxes	.	.	.	3 livres 10 sous
Gallery ('Paradis')	.	.	.	2 livres 10 sous
Pit ('Parterre')	.	.	.	2 livres 10 sous

Seats could be rented for a year at the following rates:

Front Boxes ('Timbales')	.	.	3,600 livres
Side Boxes ('Chaises de poste')	.	.	2,400 livres
Baignoires ('Crachoirs')[1]	.	.	1,000 livres

A properly regulated Box Office Agency was appointed. The responsible officials were Le sieur Levy, from whom seats for the Opera might be obtained (his orders were to reply to no letters sent unfranked), and M. de la Porte, a 'marchand perfumeur', who sold the tickets for the Opera Balls (Appendix Forty-seven).

The prices were doubled for a first performance, and quadrupled when the King attended.

In accordance with what had become almost a tradition, all was confusion on the opening night, January 26th, 1770. The police had to be reinforced; there was the usual trouble over tickets and priority of admission, and the pathetic attempt to practise the 'first come, first served' principle fell to pieces. Eventually, the Académie was given its own special troop of

---

[1] Literally 'spittoons'. We are unable to find out the reason for this description other than that the space was the official receptacle for orange peel etc. It may be a salutary thought for those who sit in these compressed places to-day!

soldiers, chosen from the élite of the Guards, and it was all they could do to stem the onrush of people who, every night, 'étaient obligés de se créer de vive force une place qui n'existait pas'.

Once inside, the audience passed the time shouting across the auditorium and making uncensored comments on the people in the more expensive seats. It was not uncommon for a person to appeal to the public for 'justice' when someone claiming the same ticket-number tried to eject him. The first-comer was usually supported so whole-heartedly that the rival claimant had to beat a hasty retreat. It would seem that the holders of tickets paid no attention to the numbers on them, but sat exactly where they wished.

Artistically, the general situation was highly favourable for the future of opera; but, alas, Rameau was dead and there was nobody capable of continuing the high standard of composition set by him. However, a striking innovation in the Académie repertoire was made in the appearance of a *Ballet-Pantomime* in an opera, *Ismène et Ismenias*, by Delaborde (or de La Borde), which was produced on December 11th, 1770. Its composer was Valet de Chambre to the King, and his contribution to music includes a weighty four-volume *Essais de la Musique*. His opera merits attention only for the introduction of *Medée ou Jason* (*Ballet-Pantomime*) by the dancer, Noverre. It was not the first attempt at the style, nor was it the first performance of the work. Noverre had previously produced it at Stuttgart. In 1755, the Duchesse du Maine had drawn up a scenario from *Horaces*, in which Horace kills Camille. This was set to instrumental music specially written for mimed interpretation. It was produced at one of the *Nuits de Sceaux*, but did not make a second appearance.

The *Ballet-Pantomime* eliminated all singing and formed the origin of what is now known simply as 'Ballet'. Its appearance as part of an opera is reflected all through the panorama of French Opera, and eventually it attained an importance second not even to the Opera of which it was part. Its omission on one occasion caused one of the biggest scandals in the history of opera.

September 7th, 1773, marks another important date in the history of French Opera as, for the first time, a composer appeared on the stage to take a call. This took place after the performance of a ballet, *L'Union de l'Amour et des Arts*, by Floquet. The twenty-five-year-old composer thus shared an honour with Voltaire, who was similarly recalled after the fall of the curtain on his tragedy *Merôpée*.

Not even *Sabinus* (February 23rd, 1774), an opera by Joseph Gossec (1734 – 1829), could alter the stagnation that had set in after the death of Rameau. Gossec was a notable composer, Belgian by birth. He had conducted Rameau's works in the house of La Pouplinière and had founded the Concerts d'Amateurs in 1770; in 1773 he had revived the Concert Spirituel. He was not, therefore, an unknown figure at the time. Later, during the Revolution, he became a leading musician in France.[1]

The story, for a while, is indeed a dull one, opera succeeding opera in humdrum routine. The period, however, saw many reforms, among which may be singled out the decree of 1776, fixing the Rights of the Composer. This regulation governed both works which occupied an entire evening and those which were part of a double or a triple bill.

In the former case, the composer received:

For each of the first twenty performances   .   200 *livres*,
For each of the next ten performances   .   150 *livres*,
For each of the next ten, up to a maximum
   of forty   .   .   .   .   100 *livres;*

In the latter:

For each of the first twenty performances   .   80 *livres*,
For each of the next ten performances   .   60 *livres*,
For each of the next ten, up to a maximum
   of forty   .   .   .   .   50 *livres.*

In both cases, the theatre became sole proprietor of the work after the fortieth performance. The composer was entitled to nothing further.

---

[1] The fact that Gossec wrote twenty-six Symphonies upon what later became known as the 'Haydn Model' before Haydn had formulated that style is usually overlooked by historians.

The Director, de Vismes, completely renewed the décors and costumes, established the principle of seven performances each week, and endeavoured to inculcate a little discipline into the permanent staff. This, as may be imagined, was resented. Under the leadership of Mademoiselle Guimard, the name of Beaumarchais (author of *The Marriage of Figaro*) was put forward to high authority as a suitable substitute for de Vismes; but the plot failed, and de Vismes remained in power. He was a man of progressive ideas and tried the experiment of lowering the house lights by means of shades reflecting the rays on to the stage. This idea came from the method in practice in the lighthouse on the Ile de Ré.

The repertoire, meanwhile, was augmented with many undistinguished works, none of which either reached the high level of those by Rameau, or fulfilled the ideal postulated by Rousseau. The situation rose to significance, however, when in 1772 Gluck arrived in Paris. Rumour maintained that he had been invited by a former pupil of his in Vienna, the Dauphine, later Queen Marie-Antoinette. He was forty-eight when he wrote his first great opera, *Orfeo ed Euridice*,[1] which had been produced in Vienna prior to his departure for Paris.

In spite of a brusque outspokenness, Gluck was a man of infinite tact when he thought it politic. Discovering the situation in Paris, and finding that the gap left by Rameau had not yet been filled, he determined first of all to placate the *Encyclopédistes*. Having appreciated the reforms which Rameau had carried out (and which approximated very closely to his own ideas), he told the Director of the Académie that he would always make a point of consulting Rousseau when further musical reforms were needed. In this way, both factions were on his side right from the beginning. The first work he wrote for the Académie was *Iphigénie en Aulide*, a *Tragédie-Opéra* in three Acts, adapted from Racine by the Bailli du Roullet. This was produced on April 19th, 1774, and for it, trombones were introduced into the Académie orchestra.

---

[1] German version, Deutsche Grammofon DGM 1843 – 4; Italian version, R.C.A. RB 16058 – 60; French version, Columbia 33cx 1520 – 1. Minuet and Dance, H.M.V. 7er 5052. *Dance of the Furies; Dance of the Blessed Spirits*, Deutsche Grammofon DG 17062.

The performance lasted for five and a half hours after the entry of the Dauphin (afterwards Louis XVI), the Dauphine, and the Comte de Provençe (later Louis XVIII), the author of at least two opera libretti. The scene was one of the utmost splendour. Although etiquette demanded that there should be no applause unless led by the royal party, the Overture[1] made such an impression through its dramatic import, that the audience broke into spontaneous acclamation. 'Jamais le public n'a montré tant d'empressement et d'enthousiasme que pour cet opéra qui doit faire époque dans la maison Françoise.' (*Mercure de France*, 1774.) After Agamemnon's first recitative, Marie-Antoinette could contain herself no longer and, giving the signal, led an applause which lasted for several minutes.

The second performance was no less splendid.

As a natural result of this success, another opera by Gluck was put into rehearsal, this being a French version of the original *Orfeo ed Euridice*. After this was performed, Rousseau remarked that such music showed him that life had something good to offer, after all. Gluck had conquered.

The absence of specialised librettists was proving a difficulty, but the Bailli du Roullet produced a translation of de Calzabigi's *Alceste*,[2] in three Acts, which was performed on April 23rd, 1776. The first and second Acts were completely successful, but the audience found the third monotonous. Immediately afterwards, Gluck left for Vienna to work on Quinault's original libretto *Armide*.

Meanwhile, a domestic crisis threatened to bring court scandal into the open. Observing that Marie-Antoinette favoured Gluck, Madame du Barry looked round for a rival, and invited a notable Italian composer, Nicola Piccinni (1728 – 1800), to come to Paris. Piccinni at first declined the invitation, but, in 1777, after the death of Louis XV, he changed his mind. He immediately set to work upon Marmontel's version of Quinault's *Roland*, now reduced to three Acts. Marmontel was none too happy about this, as he was a great admirer of Gluck.

The Abbé Arnaud waxed cynical:

---

[1] Decca LX 3063.   [2] Complete work, Decca LXT 5273 – 6.

Ce Marmontel si long, si lent, si lourd,
Qui ne parle pas, mais qui beugle,
Juge la peinture en aveugle
Et la musique comme un sourd.
Ce pendant a si triste mine,
Et de ridicule bardé,
Dit qu'il a le secret des beaux vers de Racine;
Jamais secret ne fut si bien gardé.

Marmontel replied:

Il arrive le jongleur de Bohême;
Sur le débris d'un superbe poème,
Il fit beugler Achille, Agamemnon;
Il fut hurler la reine Clytemnestre;
Il fit renfler l'infatigable orchestre;
Du coin du roi, les antiques fermeurs
Se sont émus à ses longues clameurs;
Et, le parterre éveillé d'un long somme,
Dans un grandbruit crut voir l'art d'un grand homme.

Two new factions at once sprang into being. Instead of the Lullyistes and Ramoneurs verses the *Encyclopédistes*, it was now the Gluckistes verses the Piccinnistes. Suard, Arnaud, Coqueau, and Rollet supported the former; Marmontel (perforce), La Harpe, Ginguèné and, most formidable of all, d'Alembert, the latter. This battle was even more intense than the others. The Abbé Arnaud maintained that, in *Alceste*, Gluck had recaptured the 'spirit of antique grief'; the Piccinnistes replied that they wished he had discovered that of 'modern pleasure'. A wit remarked that, while it was easy to like Gluck's music, it was very difficult to like the Gluckistes.

The new Gluck opera, *Armide*, was not a great success when it was produced on September 23rd, 1777. The purists considered that it was wrong to set new music to an already established libretto, and demanded the original work by Lully. They tried to block the second performance, but Gluck hurried off to Versailles and laid his complaint before the Queen. She took his part, and the block was dispersed. By this time, Gluck had become quite unscrupulous. Learning that Sacchini's *Olympiade* was to be produced at the Comédie-Italienne, he did all in his power to prevent it. The Parisians were furious that a foreigner should try to exert dictatorial powers over their music, particularly after so many honours had been conferred upon him. To parry this attack, Gluck declared Rameau to be the greatest composer of all time – and the battle raged more fiercely still.

Piccinni's *Roland* was eventually produced on January 17th, 1778, and was a complete success. The Queen, partly out of curiosity perhaps, and partly out of tact, attended the performance but did not applaud very much. The situation was growing tense and slightly ridiculous. The Director of the Académie, Berton, arranged a banquet, therefore, in honour of the two composers. They were placed side by side and, to everybody's astonishment, appeared to be on the best of terms. Gluck became over-heated and said to Piccinni, in a voice loud enough to be heard by everybody: 'My dear friend, the French are good people, but they make me laugh; they want us to write songs for them, but they do not know how to sing. You are celebrated all over Europe; you are anxious only to uphold your glory in writing beautiful music for them; has it got you any further? Believe me, the only excuse for living here is to make money, and nothing else'. Piccinni replied that Gluck had proved by his example that it was possible to make fame as well as money, and the two composers departed still firmer friends.

De Vismes devised the cynical scheme of giving the same subject to both composers. *Iphigénie en Tauride* was selected. Guillard wrote the libretto for Gluck, Deubreuil, that for Piccinni. In the meantime, he placated the *Encyclopédistes* by producing a large number of little Italian operas. Then, in order to prove the fatuity of maintaining a Lullyiste following, and also to prove his own complete objectivity, he revived Lully's *Thésée*. It was hissed off the stage by the occupants of the Pit. The Lullyistes retired in disorder, and one of them broke into verse:

Qu'ils me sont doux ces champêtres concerts
Où rossignols, pinsons, merles, fauvettes,
Sur le théâtre entre des rameaux verts,
Viennent gratis m'offrir leurs chansonettes!

Quels opéras me seraient aussi chers?
Là n'est point d'art, d'ennui scientifique;
Piccin[n]i, Gluck n'ont point note les airs;
Nature seule en dicta la musique,
Et Marmontel n'en a pas fait les vers.

Gluck finished before Piccinni, and his opera was produced on May 18th, 1779; Piccinni's did not appear until January 23rd, 1781, by which time Gluck was safely out of the way.

During one of the rehearsals of Gluck's work, an Inspector suddenly noticed a slim figure hiding in one of the boxes. It was a young man, faint with hunger, who said that he had spent all the day and the previous night there in order to be present at the first performance; he had no money. Gluck was struck with this manifestation of admiration and enquired the young man's name. He gave it as Étienne Méhul.

Gluck received 16,000 livres for the new opera. After its success, he began to drive bargains and asked 20,000 livres for *Echo et Narcissus*. Finally 10,000 livres was agreed upon, even this being far in excess of the standard rates paid to the French composers. In addition, Gluck received 6,000 livres from the publisher Deslauriers, of the rue Saint-Honoré, who sold no music other than his.

Echo et Narcissus was such a resounding failure that Gluck retired to Vienna in high dudgeon. He never ceased to revile the French for what he considered an insult. After September 24th, 1779, therefore, Piccinni had the field to himself.

On February 22nd, 1780, Piccinni scored one success with *Atys* (text by Marmontel, also after Quinault) and, on January 23rd, 1781, another with his version of *Iphigénie en Tauride*. The rumour reaching Gluck that he contemplated a return to Paris, he wrote to deny it, declaring that he would not come back until the French made up their minds what kind of music they really wanted.

The second performance of Piccinni's *Iphigénie en Tauride* was attended by an interesting contretemps. One of the singers, Mademoiselle Laguerre, was struck by an attack of nerves and was unable to utter a sound. It is indicative of the discipline of the Académie that she was sentenced to imprisonment in For l'évêque, coming to the theatre and returning to her cell each night under a military escort. For l'évêque must have been almost a second home to her. It was said that she represented *Iphigénie en Champagne*, not *en Tauride*.

Gluck died before finishing *Les Danaides*. At his request it was completed by his pupil, Salieri.

His philosophy may be summed up in a single sentence from a letter written to La Harpe on October 12th, 1777: 'The voices, the instruments, and all sounds, even silence itself, should have only one aim – expressiveness'. This philosophy he rigidly maintained. That his music did not sound convincing or satisfactory on the keyboard disturbed him not at all. It had come to him in terms of instruments and, as long as it sounded well in the theatre, he was content. Wagner's theories, therefore, were not original, and as they corresponded in many respects to those of Rameau, it may be said that they were obvious to the thinking operatic composer. Gluck was inconsistent only with regard to the Overture. While the Overtures to *Alceste* and *Iphigénie en Aulide* lead straight into the first Act, and that to *Iphigénie en Tauride* is simply a short Prelude (the first operatic one of its kind), that to *Orfeo* is, in reality, the Overture written by Philidor to his opera *Ernelinde*, while that to *Armide* is a movement written by Gluck in 1750 for his Italian Opera *Telemacco*. All the mature Overtures are masterpieces of classic dignity.[1]

Dignity is, indeed, the keynote of all his music. Gluck echoed Lully in his square choral writing. It has been said that while Piccinni 'sang', Gluck 'declaimed';[2] here we may see another contact with the Florentine. However, in movements such as the famous *Dance of the Blessed Spirits* he approaches very near to Rameau – and to the sublime.

His influence was universal, but it is only fair to repeat that his principles were very much those of Rameau. There was no

[1] *Alceste, Iphigénie en Aulide*, both Decca Iw 5022.

[2] *Divinités du Styx*, Decca 45–71 1100 (*Alceste*). *Vous voyez leur fureur extreme*, H.M.V. History of Music HLP 17 (*Iphigénie en Aulide*). *Che faro*, Decca Iw 5072; *Che puro ciel*, Decca Iw 5225 (*Orfeo*). *O del mio dolce ardor*, Decca LX 3112 (*Paride ed Elena*). *C'est un torrent: Un ruisselet bien clair*, Decca LX 3122 (*La Rencontre imprévue*). See *Monsieur Croche the Dilettante Hater, No. XXV* (*An Open Letter to the Chevalier W. Gluck*), Debussy (N. Douglas trans. London).

Rameau revival until 1903, when the Schola Cantorum resuscitated *Castor et Pollux*; in 1908, the Opera played *Hippolyte et Aricie*. It stands to reason, therefore, that the French composers lived in ignorance of their distinguished forbear's aesthetic theories, as they had no opportunity of seeing them in practice on the stage. French Opera underwent a period of stagnation and the French Genius disclosed itself more in the realm of *Opéra-Comique* than in that of Opera. The Gallic esprit reigned supreme in the Salle Favart, and Grétry, Méhul, Boieldieu, and the Italian-born Cherubini became standard names.

Two points are outstanding in the history of French Opera at this period.

One was the start of an invasion which brought many foreign composers and their operas to the Académie, forming the precedent for events in the nineteenth century. The list of the foreigners who found a welcome in Paris up till the time of the Revolution (when all French music became national in impulse, origin, and character) includes the Italians Pasquale Anfossi (1727 – 1797), Giovanni Guiseppe Cambini (1746 – 1825), Luigi Cherubini (1760 – 1842), Legrenzio Vincenzo Ciampi (1719 – 1762), Giovanni Paisiello (1740 – 1816), Antonio Sacchini (1730 – 1786), Antonio Salieri (1750 – 1825), Tommaso Traetta (1727 – 1779), and Niccolo Antonio Zingarelli (1752 – 1837), and the Germans Johann Christian Bach (1755 – 1782) and Johann Christoph Vogel (1756 – 1788). These were imported by de Vismes, who realised the poverty of French invention and tried to stimulate French ideas by bringing foreign ones to the Académie. It is a melancholy reflection that, with the exception of Cherubini (who later became absorbed into French musical culture when appointed Director of the Paris Conservatoire), the works of few of these composers have survived.

The other point was the obvious lack of capable specialist librettists. So barren was the soil that the Académie was driven to utilise old texts, mainly those by Quinault which, with one exception, were deprived of their Prologues and reduced to three Acts. There must have been a great deal of research among the less important scores lying on the shelves of the Académie, as several completely obscure texts were pressed into service. For instance, on July 13th, 1723, a *Ballet-Heroïque* in three Acts with Prologue entitled *Les Fêtes grecques et romaines* was produced, with libretto by Fuzelier and music by Colin de Blamont. The same book was used for the production – on March 21st, 1784 – of *Tibule et Delie ou les Saturnales*, an *Acte des Fêtes grecques et romaines*, with choreography by Gardel and music by Mademoiselle Villard de Beaumesnil.

The text used by Rameau for *Dardanus* (November 19th, 1739), written by Le Clerc de la Bruyère in five Acts with Prologue, was reduced to four Acts by de Guillard and set to music by Sacchini; the choreography on November 30th, 1784, was by Gardel the Younger, and that for the revival on January 13th, 1786, by Vestris. The book *Adèle de Ponthieu*, by Razins, was used by de La Borde for a production on December 1st, 1772, and by Piccinni on October 27th, 1781. Even hitherto unused libretti provided material. On July 26th, 1785, a *Ballet-Pantomime – Le Premier Navigateur ou le Pouvoir de l'Amour –* was produced with music drawn partly from the works of Grétry, and with choreography by Gardel. This was adapted from a work written by Fenouillot de Falbaire expressly for Philidor, but never performed.

Of the Quinault works, *Amadis de Gaule* was set *in toto* by de La Borde (November 26th, 1771); *Roland* was adapted into three Acts and set by Piccinni (January 17th, 1778); *Amadis de Gaule* was set by Johann Christian Bach (December 14th, 1779); *Atys* by Piccinni (January 31st, 1780); *Persée* by Philidor (October 27th, 1780); and *Thésée* by Gossec (March 1st, 1782).

The outstanding French composers were Candeille, Floquet, Desormery, Le Moyne, and Rodolphe; outstanding, that is, in the absence of serious competition. In spite of moderate success, particularly with *Andromaque* (June 6th, 1780), Grétry made little reputation in the Académie, and the same may be said of Cherubini, whose *Démophon* (December 5th, 1788), with a text originally intended for Mozart, did not achieve the lasting success of *Les Deux Journées*, his later *Opéra-Comique*. It may be noted that, on June 11th, 1778, a ballet by a composer named Mozart – *Les Petits Riens* – passed completely unnoticed, to the chagrin of its composer, whose name was not mentioned anywhere.

There were, therefore, no composers of the calibre of Lully, Rameau, and Gluck. The fault with the others was that their works lacked fire and impulse. They had not yet found out how to move their audiences and, for the most part, their operas were cold and uninspiring. French Opera was in the doldrums and subsequent political events did not enhance its possibilities.

CHAPTER THIRTEEN

SALLE DU PALAIS-ROYAL DESTROYED BY FIRE — NEW
THEATRE AT PORTE-SAINT-MARTIN COMMISSIONED —
RAPID COMPLETION — ACADÉMIE AT SALLE-DES-MENUS-
PLAISIRS — INADEQUACY OF STAGE — TROUBLE WITH
SINGERS — DETAILS OF NEW THEATRE — AUDIENCES TOO
HEAVY — COST OF REPAIRS AND ALTERATIONS —
FOUNDATION OF ÉCOLE DE CHANT ET DE DÉCLAMATION —
ABOLITION OF SINECURES AND PRIVILEGES — FINANCIAL
DIFFICULTIES OF ACADÉMIE — LACK OF DISCIPLINE —
PROCLAMATION OF LIBERTÉ DES THÉÂTRES — ACADÉMIE
CHANGES ITS NAME — THEATRE CONDEMNED AS UNSAFE —
LA MONTANSIER — "THE MARRIAGE OF FIGARO" — SALLE
MONTANSIER OPENED — ABONNÉS — FURTHER CHANGES OF
NAME — FURTHER FINANCIAL DIFFICULTIES

On JUNE 8TH, 1781, the Académie produced Gluck's *Orphée*,[1]
followed by *Apollon et Coronis*, composed by the brothers J. B. and
Joseph Rey.

At nine o'clock, while the audience was dispersing after the
usual four-hour performance, flames were seen rising from the
stage. The conflagration spread rapidly, in spite of the fire-proof
curtain and the two hundred hogsheads of water. Once again,
the Capucins and Recollets (who acted as fire-wardens to the
district) came to the rescue, but, by the time the regular fire
brigade arrived, the flames were beyond control. All efforts were
centred upon saving the Palais Royal itself and the neighbouring
houses. The cause of the fire was never clearly determined, but
the destruction was complete and terrifying. Twelve of the staff
perished, including two dancers named Cauguy and Beaupré;
an elderly woman, living in the Cour des Fontaines, died of fright.
All the costumes and sets were destroyed, but, as soon as the first
feelings of horror had waned, an enterprising couturière brought
out a new *mode* in a colour called 'Opera brûlé' (Appendix
Forty-eight).

---

[1] The original Italian *Orfeo*.

A letter written by the singer Sophie Arnould[1] provides a surprising instance of insularity of thought:

> Cet affreux incendie a laissé presque nues les divinités de l'Opéra. Le feu s'est communiqué aux magasins de costumes, et ce n'est pas sans miracle qu'on est parvenu à en sauver quelques-uns.
>
> La ceinture de Vénus est consumée. Les Graces iront sans voiles; le bonnet de Mercure, ses ailes et son caduce, néant! Depuis longtemps l'Amour n'avait rien à perdre à l'Opéra, aussi perd-il rien. L'Égide de Pallas et la lyre d'Apollon sont en cendres.
>
> Le char du Soleil et de la Nature, qui se tenait si gracieusement en l'air dans le très-naturel prologue d'Atys, n'a pas été épargné non plus que quantité de linons qui drapaient de grosses ombres très-palpables, et dois-je ajouter palpées . . . à quoi sert de medire? Je ne finirais pas, chère amie, si je vous contais toutes nos pertes.
>
> Mais on dit qu'avec de l'argent reparé tout.[2]

The French temperament has always been resilient. No time was lost in finding another home for the Académie, and Marie-Antoinette immediately commissioned the architect Lenoir to build another theatre at the Porte-Saint-Martin. Work began late on July 17th and the Queen ordered it to be completed by October 30th. In her commission to Lenoir, she said:[3] 'Je vous donne jusqu'au 31, et si ce jour là vous m'apportez le clef de ma loge, vous receverez en échange le cordon de Saint-Michel, et une pension de six mille livres'.

In the event of failure, Lenoir was to be fined 25,000 livres.

Lenoir set to work with a will. By employing two working parties, construction was possible for twenty-four hours a day, and he managed to complete the building with four days in hand.

Meanwhile, the Académie found refuge in the Salle-des-Menus-

---

[1] Quoted from Lasalle, *op. cit.* pp. 128, 129.

[2] Sophie Arnould remained on the stage long after her voice had run its course. On one of her last appearances the Abbé Galiani said that her voice was 'le plus bel asthme qu'on puisse entendre'.

[3] Quoted from Lasalle, *op. cit.* p. 155.

Plaisirs du Roy, which occupied the original site of the present Conservatoire National de Musique et de Déclamation,[1] and which still houses the Dramatic section of that Institution. The building was small and was used principally as a store house for the properties of the *Fêtes de Cour*. Its stage approximated in size to that of the Opera House in the Château de Versailles, and the various court performances were repeated on it for the benefit of the public. It was clearly too small for the Académie, the seating capacity being quite inadequate to cover the expenses of even a small-scale production. The charges were:

First-Row Boxes	. .	7 *livres* 10 *sous*
Second-Row Boxes	. .	6 *livres*
Parquet[2]	. . .	3 *livres*

Hitherto there had been no seats on the Parquet and the public had been forced to stand. Now they were forced to sit because the seats were immovable.

The police fruitlessly endeavoured to exercise traffic control.

The first work to be played was *Le Devin du Village*, followed by *Myrtil et Lycoris*, a *Pastorale* by Desormery. Other works included *L'Inconnue persecutée*, by Anfossi, translated from the Italian, and a *Ballet-Allégorique, La Fête de la Paix*.

The size of the theatre soon led to other troubles. Three of the male singers – Lays, Chéron, and Rousseau (not related to Jean-Jacques) – decided that it was beneath their dignity to appear under such restricted conditions. Their salaries were 9,000 livres, and they demanded 18,000. This being refused, they absconded.

Lays was recaptured in Valenciennes and thrown into prison without the formality of a trial.

Chéron lay concealed and defied all attempts to discover him.

Rousseau crossed the frontier into Belgium. The police system was in an uproar and rewards were offered for his capture. Meantime, he was earning a modest income of 360 livres a day in Brussels. The French police asked for his extradition and there was very nearly a 'diplomatic situation'. However, after much

---

[1] Now at No. 14 rue de Madrid.
[2] This was another name for the parterre, but in this instance represented our stalls.

bargaining, Rousseau was allowed to return unmolested to Paris, where he was joined by the other two defaulters. They made their submission, listened to a lengthy admonition from Monsieur de Breteuil, Master of the King's Household, and were reinstated.

When the time came for the Académie to move into its new theatre, it left some of its sets in store in the Salle des Menus-Plaisirs. In accordance with tradition, this building was destroyed by fire on April 18th, 1788, and the sets were burnt to cinders.

The Salle de la Porte-Saint-Martin was erected with such speed that the Parisians could watch it literally grow before their very eyes. The site became a favourite walking place, but pride was not unmixed with apprehension. The story of this mushroom growth was passed down from generation to generation, until it became almost like one by Perrault.

As a gesture, Lenoir placed a two-and-a-half foot doll, representing Marie-Antoinette in Gala costume, over the keystone. For this, he was rewarded with a *Privilège* authorising him to give public *fêtes* for his own benefit over a period of ten years, no limit being placed on their number. The stage was exactly the same size as that in the Salle du Palais Royal and the decorations consisted of crossed lances, lictors' fasces, and the emblems of the Gallic Cock. There were four rows of boxes.

Instead of the estimated 200,000 livres, it cost precisely double that amount; although this was hushed-up, rumours began to spread. Instead of making the best of it, the rumour-mongers endeavoured to destroy the chances of the theatre by making out that it was unsafe. The authorities were perplexed, but they finally decided to open with a gratis performance of *Adèle de Ponthieu*, an Opera in three Acts by Piccinni.

The audience began to assemble during the morning and strolled all round the building peering into every nook and cranny. Most of the time the building was holding three times the number it was built for and, by the time the performance commenced, it had sagged two inches to the right and fifteen *lignes* to the left. Fortunately, those inside had no knowledge of this.

As usual, it was a case of first come, first served. The customary scenes of confusion took place everywhere, except in the two balconies which had been reserved for the Coal Merchants' and the Fisherwomens' Guilds. The performance concluded with a magnificent Ball in which the two Guilds, the attendants, and the singers took part. Rarely has there been such interest in the opening of a new theatre.

In 1782, extensive repairs and alterations became necessary. In addition to making the building stronger, it was made larger and, according to the *Almanach de spectacles*, one tier of seats and new boxes were added on each side, the Pit was enlarged to hold a further one hundred and sixty patrons, and the Amphitheatre to hold a further thirty. The stage was widened. All this was accomplished in ten days, at a cost of 160,000 livres.

The people, however, had no confidence in the building, and, some years later, the question of a safer and more suitable theatre was discussed, the sum of 60,000 livres being allocated for the purpose. The Court appeared to have a rooted objection to rebuilding the Salle du Palais Royal. In the first place, something larger was required, and in the second, the Queen and the Duc d'Orléans[1] were not on speaking terms.

It has often been reported that Louis XVI was tone-deaf and bored by music. If this was so, it did not prevent him from taking a lively interest in the affairs of the Académie Royale de musique, for not only did he award prizes for libretti, but he also concerned himself personally with the welfare of the staff. In 1784, he founded an important École de Chant et de Déclamation, the nursery of the present Conservatoire and one of the earliest schools of music definitely intended for the training of opera singers and actors. Within the framework of the Académie the King reduced expenditure, not by cutting down wages or staff, but by abolishing all sinecures and hereditary privileges.

Until then, any parent registered on the books for a special seat in the theatre automatically handed it down to his heirs. This privilege-by-inheritance also applied to any member of a family who had once sung a role in an opera, that role being the perquisite of the singer and his heirs, regardless of an ability to sing, unless revoked by the individual concerned at any time. In 1787, Louis completely revised all the regulations and increased

---

[1] The Palais-Royal was his private house.

the permanent establishment from one hundred and fifty to two hundred. The abolition of hereditary seats naturally increased the income from places sold. For the time being, the *Abonnés* were held in abeyance.

On March 2nd, 1784, a performance in aid of the poor realised 11,567 livres, 10 sous. In the years 1787 and 1789 the receipts amounted to one million livres. Of this, 444,053 livres were taken at the door, while the annual rent for boxes brought in 415,808 livres. Twelve Opera Balls produced 34,059 livres, the rent for the café and surrounding shops, 21,000 livres, while the attendance of the Queen on one occasion brought in 240,000 livres. In addition to these sums, all the other theatres in Paris had to subscribe a percentage of their takings.

The Concert-Spirituel gave a fifth of its income, the Comédie-Italienne 40,000 livres, 2 sous (*sic*), the Variétés amusantes 46,000 livres, and the Beaujolais Théâtres de la Foire, 25,584 livres altogether.

Since 1783, it had been the custom to allow the members of the orchestra to give, for their own benefit, what were known as 'les après-soupers' when there was no operatic performance.

Even the buskers were taxed. Le sieur Nicard paid six livres *per annum* for the privilege of showing his monkey, le sieur Marigny, two sous *per diem* to show his dwarfs, while the performing fleas of le sieur Préjean cost their owner one livre *per mensem*. The Académie became a kind of licensed pirate.

The penalties for non-payment were severe. Le sieur Colon was sentenced to show his marionnettes and actors only behind a veil. Le sieur Clément d'Ornaison was forced to put his actors and singers in the wings and perform on the stage in dumb show only; he was also made to hang a gauze curtain between the stage and the auditorium.

Nevertheless, with all this assistance, the deficit in 1788 was more than 150,000 livres. The chief causes of this situation were maladministration and indifferently kept accounts. The City of Paris contributed a subsidy of 60,000 livres, but this did not ameliorate the immediate situation as most of the amount was mortgaged. In 1789, the *Droit des Pauvres* was suppressed and this eased matters to a small degree.

The singers behaved as they pleased, compelling the management to alter the rules and regulations as they thought suitable for particular occasions and circumstances. Indeed, such a state of indiscipline had been reached that the Ministre de Paris, M. Amelot, informed the Surintendant of the Menus-Plaisirs that, if a certain Mademoiselle Saint-Huberty continued to refuse to sing, he would obtain an order from the King consigning her to prison (Appendix Forty-nine).

The Director, Dauvergne, but recently appointed, was appalled at a situation over which he had no control and which, in the reign of his predecessor, had become completely out of hand. He took the easy way out and resigned. He was succeeded by a Monsieur Morel, who had never heard of the word 'scrupulous'. Morel already drew a steady income of 1,200 livres a year from the directorship of a fleet of carriages plying between Paris and Versailles. He proceeded without delay to augment his reserves at the expense of the Académie. He set up a market in opera libretti (paying the authors next to nothing) and sold them to composers under his own name. Unfortunately, he made one serious slip and included *Panurge dans l'Ile des Lanternes* and *La Caravane du Caire*, which had been written by the Comte de Provençe, afterwards Louis XVIII.

Morel's example did not improve matters. The singers, seeing themselves directed by a rogue and opportunist, behaved even worse than before and intimated that they proposed to absent themselves from three performances out of five. The King begged Dauvergne to return, which he did, and a semblance of order appeared at once.

A dossier was immediately drawn up for each member of the staff, and this disclosed some illuminating facts.

The Maître de Musique de l'Orchestre, M. Rey, and most of the singers were badly in debt. M. Rey's behaviour at the performances depended on whether he had been successful or not in the lottery. M. Vestris was reported as being 'an excellent dancer of his kind, but ugly, insolent, impudent, and one who does not take any trouble over anything'. His influence acted upon two other dancers, Mesdemoiselles Rose and Hilisberg. M. Lainez fell ill whenever he wanted a night off. M. Laurent had the 'face of a baboon', while M. Jiville spent all his time chasing debauched women in the gaming houses, in one of which he stayed for ten days. As for the women singers – Mademoiselle Maillard was up to her ears in debt and Mademoiselle Saint-Huberty was the 'naughtiest' woman who had ever been employed at the Opera.

One singer, however, was exempted from a dossier. This was Delboy, the high-tenor, whose voice was more than usually powerful. The Prince de Boix took on a wager of two hundred louis with the Comte d'Artois (afterwards King Charles X) that a high 'D' sung by Delboy on the Butte de Montmartre would be audible at Saint-Denis. The wager was accepted. The singer let loose his note and a pistol shot at Saint-Denis confirmed its arrival there.

In 1789, the Bastille was taken by the mob. The Revolution, no longer able merely to simmer, commenced in full earnest, and in the following year, the City of Paris took over control of the Académie.

On January 13th and March 2nd, 1791, the 'Liberté des Théâtres' was proclaimed. These regulations created an entirely new situation in the theatrical world of France, and the Académie no longer exercised any kind of monopoly or claim. The most important of the regulations were:

Article One. Any citizen may build a public theatre and produce pieces of all kinds, after first registering his intention so to do with the municipal authorities.

Article Two. The works of authors who have been dead for five years or more are public property and can be performed anywhere in France at any theatre.

Article Three. The works of living authors cannot be performed anywhere without their authors' written consent, the penalty for infringement of the article being the confiscation of all takings from the performances, to the benefit of the author.

Article Four. The heirs and successors of authors will be the owners of the works for five years after the death of the authors. (This was later extended to the benefit of the heirs, and the conditions of Article Two were amended).

Article Five. The 'entrepreneurs' (or general managers) of all theatres will be liable for inspection by the municipal authorities.

For the first time, the names of the actors and dancers were announced on the *affiches*. Home Rule in the theatre dates from this moment.

Two other important, though superficially minor changes affected the Académie. 'Opéra', as a genre, became known as 'Opera', reverting to the earlier custom. A decree was passed ordering that no other posters should be printed in the official yellow, and that those appertaining to the Opera and the Comédie-Française should be posted above all others. It appears, however, that this had been the custom since they were instituted in 1721, for, in his *Tableau de Paris*, Mercier wrote:

'Les affiches de spectacle ne manquent point d'être appliquées aux murailles dans le matin. Elles observent entre elles un certain rang; celle de l'Opéra domine les autres; les spectacles forains se rangent de côté, comme par respect pour les grandes théâtres. Les places pour le placage sont aussi bien observées que dans une cercle de gens du monde.'

The Royal Family continued to pay for its boxes during 1791, that for the Queen costing 7,000 livres, that for the Duc d'Orléans, 7,000 livres, and that for Madame de Lamballe, 3,600 livres.

The Académie Royale de Musique was now about to undergo a constant changing of its name. On June 24th, 1791, it became 'L'Opera', on the following June 29th, 'Académie de Musique'; then, on September 17th, it resumed its original title of 'Académie Royale de Musique'.

Louis XVI and his Queen attended the Opera for the last time on June 14th, 1791. The work performed was Candeille's curious *Castor et Pollux*, which contained several of Rameau's original movements from his *Tragedie-Lyrique* of the same name.

The King was then given something more serious to think about, for it was suddenly discovered that this utterly good, though ineffective man and his foolish, indiscreet, myopic wife were, in reality, 'tyrants'.

The Théâtre de la Porte-Saint-Martin was finally condemned as unsafe for the public. Under the aegis of La Montansier, Director of the theatre at Versailles, the King approved the erection of a new building in the rue de la Loi (now the rue Richelieu), on the site of the Hôtel Louvois (an hotel of the same name stands there to-day), opposite the Bibliothèque Nationale. One of the last productions in the old theatre was Mozart's *The Marriage of Figaro* (March 20th, 1793), with Beaumarchais' original spoken dialogue, the verses and general adaptation being by du Notaris. The opera by no means faithfully reflected the spirit of the play, for it rendered the social and political implications quite harmless, presenting them as escapades. Beaumarchais was highly indignant at this process of emasculation.

The year 1793 is of some importance in a small political way, for on January 27th of that year the composer's name was prefixed by the word 'citoyen' for the first time. Thus *La Triomphe de la République ou le Camp de Grandpré*, a *Divertissement-Lyrique* in one Act, was described as being composed by 'Citoyen Gossec'. Librettist and choreographer, however, continued to have no prefix.

The Salle Montansier was opened in 1794. It was ornate and splendid, with Doric pillars, a marble foyer, allegorical paintings, and boxes draped in crimson and gold. The Académie was transferred there and renamed the 'Théâtre des Arts', the whole administration being placed under the control of the Commune.

As it was a democratic age, seats were placed both in the pit and the gallery, giving the public equality of seating with the aristocracy and nobility, now on the way to becoming defunct. The theatre, in this way, being placed within the reach of the people-at-large, the demand for seats immeasurably exceeded the supply. The public clamoured for some control of the productions and, in the middle of all this democracy, a new aristocracy was in fact created, their privilege amounting, in time, almost to an autocracy – the *Abonnés*, originally founded by Lully.

The Revolutionary Government was quick to appreciate the value of music for propaganda purposes and for political education. Its first act, indeed, was to produce a *Mélodrame*, entitled *La Prise de la Bastille*, in Notre Dame on July 13th, 1790. This marked the disappearance of mythology and magic from the French operatic stage forever. The immediate necessity, however, was to set the Opera in order by giving it a new generic title. The disadvantages of a totalitarian system now made themselves felt, as this title changed with each alteration in aspect of the Constitution. These changes are worth tabulating, and are given in Appendix 50.

Reference has previously been made to the financial situation and the difficulties which pursued Opera even in those days. At the time of the opening of the Salle Montansier, the deficit amounted to 276,507 livres. The Comité de salut publique donated 150,000 livres and, on October 17th, 1794, the Government granted a monthly subsidy of 100,000 livres, conditional upon the theatre itself guaranteeing 680,000 francs. There is no record of this subsidy ever having been paid.

In 1797 there was a deficit of 160,000 francs. Fresh receipts brought in 60,000 francs, but the expenses amounted to 100,000 francs.[1] Forty-eight Bearer Bonds of 5,000 francs each were issued, these being redeemable in both Principal and Interest at the rate of one-twenty-fourth per month. The holders had free admission.

At this period, when Opera had become established as an element of life, still only one man had been able to make it a profitable concern – Jean Baptiste Lully.

It might justifiably be argued that the attempt to establish an Opera that was specifically French had been a complete failure. In its history, only three names were outstanding, and only one of these was French. But less than two hundred years separated *Cadmus et Hermione* and the Revolution. This is not long in the history of an art-form which starts from almost nothing and which evolves rather than grows. The theatrical antics of the Revolutionary governments called a halt to its development,

---

[1] It is as well to realise the value of the 'assignat' which became government currency. This amounted to ten centimes per 100 livres. J. G. Prod'Homme points out (*L'Opéra*, 1669–1925 – Delagrave) that the Box Office books showed fabulous returns. He quotes the figures for a performance of *Iphigénie en Tauride*, the *Hymne à la Victoire*, and the ballet *Psyché* on June 6th, 1796, as amounting to 1,071,350 livres (on paper), the actual value being 1,071 livres, 7 sous!

and the French composers had to confine themselves to Hymns, Chants and *Fêtes*. This, however, enabled them to take stock of themselves and to absorb, if only sub-consciously, the lessons put before them by the three great Geniuses.

Opera, for the moment, may have ceased to be a vital force, but this was not the case with Opéra-Comique, which flourished, advancing towards its culmination with unfaltering steps. In the circumstances, it was a useful genre. Its insistence upon 'catchy tunes' and 'happy endings' gave it an effortless popular appeal, supplying the citizens with a relaxation in dangerous times and providing a wholesome distraction to the governmental difficulties and set-backs which might otherwise have attracted attention.

Opéra-Comique, therefore, quickly established itself in the complete Gallic goût. It became an individual entity. It bore no relationship to the Italian style, save in esprit; it can hardly even be said to have been formed on the Italian model. Many of its productions would, today, be known as Musical Comedies. They were not intended to live. They were devised purely for entertainment, and they appeared with a relentless frequency. Their quality, however, was in many cases high, and, to a certain extent, they directed the style of what, towards the end of the nineteenth century, came to be recognised as 'French Music'. This happened in spite of the fact that, before then, the gap between *Opéra-Comique* and Opera was narrowed to such an extent that it became almost undetectable; even the original requirement of spoken dialogue was no longer treated as an essential element.

However, discussion of this genre and of the Revolutionary policies belongs in another place. For the moment, we may look some distance ahead and observe that the term 'spectacular opera' – as typified in the works of the post-Revolution composers, both native and foreign – is a reminder both of the long-past glories of *Circé ou le Ballet comyque de la Royne*, and of how Ballet came to be an integral part of Opera. Up till this moment, the reminder lies in the splendid, magical works of Rameau. *Circé* may be regarded as the complete French 'authority'. The fundamentals were constant; only their design, and the manner of expressing them, suffered any kind of change. Stage machinery improved as stage carpentry became more efficient. The chariots of the gods were less crude, less mechanically obtrusive, infinitely safer for the occupants. Rousseau's childish criticisms had been grossly exaggerated in order to achieve the writer's own ends. It is always easy to distort situations and conditions so that those not entirely aware of them may be convinced by the distortion; it should be remembered that Rousseau's pontifical dicta were read by a great many who had never seen an opera.

What is most significant is the fact that the greater part of the operatic paraphernalia of the seventeenth and eighteenth centuries became permanent. It can be seen to-day in Pantomime, not quite such a lofty ideal, perhaps, as Opera, but equally important in theatrical history and continuity. Time and sophistication made many theatrical elements, once considered as marvels, appear puerile or merely sensational. A mythological opera produced to-day as it was in the past would be intolerable, and whenever there is such a revival, nearly everything has to be touched up and adjusted, to say nothing of ruthless cutting.[1] As a rule, such revivals and reconstructions are completely successful, as in the case of *Les Indes galantes*.

The orchestration of neither Lully nor Rameau can be played in its original state. It is significant of the importance of Gluck that his works, and those of the post-Revolution French composers, can be allowed to stand in their original condition. It would be sacrilege to re-score Gluck; to re-score Rameau, Lully, and their contemporaries, is essential. The quality of the music remains; its quantity has to be reconsidered.

These pages have shown that French composers learned what to do from their Italian visitors. How they did it was quite different, and it is important to note that instinctively they used their own language and remained faithful to their own natural *esprit*. This continued to be the case, and history reveals that they even evolved their own style of coloratura opera in the face of Italian influences. French Opera showed a steady and consistent evolution; its further development was to be even steadier and more consistent.

---

[1] It was the performance of two acts of *Castor et Pollux* at the Schola Cantorum, and Vincent d'Indy's edition and production of *Hippolyte et Aricie* at the same school in 1908, which opened Debussy's ears to the Gallicism and other merits of Rameau, a performance of Gluck's *Iphigénie en Aulide* prompting his famous *Open Letter to the Chevalier W. Gluck*.

APPENDICES

The text of the old documents has been followed
strictly, in spite of the fact that certain words are
spelt differently from time to time.

Appendix One

Lettres Contenant des Statuts pour la Communauté des Ménestriers ou Ménstrels[1]

Paris 24 avril 1407

Nous avoir receu l'umble supplication du roy *des Ménestriers* et des aultres ménestrierz, jouers d'instrumens, tant haulx comme bas[2], en la ville, viconte et dyocèse de Paris et des aultres de nostre royaume, contenant comme dès l'an mil trois cent quatre vingt seize (1396), pour *leur science de ménestrandise* faire et entretenir selon certaines ordannances par eulx autreffois faictes et que, en temps passé, estoit accoutumez de faire, et par l'advis et délibéracion d'eulx et de la plus grant et saine partie d'entreulx eussent et ayent fait certaines instruccions et ordannances, dont la congnoissance des amendes qui ycelles enfraindroit en aucune manière, en tant qu'il touche ycelle science, appartiendroit moitié à appliquier à nous et l'aultre moitié à l'ospital Saint-Julien, assiz à Paris en la rue Saint-Martin, et audict roy des Ménestrierz, et que tous Ménestrelz, tant joueurs de haulx instrumens comme de bas, soit estranges ou de nostre royaume, *sont et seront tenuz de aler pardevers* ledict roy des Menestrierz ou ses députez, pour faire serment d'accomplir et parfaire toutes les choses ci-aprez déclaréez, à paine de XX solz d'amende, moitie a nous a appliquier et l'aultre moitie ausdis hospital Saint-Julien et roy des Ménestrelz, pour chacun article qu'ils seront trouvez faisants le contraire, sans le congié ou licence dudit roy ou de ses députez, en la manière qui s'en suit c'est assavoir, se aucun desdiz ménestrelz font marchié d'aler à aucune feste ou nopces, ilz ne les pourront laisser jusques à ce qu'ilz auront parfait leurdict marchie pour aler à aultres, ne y envoyer pour eulx aultres personnes, se ce n'est en cas de maladie, de prison ou d'aultre nécessité, sur paine de ladicte amende de XX solz parisis: et avec ce, ne peuvent et ne pourront yceulx ménestrelz aler en ladicte ville de Paris ne dehors, pour eulx présenter à festes ou à nopces, pour eulx ne pour aultres, ne faire parler par aultres personnes pour avoir lesdictes festes ou nopces, se première-ment et d'aventure on ne leur demande, sur ycelle paine; et se aucune personne aloit en la rue d'yceulx ménestrelz à Paris, pour eulx louer, que sur le premier que ycelle personne appellera ou s'adrecera pour louer, aultre ne se peut embattre ne parler à ycelle personne jusque à ce qu'elle soit départie, sur ladicte paine; et aussi nulz desditz ménestrelz ou apprentiz ne se pourront louer à festes ou nopces jusque à ce qui ycelui roy des Ménestrelz ou sesdiz députez les ayent une fois *veuz, visitez et passez pour souffisans*; à laquelle visitacion cellui ou ceulx qui seront passez et retenuz de paier vint solz parisis d'entrée

---

[1] Letters Patent authorising the Confrères de la Passion to perform Mystères had been issued in December 1402.

[2] *i.e.* violins and basses.

audit ospital et audit roy des Ménestrelz; et est *ladicte science deffendue aux nonsouffisans*, à nopces ne assembléez honorables sur paine de ladicte amende de XX solz, qui doibt estre convertie, moitié à nous, et l'aultre moitie audit roy des Ménestrelz et audit hospital; et avec ce que nulz menestrelz ne peuvent prendre ou louer aprentis, *se ilz ne sont souffisans pour leur monstrer*, ne prendre lesdiz apprentiz, *à moins que de six ans*, sur paine de privacion de ladicte science, an et iour, se ce n'est par le congié et licence desdiz roy ou députez; et se aucun ménestrel estrangier veut jouer desdiz instrumens en la ville de Paris ou ailleurs es-lieux dessusdiz, pour soy allouer ou gaingnier argent, ycellui roy des Ménestrelz ou ses députez lui peuvent *défendre ladicte science*, iusque à ce qu'il ait juré par la foy et serment de son corps, à tenir et garder l' ordonnance dessuasdicte, sur paine d'estre banni de ladicte science, par an et jour, et de l'amende dessusdicte, se ce n'est à la voulonté desdiz roy ou députez; laquelle science ycellui roy ou députez *pourront deffendre à tous menestrelz qui vivront de deshonnête vie*, sur paine de ladicte amende, et d'estre banni an et iour d'ycelle science et aussi ne peuvent ou doivent yceulx ménestrelz commencer escole pour monstrer ne aprendre Ménestrandise, se ce n'est par le congié et licence desdiz roy ou députez. Et pour ce que ledit hospital St. Julien qui est fondé desdictz ménestrelz et n'a aultres rentes, sinon des aumonsnes des bonnes gens, yceulx ménestrelz sont et seront tenuz de demander à sueillir l'aumosne St. Julien aux nopces ou ils seront louez et par dons[1] accoustumez – Et se aucune personne demande à yceulx menestrelz aucuns desdiz ménestrelz par leurs noms, ils sont et seront tenuz les enseigner, sur paine de ladicte amende. Et ne peut aucun desdiz ménestrelz prendre aucun marchié, excepté pour lui et ses compaignons jouans en sa compagnie, pour la journée, sur paine de ladicte amende; et se il advient que un tout seul prengne aucun marchié avec aucune personne pour faire aucunes nopces ou festes et il en prend un, deux, ou trois qui lui permettent estre avec lui, ilz ne s'en pourront départir jusque à ce que ycelles nopces ou festes seront faites, sur paine de l'amende; et aussi nulz d'yceulx ménestrelz qui ait prins à faire festes ou nopces ne peut prendre aultres compaignons *pour gaignier sur eulx*, sur paine de ladicte amende; en nous umblement suppliant que comme ycelles ordannances et instruccions ilz aient faictes, pour le bien et prouffit d'entre eulx et pour eschever à sucuns grants dommaiges qui leur en pourroyent ensuir, se ycelles n'estoient tenuês et gardées, nous veuillons ycelles instruccions et ordonnances confermer pourquoy nous, ces choses considerées, inclinans favorablement à leur supplicacion etc.

Donné à Paris le 24e iour d'avril, l'an de grâce 1407 et de nostre règne le vingt-septième.

Signé:

CHARLES

---

[1] *i.e.* Religious Festivals ('Pardons').

('*Recueil général des anciennes lois françaises*' établi par *Isambert et Decrusy, Vol. VII, pp. 136–139 – Paris, Belin Leprieur, 1825. Cote de la Bibliothèque nationale 8° F 4150.*)

Appendix Two

IN THE reign of Louis XIII the 'King' was L. Constantin, one of the Court violinists. He was succeeded by 'Kings' Dumanoir I and II, who gave place to Guillaume I and II. The last-named tried to make all musicians join the Union, but the organists, especially those at the Cathedrals and Chapelles-royales formed their own Union in 1707, having applied for their Charter as far back as 1695. This absolved them from paying a large sum in lieu of joining the original Union, a fine extorted by personal force. Peace reigned for over forty years; then 'King' Guignon demanded a general levy and drew up a code of twenty-eight articles which stated his right to rule over all the musicians in the Kingdom. He appointed deputies in the principal cities and towns and levied fees of twenty livres to be given to Saint-Julien and a hundred to himself. The organists, being men of spirit, flatly refused to pay. On May 30th, 1750, Parliament stepped in and granted a separate charter to the composers. Guignon was deposed, his office being considered a hindrance to the progress of musical art, and he died at Versailles on January 30th, 1774. This 'Kingdom' had lasted for five centuries in name if not in fact and deed, and was the first instance of a Trade Union as opposed to a Guild or City Company. Dissolution was inevitable under the circumstances, but the system might have survived had the organists not refused to be brow-beaten, and, with the composers, not insisted on their own autonomy.

Appendix Three

DECLARATION ON THE SUBJECT OF COMÉDIENS MADE BY
LOUIS XIII ON APRIL 16, 1641

LOUIS, par le Grâce de Dieu, Roy de France et de Navarre: A tous ceux qui ces présentes Lettres verront, Salut. Les continuelles bénédictions qu'il plait à Dieu épendre sur notre Règne. Nous obligeant de plus en plus à faire tout ce qui depend de Nous pour retrancher tous les deriglemens par lesquels il peut être offensé.

Le crainte que Nous avons que les Comédies qui se représentent *utilement* pour le divertissement des Peuples sont quelquefois accomoagnées de représentations peu honnêtes, qui laissent de mauvaises impressions sur les espirits, fait que Nous sommes resolu de donner les ordres requis pour éviver tels inconvénients . . . . . A CES CAUSES Nous avons fait et faisons très expresses inhibitions et deffenses par ces Présentes, signées de nôtre main, à tous Comédiens de représenter *aucunes actions malhonnêtes,* ni *d'user d'aucunes paroles lascives ou à double entente,* qui puissent blesser l'honêteté publique, *et sous peines d'être déclarés infâmes* et autres peines qu'il y a: Enjoignons à nos Juges, chacun à son district, de tenir le main à ce que nôtre volonté soit réligieusement executée.

Et, en cas que lesdits Comédiens contreviennent à *Nôtre présente Déclaration*, Nous voulons et entendons que nosdits Juges *leur interfisent le Théâtre* et procedent contre-eux par telles voyes qu'ils aviseront à propos selon la qualité de l'action, sans néamoins qu'ils puissent ordonner plus grandes peines qui l'amende et le Banissement. Et en cas que lesdits Comédiens *règlent tellement les actions du Théâtre, qu'elles soient du tout ecemptes d'impureté*, Nous voulons que leur exercice qui peut *innoucement divertir nos Peuples de diverses occupations mauvaises, ne puisse leur estre imputé à blâme, ni préjudicier à leur réputation dans le commerce public;* ce qui Nous faisons, afin que le désir d'éviter le reproche qu'on leur a fait jusques ici leur donne autant de sujet de se contenir dans les termes de leur devoir des représentations publiques qu'ils feront, que la crainte des paines qui leur seroient inévitables, s'ils contrevenoient à la présente déclaration. Si donnons en mandement à nos amez er . . . . Conseilles, les gens tenans notre Cour de Parlement à Paris que ces presentes ils ayant à faire verifier et enregistrer et du contenu en icelles faire jouir et used lesdits Comédiens, sans permettre qu'il y soit contrevenu en aucune forte et manière que ce soit. CAR TEL EST NOSTRE PLAISIR.

Donné à Saint-Germain-en-Laye le 16e jour d'Avril, l'an de grâce 1641 et de notre Régne le 31er.

Signe LOUIS et sur le repli par le Roy DE LOMENIE et scellees di grand sceau sur simple queue de cire jaune.

Registré,   le Procureur General du Roy pour estre executées selon leur forme et teneur.

A Paris, en Parlement le 24er jour d'Avril 1671. Collationné, Signe DU TILLET.
de l'imprimerie de Sevestre, Pont Saint-Michel.

(*This text appears in a collection of essays on the theatre* [*1671–1720*], *bequeathed to the Bibliothèque nationale in the name of Don Ravenal.*)

Appendix Four

THE PETIT-BOURBON stood at the east end of the Louvre and occupied the present space between the Château and Saint Germain l'Auxerrois. It was originally the property of the Constable de Bourbon. It was used for all Court functions and for the Assemblies of the States-General. It was demolished in 1670 when the Colonnade of the Louvre was constructed.

Appendix Five

THE LOUVRE, originally a hunting box, served to house distinguished visitors. It did not become a royal residence until the reigns of Charles IX and Henri III. Demolition started in 1527 when the Donjon was destroyed; reconstruction, however, did not commence until 1541 under François I, but this King died before very much had been accomplished. Its condition at the time of the present narrative was due to Henri II, who erected the main hall known as the 'Tribune' or 'Salle des Cariatides'. This contained a dais which served as a stage for the *Fêtes* and *Ballets*, a throne being placed on it for the King when he received foreign visitors. The window from which Charles IX is supposed to have fired at the Huguenots on the river bank did not exist at that time – presumably the plaque was placed in its present position for reasons of symmetry, like that commemorating the execution of Charles I of England outside the Palace of Whitehall. The only window in his private apartments from which Charles IX could have fired would have necessitated the bullets' turning a corner.

Appendix Six

THE MONASTERY of Saint Germain-des-Prés was one of the ecclesiastical wonders of the 16th century. It received its name from the expanse of fields which bordered the south side of Paris in the time of Henri III. It consisted of churches, palaces, cloisters, gardens and battlements; its area covered the Rues de l'Echaude, Jacob (then Colombier), and Saint-Benoit. The view from the top of the church tower covered the whole of Paris, and it was from there that Henri IV examined the dispositions of the opposing armies when he was enforcing his claim to the throne. It was beneath its walls that duels were usually held, those duels so graphically described by Alexandre Dumas (père) in his Musketeer novels.

The Abbey was demolished, and also a turret which stood in what is now the Rue Jacob. The present Hotel d'Angleterre in this street (and, therefore, within the confines of the Monastery) was for many years, during the period under discussion, the English Embassy.

Appendix Seven

THE Palais des Tuileries was commenced by Catherine de Medici in 1564. It took its name from the brick-kilns which originally occupied the site. After Catherine's death it fell into a state of disrepair and neglect, although Henri IV continued the work by uniting it with the Louvre. The Arc de Carrousel, erected by Napoleon I, marks the main entrance. It was constructed in the form of three sides of a square, the Jardin des Tuileries occupying the centre. A drawbridge led into the present Place de la Concorde.

Appendix Eight

THE PRESENTATION OF THE GIFTS

THIS custom originated in Spain and Italy. The gifts, known as *Zapates*, consisted of subtle little presents offered in various ways and usually produced from unexpected places. These gifts ranged from single diamonds to the collars of Orders presented by the Sovereign, but they often had a symbolical import applicable to the recipient. The custom resembled that of the Easter Egg and the Valentine, but without the latter's mystery. Its authority came from the story of St. Nicholas who, hearing a poor woman lamenting that she was too poor to give her three children presents, threw a purse of gold through the door.

Among the most costly of these gifts recorded in history were a golden shield decorated with heraldic devices, presented by Catherine de Medici to Henri III when he was elected King of Poland; a victory palm-tree in gold and green enamel, given to the Emperor Charles V by the Queen of Hungary; and an enamelled golden effigy of the sun given to Catherine de Medici by her twelve Maids of Honour (her famous 'Flying Squad' who, in the most natural manner in the world, were always able to worm secrets out of courtiers). Ordinary folk practised the custom in accordance with their means.

Appendix Nine

AD LEONORAM ROMAE CANENTEM

by John Milton

Angelus unicuique suus (sic credite gentes)
    Obtigit aethereis ales ab ordinibus.
Quid mirum? Leonora tibi si gloria major,
    Nam tue praesentem vox sonat opsa Deum.
Aut Deus, aut vacui certe mens tertia coeli
    Per tua secreto guttura serpit agens;
Serpit agens, facilisque docet mortalia corda
    Sensim immortali assuescere posse sono.
Quod si cuncta quidem Deus est, per cunctaque fusus,
    In te una loquitur, caetera mutus habet.

Appendix Ten

REPORT ON 'NICANDRO E FILENO' (?)
IN THE GAZETTE DE PARIS

LE 28 (Février) Le Roy donna un disner à la Reine d'Angleterre, à la Reine, à Monsieur le Duc d'Anjou, à Monseigneur le Duc d'Orléans, oncle de sa Majesté et à Mademoiselle. Sur le soit il y eut une comédie italienne dans le Grande Salle et un ballet dansé par plusieurs seigneurs de la Cour. Après lequel la Reine donna un souper dans son grand cabinet à la Reine d'Angleterre[1] et à son Altesse Royale [sic].[2]

Appendix Eleven

REPORT ON 'LA FINTA PAZZA'
IN THE GAZETTE DE PARIS

LE 14 de ce mois, la Reine avec unde grande partie dela Cour se trouvé à la comédie que la Compagnie des Italiens représenta sous le titre de 'Finta Pazza' de Juillio Strozzi, dans le grande Sale [sic] du Petit-Bourbon, toute l'assistance d'estrant pas moins ravié des récits de la poesie et de la musique, qu'elle l'estoit de la décoration du théâtre, de l'artifice de ses machines et de ses admirables changemens de scenes, jusques à present inconnus à la France et qui ne transportent pas moins les yeux de l'esprit que ceux du corps par des mouvements imperceptibles: invention du sieur Jacques Torelli de mesme nation: qui furent suivis de balets [sic] fort industrieux et recréatifs, inventez par le sieur Jean Baptiste Balbi: dont vous verrez ailleurs de détail.

Appendix Twelve

REPORT BY LEFÈVRE D'ORMESSON
ON 'LA FINTA PAZZA'

. . . . J'ALLAI, après le disner, avec M. de Fourcy, à la comédie italienne, ou je vis cinq faces de théâtre différentes, l'une représentant trois allées de cypres, longues à perte de vue; l'autre, le port de Chio, ou le Pont-Neuf et la place Dauphine estoient représentés admirablement; la troisième une ville; la quatrième, un palais ou vous voyez des appartemens infinie; la cinquième, un jardin avec de beaux pilastres. En toutes ces facez différentes, la perspective estoit si bien observée, que toutes ces allées paroissent à perte de vue, quoyque le théâtre n'eust que quatre ou cinq pieds de profondeur. Parmi

---

[1] Henrietta Maria.
[2] Afterwards Charles II.

la pièce qui estoit la 'Descouverte d'Schille par les Grecs', ils dansoient un ballet d'ours et de singes, un ballet d'autruches et de nains, et un ballet d'Ethopiens et de perroquets. D'abord, l'Aurore s'elêvoit de terre sur un char insensiblement et traversoit ensuite le théâtre avec une vitesse merveilleuse. Quatre zephirs estoient enleves au ciel de mesme, quatre descendoient du ciel et remontoient avec mesme vitesse. Ces machines meritoient estre vues.

Appendix Thirteen

Justification for the use of Music in Corneille's 'Andromède'[1]

CHAQUE acte, aussi bien que le prologue, a sa décoration particulière, et du moins une machine volante, avec un concert de musique, que je n'ai employé qu'a satisfaire les oreilles des spectateurs, tandis que leurs yeux sont arrêtés à voir descendre ou rémonter une machine où s'attachent à quelque chose qui les empêche de prêter attention à ce que pourraient dire les acteurs. Mais je me suis bien gardé de faire rien chanter qui fut nécessaire à l'intelligence de la piece parce que, communement, les paroles qui se chantent étant mal entendues des auditeurs pour la confusion qu'y apporte la diversité des voix qui les prononcent ensemble, elles auraient fait une grande obscurité dans le corps de l'ouvrage, si elles avaient eu à l'instruire de quelque chose qui fut important.

Appendix Fourteen

Voltaire's Opinion of 'Andromède'

CE FUT Boissette qui mit ces choeurs en musique. On ne connaissant guère en ce temple-là qu'une espèce de faux-bourdon, qu'un contrepoint grossier; c'était une espèce de chant d'église, c'etait une musique barbare en comparaison de celle d'aujourd'hui. Ces paroles: 'Reine de Paphe et d'Amathonte' sont aussi rediculés que la musique. Il n'y a rien du moins musical, de moins harmonieux que: 'D'ou le mal procêde part aussi le remédé . . . . .' L'Opéra fit tomber absolument toutes les pièces de ce genre.

(*'Commentaires' on Corneille.*)

---

[1] 'Préface'.

Appendix Fifteen

LORET'S OPINION ON THE STAGE MACHINERY
IN 'NOZZE DI PELEO E DI THETI' IN THE
MUZE HISTORIQUE

Jamais dans le vague des airs
On n'ouit de si doux concerns,
Soit de luts, soit de voix humaines,
Qui du moins étoient deux douzaines.

Appendix Sixteen

LE GRAND COMMUN AND LE POTAGER

THE *Grand Commun* of the Château de Versailles was an enormous building capable of housing some thousands, the Château itself having an almost equal capacity. The combined premises constituted a small town on their own. Very little check seems to have been kept on the occupants of the Grand Commun, and since admission was obtained by virtue of wearing a hat and 'épée de ville' (the equivalent of the 20th century City Gent's bowler hat, gloves and rolled umbrella) it is reasonable to suppose that comparatively few of the inmates really occupied positions on the establishment. Matters reached their climax in the reign of Louis XVI when a census was taken. The figures are astonishing: in the household of the King, 4,000 persons; the Queen, 500; Monsieur, 420; Comte d'Artois, 456; Madame, 256; Comtesse d'Artois, 239; King's Aunts, 210. One may indeed ask what their duties may have been.

The original building is now the Military Hospital of Versailles.

The cooking was done in the *Potager*, so called because of the great stoves which it contained. At Versailles it was situated at an unusual distance from the Château, the dishes being carried along a covered way under strong escort; onlookers raised their hats. The catering department was known as 'la bouche du Roi'.

The building now houses the École d'Horticulture and stands slightly to the right of the Cathédrale-de-Saint-Louis.

Appendix Seventeen

MOLIÈRE'S 'ILLUSTRE THÉÂTRE'

THIS WAS originally the 'Jeu de Paume des Metayers'. It occupied Nos. 10, 12, and 14 of the Rue Mazarine and backs on to the Rue de Seine, just behind the Institut. Molière rented it for three years and, with the assistance of Aubry, the Master Roadmender to the

King, constructed a sweeping approach round the side of the building to accommodate the carriages which he hoped would bring large audiences to his productions. This is now a gravelled pleasaunce from which one can form some idea of the original interior from the trellis-work marked on the outside wall.

The auditorium was eighteen metres long, the stage, nine, and the *arrière-scène*, four. The floor was constructed of stone, and the walls, in common with those of all tennis courts, were painted black.

The venture was a failure, and on December 20th 1644, ten days short of twelve months after the opening performance, Molière moved to a better-class neighbourhood at the Porte-Saint-Paul, the building being the 'Jeu de Paume de la Croix Noire'. This building occupied the site of what is now No. 6 Rue des Jardins, next door (No. 8) to which Rabelais had died in 1553.

Paris seems to have been full of Tennis Courts at this period and it would be interesting to find out in what ways they were so suitable for adaptation as theatres.

Appendix Eighteen

La Salle des Tuileries

Le corps de la Salle est partagé en deux parties inégales. La première comprend le théâtre et ses accompagnemens. La séconde contient le parterre, les corridors et loges, qui font face au théâtre et qui occupent le reste du Salon de trois cotez, l'un qui regarde le Court, l'autre le jardin et le troisième le corps du Palais des Thuileries. . . . [the theatre itself] a de profondeur vingt-deux toises. Son ouverture est trente-deux pieds sur la largeur ou entre les corridors et chassis qui regnent des deux costez. La hauteur ou celle des chassis est de vingt-quatre pieds jusques aux nuages. Par-dessus les nuages, jusqu'au tiran du comble, pour le rétraite ou pour le mouvement des machines, il y a 37 pieds. Sous le plancher ou parquet du théâtre, pour les Enfers ou pour les changemens des Mers, il y a quinze pieds de profond . . . . . La séconde partie ou celle du Parterre qui est du coste de l'apartement des Thulieries a de largeur entre les deux murs 63 pieds, entre les corridors 49. Sa profondeur . . . . . est 93 pieds. Chaque corridor est de six pieds et la hauteur du parterre jusqu'au plafond est 49 pieds.

('*Idées des Spectacles*' – *Michel de Pure*)

Appendix Nineteen

LORET'S CRITICISM OF 'SERSE'

Enfin, il faut que je die,
Les Balets et la Comédie
Se pouvoient nommer, sur moy-foy,
Un divertissement de Roy:
Mais, à parler en conscience,
J'us bien bezoin de patience:
Car moi, qui suis Monsieur Loret,
Fus sur un siége assez duret,
Sans aliment et sans bruvage,
Plus d'huit heures et davantage.

Appendix Twenty

ACCOUNT OF 'PASTORALE' AT ISSY WRITTEN
BY LORET (MUZE HISTORIQUE)

L'allay, l'autre jour, dans Issy,
Village, peu distant d'icy,
Pour oüyr chanter en muzyque
Une Pastorale comique,
Que Monsieur le duc de Beaufort,
Étant prezant, écouta fort,
Et, pour le moins, trois cens personnes,
Y comprizes plusieurs mignonnes
Aimables, en perfection,
Les unes, de condition,
Les autres, seulement bourgeoizes,
Qu'a peine voit-on dans les cours
Des objets si dignes d'amours.
L'auteur de cette Pastorale
Est à Son Altesse Royale
Monseigneur le Duc d'Orléans,
Et l'on l'estime fort, céans:
C'est Monsieur Perrin qu'il se nomme,
Très-sage et sçavant gentil-homme,
Et qui fait aussi bien des vers
Qu'aucun autre de l'univers
Cambert, maitre par excellence
En la muzicale science,
A fait l'*ut-ré-mi-fa-sol-la*
De cette rare pièce-là,
Dont les acteurs et les actrices
Plairoient a des impératrices:

Et, sur tout, la Sarcamanan[1]
Dont grosse et grasse est la maman,
Fille d'agréable vizage,
Qui fait fort bien son personage,
Qui ravit l'oreille et les yeux,
Et dont le chant melodieux,
Ou mille douceurs on découvre,
A charmé, pluzieurs fois, le Louvre.
Enfin, j'allay, je vis, j'ouys,
Et, mesmement, j'us deux oranges
Des mains de deux vizibles anges
Dont, à cauze qu'il faizoit chaud,
Je me refraîchis comme il faut.
Puis, l'action etant finie,
La noble et grande compagnie
Se promena dans le jardin,
Qui, sans mentir, n'est pas gredin,
Mais aussi beau que le peut être
Le jardin d'un logis champêtre.

Appendix Twenty-One

Account of 'Pastorale' at Vincennes written by Loret (Muze Historique)

Le Cour a passé dans Vinceine
Cinq ou six jours de la semeine,
Château, certainement royal,
Où Monseigneur le Cardinal
(Dont la gloire est, par tout, vantée)
La parfaitement bien traitée.
Leurs Majestez, à tous momens,
Y goûteoient des contentemens
Par diverses rejouissances,
Sçavoir des bals, balets et dances, (*sic*)
A faire soldats exercer,
A se promener et chasser,
Et voir mainte piece comique,
Et la Pastorale en muzique,
Qui donna grand contentement
Et finit, agréablement,
Par quelques vers beaux et sincères,
Que la plus belle des bergères
Avec douceur et gravité
Chants devant Sa Majesté,

---

[1] La Sarcamanan – mother and daughter, two distinguished singers of the period.

Qui, la regardant au vizage,
Les écouta, de grand courage.
Ces quatre ou vers etoient faits
Sur le cher sujet de la paix[1]
Et plùrent, fort, à l'assistance,
Quoy qu'ils ne fissent qu'une stance.

Appendix Twenty-Two

ACCOUNT OF 'LA TOISON D'OR' BY VOLTAIRE (COMMENTAIRES)

LA PARTIE fabuleuse de cette histoire semble beaucoup plus convenable à l'opera qu'a la tragédie. Une toison d'or gardée par des taureaux qui jettent des flammes, et par un grand dragon: ces taureaux attachés à une charrue de diamant, les dents du dragon qui font maître des hommes armés, toutes ces imaginations ne ressemblement guère à la vraie tragédie, qui, après tout, doit être la peinture fidèle des moeurs, Aussi Corneille voulut en faire une espèce d'opera, ou du moins une pièce de machines, avec un peu de musique. C'était ainsi qu'il en avait usé en traitant le sujet d'*Andromède*. Les operas français ne parurent qu'en 1671, et *La Toison d'Or* est de 1660. Cependant un an avant la représentation de la pièce de Corneille, c'est-a-dire en 1659, on avait executé à Issy une pastorale en musique; mais il n'y avait que peu de scènes, nulle machine, point de danse; et l'opera s'établit ensuite en reunissant tous ces avantages, Il y a plus de machines et de changements de decorations dans *La Toison d'Or* que de musique: on y fait seulement chanter les Sirènes dans un endroit, et Orphée dans un autre; mais il n'y avait point, dans ce temps-là, de musicien capable de faire des airs qui répondissent à l'idée qu'on s'est faite du chant d'Orphée et des Sirènes. La mélodie, jusqu'a Lulli, ne consista que dans un chant froid, trainant et lugubre, ou dans quelques vaudevilles tels que les airs de nos noëls, et l'harmonie n'était qu'un contrepoint assez grossier. En général, les tragédies dans lesquelles la musique interrompt la déclamation, font rarement un grand effet, parce que l'une étouffe l'autre. Si la pièce est interessante on est fâché de voir cet intérêt détruit par des instruments qui detournent toute l'attention. Si la musique est belle, l'oreille du spectateur retombe avec peine et avec dégoût de cette harmonie au recit simple. Il n'en était pas de même chez les anciens, dont la déclamation, appelée *melopée*, était une espèce de chant; le passage de la mélopée à la symphonie des choeurs n'étonnait point l'oreille et ne rebutait pas. Ce qui surprit le plus dans la représentation de *la Toison d'Or*, de fut la nouveauté des machines et des décorations, auxquelles on n'etait point accoutumé.

---

[1] France, England and the United Provinces had signed the Treaty of La Haye on May 21st, 1659.

Appendix Twenty-Three

Privilège accordé au Sieur Perrin pour l'etablissement d'une académie d'opera en Musique et verbe François du 28 juin 1669.

Lettres patente du Roy, pour establir, par tout le royaume, des Académies d'Opera, ou representations en Musique en lange françoise, sur le pied de celles d'Italie.

LOUIS, par le grace de Dieu, Roy de France et de Navarre, à tous ceux qui ces présentes Lettres verront, Salut. Notre bien-amé et féal Pierre Perrin, conseiller en nos conseils, et Introducteur des ambassadeurs près la personne de feu nostre très-cher et bien-amé oncle le duc d'Orléans, nous a très-humblement fait remonstrer, que depuis quelques années les Italiens ont estably diverses Académies, dans lesquelles il se fait des représentations en musique, qu'on nomme Opera; que ces Académies estans composées des plus excellens musiciens du Pape et autres Princes, mesme de personnes d'honneste famille, Princes, Nobles et Gentilshommes de naissance, très-sçavans et experimentez en l'Art de la Musique, qui y vont chanter, font à present les plus beaux spectacles et les plus agréables divertissemens non seulement des Villes de Rome, Venise, et autres Cours d'Italie, mais encore ceux des Villes et Cours d'Allemagne, et Angleterre, ou lesdites Académies ony este pareillement establiés à l'imitation des Italiens; que ceux qui font les frais nécessaires pour lesdits représentations; faisant très-expresses inhibitions et deffences à toutes personnes de quelque qualité et condition qu'elles soient. mesme aux Officiers de nostre Maison, d'y entrer sans payer, et de faire chanter de pareilles *Opera* ou représentations en Musique en Vers François, dans toute l'etendue de nostre Royaume pendant douze années, sans la consentement et permission dudit Exposant; à peine de dix mil livres d'amende, confiscation des Thèatres, Machines et Habits, applicables un tiers à Nous, un tiers à l'Hôpital Général, et l'autre tiers audit Exposant. Et attendu que lesdits *Opera* ou Représentations sont des Ouvrages de Musique tous différents de Comédies recitées et que nous les erigéons par cesdits présentes sur le pied de celles des Académies d'Italies, ou les gentilhommes chantent sans deroger.

VOULONS ET NOUS PLAIST, que tous Gentilshommes, Damoiselles, et autres persons, puissent chanter auxdites *Opera*, sans que pour de ce ils derogent au tiltre de Noblesse, ny à leurs Privilèges, Charges, Droits et Immunitez. Révocquons par ces présentes toutes Permissions et Privilèges que Nous pourrions avoir cy-devant donnez et accordez, tant pour raison desdites Opera que pour réciter des comédies en musique, sous quelques noms, qualitez, conditions, et prétextes que se puisse estre. SI DONNONS EN MANDEMENT à nos amez et féaux Conseillers les Gens tenans nostre Cour de Parlement à Paris, et autres nos Justiciers et Officiers qu'il appartiendra, que ces présentes ils ayent à faire lire, publier et enregistrer, et du contenu en icelles, faire jouer et user ledit exposant pleinement et paisiblement, cessant et faisant cesser tous troubles et empêchemens au contraire, CAR tel est nostre plaisir.

DONNÉ à Saint-Germain en Laye le vingt-huictiesme jour de juin mil six cens soixante neuf. Et de nostre Règne le vingt-septiesme. Signé LOUIS et sur le Reply, par le Roy: Colbert. Et Scelle du grand Sceau de cire jaune.

(Manuscrit anonyme. Bibliothéque de l'Opéra, C.954)

This may be the place to discuss the various *Académies* which came into being at the period under discussion. In England such institutions would be described as 'Societies', the term 'Academy' having a somewhat different connotation.

In 1636 Cardinal Richelieu founded the 'Académie Française' and in 1655 Cardinal Mazarin established an 'Académie de peinture et du sculpture'. Encouraged by Colbert, Louis XIV added the 'Académie de danse' in 1661, following it by the 'Académie des inscriptions et belles lettres', in 1666 by the 'Académie des sciences', and, finally, by the 'Académie d'architecture'. Collectively these 'Académies' became known as the 'Institut (de France)' whose present constitution is

Académie Française
Académie des inscriptions et belles-lettres
Académie des sciences
Académie des beaux-arts
Académie des politique et morale sciences.

The last-named was founded as a means of honouring distinguished men whose qualifications do not apply to the previous four. Thus, while being severally autonomous, the learned Societies of France are united beneath one roof, the members describing themselves as being 'de l'Institut'. Music, Painting, Sculpture and Architecture are represented in the 'Académie des beaux-arts'.

Foreigners may be elected 'Membres étrangers' and 'Membres correspondants' to all the Académies except the 'Académie Française' which is exclusively and entirely French. The 'Membres étrangers' are honorary and play no part in the functions and activities of their respective Académies, but the 'Membres correspondants' may be called into consultation by their Académies over matters relevant to France and their respective countries, the one stipulation being that they do not live permanently in Paris. Few to-day wear the distinctive uniform owing to the high cost (nearly a thousand pounds) but on occasions a deceased member's uniform may become available according to size. The process of election as a French-born citizen consists in the first place of formal visits to members in order to solicit votes. Originally this was carried out in full evening dress, a sight to which the French are fully accustomed whether in the morning, afternoon, or evening. This rule has now been waived. Foreigners, incidentally, do not solicit patronage and any attempt to do so would be met with refusal. Election here is entirely in the hands of the Academicians.

Once each year the Académies unite beneath the 'Coupole de l'Institut de France', the building known originally as the 'Collège' and later the 'Palais Mazarin'. Mazarin himself was buried beneath the cupola, but during the Revolution his body was reported to have been dug up and thrown into one of the many ditches to which the childishness of the revolutionary authorities consigned nearly all France's great historical figures. Charles Marie Widor (1845 – 1937) when 'Secrétaire perpétuel' (*i.e.* for life) was of the opinion that the body had escaped attention, but close search and careful sounding of floors and walls revealed nothing.

Widor was instrumental in putting one traditional custom into abeyance. The Secrétaire perpétuel from time to time makes reports to the President of the Republic on the condition of France's national buildings, for which purpose he dons his uniform and proceeds to the Elysée in a coach hundreds of years old, drawn by four horses. Widor did not object to the uniform or, in principle, to the coach, and was prepared to face the amazed amusement of the Parisians; but the coach was neither sprung nor slung and the cobbles of Paris threw the occupant up and down and sideways. Although injury amounted to no more than excessive bruising of an awkward part of the body, Widor felt that this was carrying tradition rather too far and the visit is now made in a more prosaic but more suitable car.

The main purpose of the 'Institut' is research, the 'Académie Française' being charged with the official French Dictionary, and the 'Académie des beaux-arts' with the care of all France's national monuments and buildings; it also awards the annual Prix de Rome in all its branches and is responsible for the good running of the 'Académie de France à Rome' (the Villa Medici), which was founded by Colbert. Each Académie carries out its business in its own fashion and, judging from the Privilège authorising the foundation of the 'Académie de danse', some hilarious meetings must have taken place:—

LETTRES PATENTES DU ROY

Pour l'etablissement d'une Académie Royale de Danse en la ville de Paris.

LOUYS PAR LA GRACE DE DIEU, ROY DE FRANCE ET DE NAVARRE.

A tous présens et à venir, Salut.

Bien que l'art de la danse ait toûjours esté reconnu l'un des plus honnestes et plus nécessaires à former le corps, et luy donner les premières et plus naturelles dispositions à toute sorte d'exercices, et entre autres à ceus des armes, et par consequent l'un des plus avantageux et plus utiles à nostre Noblesse, et autres qui ont l'honneur de nous approcher, non-seulement en temps de guerres dans nos armées, mais même en temps de paix dans le divertissement de nos Ballets: néanmoins il s'est, pendant les désordres et la confusion des dernières guerres, introduit dans ledit Art, comme en tous les autres, un si grand nombre d'abus capables de les porter à leur ruïne irréparable, que plusieurs personnes, pour ignorans et inhabiles qu'ils ayent esté en cet Art de la Danse, se sont ingérés de la montrer publiquement; en sorte qu'il y a lieu de s'étonner que le petit nombre de ceux qui se sont trouvez capables de l'enseigner, ayent par leur etude et par leur application si longtemps resisté aux essentiels défauts dont le nombre infiny des ignorans ont tâché de la défigurer et de la corrompre en la personne de la plus grande partie des gens de qualité. Ce qui fait que nous en voyons peu dans nostre Cour et Suite, capables et en estat d'entrer dans nos ballets et autres semblables divertissements de Danse, quelque dessin qui nous cussions de les y appeler. A quoy estant nécessaire de pourvoir et désirons restablie ledit Art dans sa première perfection et l'augmenter autant que faire se pourra: Nous avons jugé à propos d'établir dans nostre bonne ville de Paris, une Académie Royale de Danse, à l'exemple de celles de Peinture et Sculpture composée de treize des Anciens et plus experimentez au fait dudit Art pour faire par eux, en tel lieu et maison qu'ils voudront choisie dans ladite ville, l'exercisce de toute sorte de Danse, suivent les statuts et réglements que nous en avons fait dresser en nombre de douze principaux articles. A CES CAUSES, et autres bonnes considérations, à ce nous mouvons, nous avons par ces présente signées de nostre main et de nostre pleine puissance et autorité Royale, dit, statué et ordonné, disons, statuons et ordonnons, voulons et nous plaist, qu'il soit incessament étably en nostre dite ville de Paris, une Académie Royale de Danse que nous avons composée de treize des plus experimentez dudit Art et dont l'adresse et la capacite nous est connue par l'expérience que nous en avons souvent faite dans nos Ballets où nous leur avons fait l'honneur de les appeler depuis quelques années, sçavoir de François Galland; sieur du Desert, Maistre ordinaire à danser de la Reine nostre très-chère Epouse; Jean Renauld, Maitre ordinaire à danser de nostre très-cher et unique frère le duc d'Orléans; Thomas le Vacher; Hilaire d'Olivet; Jean et Guillaume Reynal, frères; Guillaume Queru; Nicolas de l'Orge; Jean-Francois Piquet; Jean Grigny; Florent Galand-Désert, et Guillaume Renaud: lesquels s'assembleront une fois le mois, dans tel lieu ou maison qui sera par eux choisie et prise à frais communs, pour y conférer entre eux du fait de Danse, aviser et délibérer sur les moyens de la perfectionner, et corriger les abus et défauts qui y peuvent avoir esté ou estre cy-après introduits; tenir et regir ladite Académie suivant et conformement ausdits Statuts et Réglemens cy attachez sous le contresol de nostre Chancellerie: lesquels nous voulons estré gardez et observez selon leur forme et teneur. Faisant très expresses défenses a toutes personnes de quelque qualité qu'elles soient d'y contrevenir, aux peines y contenües et de plus grande s'il y écheoit. Voulons que les susnommez et autres qui composerent ladite Academie jouissent à l'instar de ladite Académie de Peinture et Sculpture de droit de Committimus, de toutes leurs causes personnelles, passessoires, hypothéquaires ou mixtes, tant en demandant que défendant, par devant les Maistres des Requestes ordinaires de nostre Hostel ou aux Requestes de Palais à Paris, à leur choix; tout ainsi qu'en jouissent les Officiers commenseaux de nostre Maison et décharge de toutes Tailles et Curatelle, ensemble de tout Guet et Garde. Voulons que ledit Art de Danse soit et demeure pour toujours exemp de toutes Lettres de Maitrises, et si par surprise ou autrement en quelque manière que ce soit, il en avait esté ou estoit cy-apres expédié aucune. Nous les avons dès à présent révoquées, déclarées nulles et de nul effet; faisant trèsexpresses défenses à ceux qui les auront obtenües de s'en servir à peine de quinze cens livres d'amende et autant de dommages et intérests, applicables à ladite Académie. SI NOUS DONNONS EN MANDEMENT à nos amez et féaux les Gens tenons nostre Cour de Parlement de Paris, que ces présentes ils ayant à faire lire, publier, registrer et du contenu en icelles faire jouïr et user ledit Desert, Renauld et autres de ladite Académie Royale, cessant et faisant cesser tous troubles et empeschemens contraire: CAR TEL EST NOSTRE PLAISIR. Et afin que ce soit chose ferme et stable à toujours nous avons fait mettre notre scel à cesdites présentes, sauf en autres choses nostre droit et l'autruy en toutes.

DONNÉ à Paris au mois de Mars, l'an de grâce 1661 et de nostre règne la dix-neuvième.

Signe LOUYS et sur le reply par le Roy, DE GUENEGAUD pour servis aux lettres pour l'etablissement d'une Académie Royale de Danse. Visa SEGUIER

Registrées oui à ce consentant le Procureur Général du Roy, pour jouir par les impétrans de l'effect et contenu en icelles, aux charges portées par l'Arrest de Vérification de ce jour, à Paris, en Parlement le 30 Mars 1662. DU TILLET

(*Text from a collection of essays concerning the theatre printed, at the time, in the Bib: Nat: cote Inv. 7f 328–329 – 'à Paris, chez Pierre le Petit, imprimeur et Libraire ordinaire du Roy, rue Saint-Jacques, à la croix d'or. MDCLXIII avec privilège du Roy'.*)

Completing the story as far as it applies to the present context, Louis founded 'Académies de beaux esprits et des sciences' in Arles (1669), Soissons (1675), Mismes (1682), Angers (1685), Villefranche-en-Beaujolais (1687), Caen and Montpellier (1706) and Bordeaux (1713). In 1694 he founded the 'Jeux floraux de Toulouse en Académie'. All this cultural enterprise cannot be too highly admired, but, at the same time, due credit must be given to Colbert as the main instigator.

Appendix Twenty-Four

BAIL DU 8 OCTOBRE 1670 POUR LA LOCATION DE LA SALLE
DU JEU DE PAUME DE LA BOUTEILLE

PAR DEVANT les notaires gardenottes du Roy au Chastelet de Paris
soussignez, fut present Maximilien de Laffemas, escuyer, Sr de
Sérocourt, conseiller et maistre d'hostel ordinaire du Roy, demeurant
à Paris, rue du Chaulme, paroisse Saint-Jean en Grève, tant en son
nom que comme se faisant et portant fort de Messieurs et Dames ses
cohéritiers dans la succession du deffunt Mr. Isaac de Laffemas,
leur père, vivant conseiller du Roy en ses Conseils, doyen de Messrs
les maistres des requestes ordinaires de l'hostel du Roy . . . . .
lequel, ès dits noms, a réconnu et confessé avoir baillé et délaissé par
ces présentes, à tiltre de loyer et prix d'argent, du premier jour du
présent mois d'octobre jusques et pour cinq ans prochains . . . . .
à hault et puissant seigneur Mre [*i.e.* Maître] Alexandre de Rieux,
chevalier, seigneur marquis de Sourdéac et autres terres et à Laurent
de Bersacq de Fondant, escuyer, seigneur de Champeron, demeurant
à Paris, sçavoir ledit seigneur marquis de Sourdeac en son hostel, au
faubourg Saint-Germain, rue Garanacière, et ledit Sr de Champeron,
rue des Fossez de Nesle, paroisse Saint-Sulpice, à ce présents et
acceptans, prenans et rétenans pour eux au dict tiltres durant le
dict temps, c'est assavoir le jeu de paulme où est pour enseigne *la
Bouteille*, seize rue des Fossez de Nesle, ayant *sortie par le rue de Seine*,
ledict jeu de paulme clos de murs, couvert de tuille, garni de ses
auges, au pourtour de charpenterie gallèrie dans ledict jeu d'un
costé couvert d'ais, les murs d'appuy de pierre de taille avec de petites
colonnes de charpenterie qui portent le couvert de laditte gallèrie,
iceluy jeu de paulme pavé de pierres de Can; deux cours au costé
du duct jeu et deux corps de logis ayant fasse sur le dicte rye, apliquez
au rez de chaussée, à salles à cheminée allée de passage et cuisine,
escurie ou apertis, plusieurs estages au nombre de trois, chambres
à cheminées et grenier au dessus, monté dans oeuvre, leurs aisances,
appartenances et dépandances; les dicts lieux ainsy qu'ils s'estendent,
poursuivent et compartent, sans en rien excepter, retenir ni réserver,
avec partie de la place du chantier du costé de la rue de Seyne,
occupe par Mr Levasseur, maistre charon à Paris, à prendre quatre
toises et un pied du devant du mur dudict jeu de paulme cy devant
déclaré, jusques au dehors du mur que les dicts sieurs preneurs
pourront faire faire, à leurs despens, pour séparer le dict chantier
d'avec la dicte place; lequel mur sera faict en l'estendue du dict
chantier et de pareil le construction en espoisseur que ceux du dict
jeu, jusques à la hauteur des autres murs du duct jeu, ainsy qu'ils
sont à présent; au dessus de quel mur les dicts sieurs preneurs pourront
faire faire telle eslévation que bon leur semblers, soit de maçonnerie
que de charpenterie, pour porter la charpent et couverture du comble
qu'il désirent faire, le tout à leurs frais et despens; et pourront aussy

les dictz srs preneurs eslever telle quantité de travées du dict jeu de paulme que bon leur semblers pour leur commodité, en faisant par eux servir les bois que se trouveront bons et en mettant de neufs au deffault. Mesme en faisant par eux faire les couverture et fournissant le fer qu'il conviendre, et sans estre par le dit sr bailleur, es dictz noms, tenu de faire mettre aucun bois en ce qui se trouveroit pourry ou rompu en l'endroit où ils feront les dictes eslevations, pour la construction d'un Theastre qu'ils entendent faire faire du costé du dict chantier, pour les représentations en musique nommées *opera*, en consequence de la permission et privilège qu'ils en ont obtenus par les lettres patentes de Sa Majesté, sous le nom du Sr Perrin, le vingt huit juin mil six cens soixante neuf; pour lesquelles représentations les dictz sieurs preneurs feront faire à leurs despens, dans les dictz lieux, telles loges, amphitheastre et autres accommodements que bon leur semblers, en restablissant par eux les dégradations qui se trouveront faittes aux dictz murs, lorsqu'ils sortiront des dictz lieux . . . . Ce présent bail faict moyennant deux mil quatre cent livres de loyer pour et part chacune des dictes cinq années . . . . Payeront les dictz sieurs preneurs les deniers à quoy les dictz lieux baillez sont et pourront estre, durant le dict temps, taxées et cottizées pour les fortiffications de cette ville et faulxbourgs de Paris, pauvres, boués, chandelles, lanternes, et autres charges de ville et police. Faict et passé à Paris en la maison du dict sieur de Sérocourt sus declarée, l'an mil six cens soixante dix, le huitiesme jour d'octobre, avant midy; et ont signé la minute des présentes, demeurée vers Raveneau, qui a delivré ces présentes pour coppie collationnée sur la ditte minute, ce jour d'huy vingt cinq juin mil six cens quatre vingt sept pour servir aux dictz Srs de Champeron et de Sourdéac.

(*Quoted in 'Les débuts de l'opéra', by Arthur de Boislisle, Paris, 1875, pp. 8–10.*)

Appendix Twenty-Five

PROLOGUE TO 'POMONE'

LA NYMPHE DE LA SEINE:

Toy qui vis autres fois la fleuve des Romains
Triompher des humains,
Et porter le sceptre du monde,
Vertune, que dis-tu de ma rive féconde?

VERTUNE:

J'admire tes grandeurs et la félicité
De ta belle cité:
Mais ta merveille la plus grande
C'est la pompeuse Majesté
Du Roy qui la commande.
Dans l'august LOUIS je trouve un nouveau Mars,
Dans sa ville superbe une nouvelle Rome:
Jamais, jamais un si grand homme
Ne fut assis au thrône des Césars.

LA NYMPHE DE LA SEINE:

Assis sur la terre et sur l'onde,
De monarque puissant ne fait point de projets
Que le ciel ne seconde:
Il est l'Amour.

ENSEMBLE:

Il est l'Amour et la terreur du monde,
L'effroy de ses voisins, le coeur de ses sujets,

LA NYMPHE DE LA SEINE:

Mais quel dessein t'amene
Sur le bord de la Seine?

VERTUNE:

Moy qui forge les visions,
Je viens tromper ses yeux de mes illusions
Et lui montrer mes anciennes merveilles

ENSEMBLE:

Sus donc, par nos accords amoureaux et touchante,
Commençons de charmer son coeur et ses oreilles:
Meslons nos voix, et remplissons les champs
Du doux bruit de nos chants

T

Appendix Twenty-Six

DEDICATION OF 'POMONE' TO THE KING

SIRE,

Aprèz avoir rendu vostre estat victorieux, tranquille et bien-heureux, il ne restoit plus à V.M. qu'a le rendre riche, brillant et magnifique. C'est dans ceste voue qu'elle a transplante dans son royaume les arts liberaux, le commerce et les manufactures, et qu'elle s'est appliquée avec tant de soin à l'embellissement de ses maisons et de sa ville capitale: C'est cet esprit de grandeur et de magnificence, dont Vostre ame royale est entièrement possedée, qui a fait sortir de terre ces grands palais de Louvre et de Versailles, et qui les a comblez de cette profusion admirable de meubles et de richesses: C'est luy qui a donné à la France tant de beaux divertissemens, et nouvellement ce superbe ballet qui a fait l'étonnement de toute l'Europe. Toutes ces choses m'ont persuadé, Sire, que V.M. auroit agréable que l'on introduisit dans son royaume le seul spectacle et l'unique divertissement dont il estoit privé, qui est celuy des opera, que l'Italie et l'Allemagne avoient de particuliers, et sembloient nous reprocher tous les jours. V.M., Sire, a eu la bonté d'approuver mon dessein, et de l'appuyer de son authorité, et j'ay eu le bonheur d'estre assisté dans cette enterprise des soins et de la dépense d'un des plus grands seigneurs tout ensemble et des plus beaux génies de vostre royaume. Avec cela, Sire, V.M. trouvera sans doute que nous avons mal repondu à la grandeur de ses illustres desseins, et à la magnificence de ses ballets: mais quelle proportion y peut-il avoir entre le soleil et les étoiles, entre de foibles sujets et le plus grand des roys? Le courage, Sire, nous manque mouns que les forces; elles rédoubleront, si V.M. honore nos représentations de sa royale présence, et nostre Académie de sa toute-puissante protection: Nous luy demandons très-humble-ment l'un et l'autre. Pour moy, Sire, je suis déjâ plus que content d'avoir témoigne par cet effort téméraire le zêle passionne que j'ay pour l'avancement de vostre gloire, et la profonde vénéra-tion avec laquelle je suis,

SIRE,

de V.M.

Le très-humble, très obéissant
et Très-fidèle sujet et serviteur,

PERRIN

Appendix Twenty-Seven

PAR LE ROY ET MONSIEUR LE PREVOST DE PARIS

au Monsieur le lieutenant criminel

A TOUS ceux qui ces presentes lettres verront: Achilles du Harlay, conseiller du Roy en ses Conseils, son procureur general au Parlement de Paris, garde de la ville, prévosté et vicomté de Paris, le siége vacant, SALUT. Sçavoir faisons que, sur de qui nous a esté remontré par le Procureur du Roy que, Sa Majesté, ayant bien voulu honorer d'une protection toute singulière l'etablissement en cette ville de son Académie royale des Opera, elle auroit estimé à propos d'en deffendre l'entrée à ceux de sa Maison qui sont admis ordinairement dans les Comédies sans payer aucuns droits, comme aussi à tous pages, lacquais et gens de livrées pour empescher les désordres et les querelles qui arrivent le plus souvent par le concours et la confusion du toutes sortes de personnes. Et bien que les officiers préposez à la police ayent employe leurs soins pour les exécutions des ordres de Sadite Majesté, néantmoins ils n'auroient pû empescher la violence de plusieurs lacquais attroupez au mois du mars dernier dans le rue des Fossez de Nesle, lesquels s'etant présentez à la porte de ladite Académie pour y entrer, et cette liberté leur ayant esté refusée suivant l'intention du Roy, ils auroient passé jusques à cet excès d'insolence que d'en vouloir briser les portes et forcer les gardes, aucuns desquels auroient esté grièvement blessez à coups de pierre et de bastons, dont lesdits lacquais estoient armez; aucuns desquels auroient esté arrestez sur le champs et conduits prisonniers au Grand Chastelet, auxquels l'on instruit le procès. Et d'autant qu'il importe pour le seureté publique qu'une semblable violence, et dont les suites sont d'une très-grande conséquence, soit reprimée par l'autorité de la justice, et ceux qui s'en trouveront auteurs ou complices punis selon la rigueur des ordonnances, réqueroit ledit procureur du Roy luy estre sur ce pourveû. NOUS, ouï le procureur du Roy, et faisant droit sur ses conclusions, avons ordonné et ordonnons que les informations encommencées contre les accusez de ladite violence seront incessamment continuées, et leur procés à eux fait et parfait jusques à sentence définitive inclusivement. Et cependant avons fait inhibition et deffences à tous pages, lacquais, gens de livrées et tous autres, de quelque qualité ou condition qu'ils puissent estre, de se présenter aux portes de ladite Académie royale des Opera, pour y entrer sans payer, ny s'attrouper, et faire aucunes violences, pour raison de ce, à main armée, ou autrement excéder ny outrager les gardes préposez pour le sureté desdites Académies royales; le tout à peine des gallères, ou autre, s'il y échet, contre les contrevenans et ceux qui seront pris en flagrant délit; enjoignant aux commissaires du Chastelet de se transporter dans le quartier et ès environs de ladite Académie royale, les jours de représentation faire conduire ès prisons du Grand Chastelet les auteurs et complices desdites violences, et pour cet effet se faire assister de tel nombre d'huissiers, sergens, archers et autres officiers de justice qu'ils aviseront, lesquels seront tenus de leur obeïr au premier commandement; comme aussi aux bourgeois dudit quartier et des environs de prester main forte ausdits commissaires, quand ils en seront requis, avec deffences à eux de donner retraite et recevoir en leurs maisons aucuns desdits délinquans, à peine de cent livres d'amende, et de répondre civilement des dommages et intérests. Et sera nostre présente ordonnance leuë, publiée et affichée à la porte de ladite Académie royale des Operas, lieux et endroits accoûtumées de cette ville et fauxbourgs de Paris, et exécutée nonobstant oppositions ou appellations quelconques, et sans préjudice d'icelles. Ce fut fait et donné en la Chambre criminelle du Chastelet par messire JACQUES DEFFITA, conseiller du Roy en ses Conseils d'Estat et privé et lieutenant criminel de la ville, prévosté et vicomté de Paris, le vingt-troisième jour de may mil six cens soixante-onze.

Signé,

DEFFITA

DE RYANTZ
LE COINTRE, greffier

Collationné

(*Quoted in 'Les débuts de l'opéra', by Arthur de Boislisle, Paris, 1875, pp. 16–18.*)

Appendix Twenty-Eight

Extract from Perrin's Answer to his Critics

Je le demande après cela qu'ils attaquent la place en galants hommes, c'est-a-dire en soldats et par les formes, et non pas en frondeurs en escarmouchant, et je leur declare que s'ils continuënt de la faire par satyrs et par invectives, je leur répondray par un doux silence, et que je donneray toute mon application à composer de nouvelle pièces pour continuer à les divertir.

Au reste le champ est ouvert pour mieux faire, et si quelqu'un veut travailler sur cette matière, et faire l'honneur à l'Académie de luy presenter un opera, je luy dy de sa part qu'après qu'il aura esté examine par des gens habiles et non suspects, s'il est par eux jugé digne d'estre réprésente, il le sera bonne foy avec tous les soins et tous les ornemens possibles, et mesme si c'est une personne d'intérest, on lui promet une honneste reconnoissance.

Appendix Twenty-Nine

DEDICATION OF 'LES PEINES ET LES PLAISIRS DE L'AMOUR' TO COLBERT

MONSEIGNEUR,

Je prens la liberté de vous dédier cet ouvrage, que je souhaiterois qui fut mon chef-d'oeuvre, pour estre plus digne de vostre protection: je ne puis l'addresser à personne plus justement qu'a vous, Monseigneur, qui prenez le soin sous les ordres du Roy, de faire fleurir en France les sciences et les arts. Après avoir etably des Académie pour la physique, l'astronomie, la peinture et l'architecture, vous avec fait dessein d'en etablir une pour la musique, qui a cet avantage sur les autres arts, d'exercer un empire presque absolu sur les passions des hommes. Un ancien roy d'Arcadie ne pouvant adoucir par ses loix les esprits farouches de ses sujets, ni les retenir dans le devoir, fit venir des villes de Grèce les plus excellens musiciens, qui par les charmes de leur art firent de cette nation rude et sauvage un peuple civil et obeissant. Peut-estre, Monseigneur, que cette histoire que raconte Polybé vous a fait naitare la pensée d'etablis l'Académie de l'Opera, non pour adoucir l'esprit des François, mais pour les entretenir dans les beaux sentimens ou ils sont nez, et pour achéver par cette belle science ce que la nature à si bien commence. Si l'establissement de l'Académie françoise, dont la principale fin est la politesse du langage, a donné tant de gloire au cardinal Richelieu, celuy de l'Académie de la musique qui a pour but d'adoucir et de polir les moeurs, ne sera pas moins glorieux à son protecteur. Je scay bien que ces beaux esprits qui composent la première ont une aussi parfaite connoissance des choses que des paroles, comme il paroist par tant d'cuvrages merveilleux qu'ils ont mis en lumière, et particulièrement par des comédies, dont ce grand ministre fascit son plus agréable divertissement. Mais bien que ces pièces de théâtre ayant este admirées de toute la France, et des nations etrangères: je ne puis m'empescher de dire que la musique est une beauté essencielle qui leur manque, et qui est le plus grand ornement de la scène. Les Grecs qui sont les inventeurs du poème dramatique ont finy tous les actes de leurs tragédies par les choeurs de musique, ou ils ont mis ce qu'ils ont imagine de plus beau sur les moeurs. Les inventeurs de l'Opera ont enrichy sur les Grecs, ils ont meslé la musique dans toutes les parties du poème pour le rendre plus accomply, et donner une nouvelle ame aux vers. Que si ces esprits ingenieux ont merité une estime générale, c'est à vous, Monsigneur, que la principale gloire en est deue; puisque vous avez bien daigné les encourager, et qu'ils n'ont rien entrepis que sur l'assurance de votre protection. Il est juste que le public apprenne cette nouvelle obligation qu'il vous a, et qu'il connoisse par cet exemple, aussi bien que par tant d'autre infiniment plus importans, que vous faites sans faste et sans bruit les choses mesme les plus louables.

Que ne dirois-je point sur un sujet si riche, si je ne scavois que les louanges du Roy vous plaisent incomparablement plus que les vostres. Je finis, donc, Monseigneur, pour vous laisser voir ce que la renommée dit de ce grand monarque dans le prologue de cette pièce, après vous avoir assure que je suis, avec la soumission et le respect que je dois.

Monseigneur,
Vostre très-humble et très-obéissant serviteur
GILBERT

Appendix Thirty

PROLOGUE TO
'LES PEINES ET LES PLAISIRS DE L'AMOUR'

(Vénus paroist dans un char tiré par des colombes avec le Renommée et deux petits Amours.)

VÉNUS:

Un nouvel Apollon dans la France m'amène,
Le Soleil des François
Qui dans le champ de Mars soûmet tout à ses loix
Et dans un char pompeux en vainqueur de promène.

LA RENOMMÉE:

Il n'a que de nobles désirs,
Et la gloire fait des plaisirs.

VÉNUS:

Des Dieux et des héros illustre messagère,
Va d'une aisle légère
Dire en publiant ses exploits,
LOUIS est le plus grand des rois.

LA RENOMMÉE:

J'ay fait voler son nom des rives de la Seine
Jusques où le soleil recommence son tour,
Et l'Inde quelque jour
Sera de son domaine.

VÉNUS:

Puisque de grand monarque un jour
De tout cet univers ne fera qu'une cour,
Allez, petits Amours, sur le terre et sur l'onde
Dire qu'il a conquis les coeurs de tout le monde.

(*à la Renommée*)

Et toy ne te lasse jamais
Ne vanter partout ses hauts faits.

LA RENOMMÉE:

Desjà les habitans et du Nil et du Tage
Et les plus éloignez de l'Empire François,
Les sauvages sans loix
Viennent luy tendre hommage.

LES NATIONS (*paraissent sur la terre*):

Charmez de sa valeur, nous venons dans ces lieux
Pour divertir en paix ce Roy victorieux.

Appendix Thirty-One

LETTER FROM COLBERT TO M. DE HARLAY, PROCUREUR-
GÉNÉRAL AU PARLEMENT DE PARIS, NOTIFYING HIM OF
THE TRANSFER OF THE PRIVILÈGE FROM PERRIN TO LULLY

Versailles, 24 Mars 1672

LE ROY avant accordé au sieur Lully, intendant de la musique de
sa chambre, la privilège des operas en musique que Sa Majesté avoit
donné auparavant au sieur Perrin, ledit sieur Lully a representé
à Sa Majesté que les Marquis de Sourdéac et de Champerron et les
sieurs de Sablières et Guichard se sont opposés a l'enrégistrement
de ses lettres, quoyque les sieurs de Sourdéac et de Champerron
n'ayent aucun droit dudit Perrin et que les autres soyent porteurs
d'un écrit fait entre Perrin et eux qui ne leur donne aucune part en
ce privilège et est mesme detruit par une contre-lettre.

Le Roy estany persuadé que si la sieur Lully veille à la conduite
de cette Académie, Sa Majesté et la public en pourront avoir de la
satisfaction, m'a ordonné de vous faire sçavoir qu'il souhaite que
cette affaire soit jugée le plus tost qu'il sera possible et que vous luy
donniez des conclusions favorables autant que la justice vous le
pourra permettre.

Signé COLBERT

(*Lettres, Instructions, et Mèmoires de Colbert par Pierre Clement, Paris, Imprimerie Impériale,
1868, Vol. V.*)

Appendix Thirty-Two

PRIVILÈGE POUR L'ETABLISSEMENT DE L'ACADÉMIE ROYALE
DE MUSIQUE, EN FAVEUR DE MONSIEUR DE LULLY

à Versailles au mois de Mars 1672

LOUIS, par la grace de Dieu, Roy de France et de Navarre, à tous presens et à venir, Salut. Les Sciences et les arts étant les ornemens les plus considérables des Etats, Nous n'avons point eu de plus agréables divertissemens, depuis que Nous avons donné la paix à nos peuples, que de les faire revivre, en appelant auprès de Nous tous ceux qui se sont acquis la réputation d'y exceller, non seulement dans l'etendüe de notre Royaume, mais aussi dans les païs étrangers: et pour les obliger d'avantage à s'y perfectionner, Nous les avons honorés des marques de notre estime et de notre bienveillance; et comme entre les arts liberaux, la Musique y tient un des premiers rangs, Nous aurions dans la dessein de la faire réüssir avec tout ses avantages, par nos lettres patentes du 28 juin 1669, accordé au Sieur Perrin une permission d'établir en notre bonne ville de Paris et autres de notre Royaume, *des Académies de Musique* pour chanter en public des pièces de théâtre, comme il se pratique en Italie, en Allemange, et en Angleterre, pendant l'espace de douze années. Mais ayant depuis été informé que les peines et les soins que ledit sieur Perrin a pris pour cet etablissement n'ont pu seconder pleinement notre intention, et élever la musique au point que Nous nous l'étions promis, Nous avons cru pour y mieux réüssir qu'il étoit à propos d'en donner la conduite à une personne dont l'expérience et la capacité nous fussent connues, et qui eut assez de suffisance pour former des élèves tant pour *bien chanter* et *actionner sur le theatre,* qu'dresser des bandes de violons, flutes et autres instrumens. A ces causes, bien informé de l'intelligence et grande connoissance que s'est acquise notre cher et bien-amé *Jean Baptiste de Lully,* au fait de la Musique, dont il Nous a donné et donne journellement de très-agréables preuves, depuis plusieurs années qu'il s'est attaché à notre service, qui nous ont convie de l'honorer de la Charge de notre service, qui nous ont convie de l'honorer de la Charge de *Surintendant et compositeur de la Musique de notre Chambre;* Nous avons audit Sieur de Lully permis et accordé, permettons et accordons par ces présentes, signées de notre main, d'etablir une *Académie royale de Musique* dans notre bonne ville de Paris qui sera composée de tel nombre et qualité de personnes qu'il avisera bon être, que Nous choisirons et arrêterons, sur le rapport qu'il nous en fera, pour faire des représentations devant Nous, quand il nous plaira, des *pièces de musique* qui seront composées, tant *en vers françois qu'autres langues étrangères,* pareilles et semblables aux Académies d'Italie, pour en jouir sa vie durant, et après lui celui de ses enfans qui sera pourvu et reçu en survivance de ladite charge de Surintendant de la Musique de notre Chambre; avec pouvoir d'associer avec lui qui bon lui semblera, pour l'establissement de ladite Académie, et pour le dédommager des grands frais, qu'il conviendra faire pour lesdites représentations, tant à cause des Théâtres, Machines, Décorations, habits, qu'autres choses nécessaires, Nous lui permettons de donner au public toutes les piéces qu'il aura composées, mêmes celles qui auront été représentées devant Nous, sans néanmoins qu'il puisse se servir pour l'execution des dites piéces, des Musiciens qui sont à nos gages; comme aussi de prendre telles sommes qu'il jugera à propos, et d'établir des gardes et autres gens nécessaires aux portes des lieux ou se feront lesdites représentations; faisant très-expresses inhibitions et deffenses à toutes personnes de quelque qualité et conditions qu'elles soient, même aux officiers de notre Maison, d'y entrer sans payer; comme aussi de faire chanter aucune piece entière en Musique, soit en françois ou autre langue, sans le permission per écrit dudit Sieur de Lully, à peine de dix mille livres d'amende et de confiscation de Thèatre, Machines, Décorations, habits et autres choses, applicables, un tiers à Nous, un tiers, à l'hôpital-général, et l'autre tiers audit Sieur de Lully, lequel pourra aussi établir des *écoles particulières de musique* en notre bonne ville de Paris et partout ou il jugéra nécessaire pour le bien et l'avantage de ladite *Académie royale*, et d'autant que Nous l'érigeons sur le pied de celles sur le pied des Académies d'Italie où les Gentilhommes chantent publiquement en musique sans déroger, Nous voulons et nous plait que tous Gentilhommes et Damoiselles puissent chanter auxdites pièces et representations de notre dite *Académie royale*, sans que pour ce ils soient censés déroger audit Titre de Noblesse, ni à leurs privilèges, charges droits et immunites. Révoquons, cassons, et annullons par ces présentes toutes provisions et privilèges que nous pourrions avoir cydevant donnés, ou accordés, même celui dudit sieur Perrin, pour raison desdites pièces de Théâtre en Musique, sous quelque nom, qualité, condition et pretexte que ce puisse être. SI DONNONS EN MANDEMENT à nos amés et deaux Conseillers, les gens tenans notre Cour de Parlement à Paris, et autres nos justiciers et officiers qu'il appartiendra, que ces présentes ils ayant à faire lire, publier et enregistrer; et du contenu en icelles, faire jouir et user ledit exposant pleinement et paisiblement, cessant et faisant cesser tous troubles et empêchemens au contraire. CAR TEL EST NOTRE PLAISIR. Et afin que ce soit chose ferme et stable à toujours; Nous y avons fait mettre notre scel.

Donné à Versailles, au mois de mars, l'an de grace 1672 et de notre régne le vingt-neuvième.

Signé :

LOUIS

Et plus bas: COLBERT

(*Manuscrit anonyme C 954, Bib : de l'Opéra.*)

Appendix Thirty-Three

LETTER FROM THE KING TO M. DE LA REYNIE,[1] LIEUTENANT
OF THE POLICE, TO STOP PERFORMANCES OF THE OPERA
BECAUSE OF LULLY'S PRIVILÈGE

A Versailles, le 30 Mars 1672

MONSIEUR de la Reynie, ayant revoqué le *privilège* des *Opera*, que j'avois cy-devant accordé au Sieur Perrin, je vous écrit cette lettre, pour vous dire que mon intention est, qu'a commencer du premier jour du mois d'avril prochain, vous donniez les ordres nécessaires pour faire cesser le *représentations* que l'on a continué de faire desdits opera, et vertu de ce *privilège*. A quoi me promettant que vous satisfere bien ponctuellement, je prie Dieu qu'il vous ait, M. de la Reynie, en sa sainte garde. Ecrit à Versailles le 30 Mars 1672.

Signé:

LOUIS

et plus bas COLBERT

(Manuscrit anonyme C 954, Bib: de l'Opéra, where it follows immediately Appendix Thirty-One.)

Appendix Thirty-Four

PETITION TO THE PARLIAMENT OF PARIS BY THE MARQUIS DE
SOURDÉAC AND LAURENT DE BERSAC DE FONDANT

A Nosseigneurs du Parliament

SUPPLIANT humblement Alexandre de Rieux, chevalier, marquis de Sourdéac, et Laurens de Bersac de Fondant, escuyer, sieur de Champeron, disans qu'il a pleu au Roy par ses lettres pattentes du vingt huictiesme juin 1669 leur accorder soubz le nom de Pierre Perrin permission d'establir en cette ville de Paris et autres du royaume des académyes pour y faire des opperas et representations des pièces de théastre en musique en vers françois, pareilles à celles d'Italie, et de prendre du publiq telles sommes qu'ils adviseroient pour les desdomager des grands frais qu'il conviendra faire pour les théastres, machines, décorations, habitz et autres choses nécessaires, avec deffences à toutes personnes de faire de pareilles représentations,

---

[1] It was M. de la Reynie who gave Paris her first claim to the description 'Ville lumière', for his street lighting (6,000 candle-burning lanterns) was the first serious attempt at such a thing in Europe. He amassed a vast library, this including all Molière's original manuscripts. (*The Police of Paris* – Philip John Stead, Staples Press, 1957, pp. 28 and 32 respectively.)

sans leur consentement et permission, pendant les douze années portées par lesdites lettres, soubz les peynes y contenües; au quel establissement les supplians ayans travaillé sans discontinuation depuis le dit temps, à grands frais, et couru risque plusieurs fois de perdre des sommes considérables qu'ilz y avoient réussy avec applaudissement et satisfaction du publiq, pour s'aproprier ce qui leur appartient et les en frustrer auriot aupose à Sa Majeste qué n'y ayans peu reussir audit establissement et soubz ce prétexte se seroit fait accorder la mesme permission d'establir des oppera par lettres du mois de mars 1672 avec révocation de celles accordées aux supplians, lesquels en ayans eu advis et que ledit sr Lully en vouloit poursuivre l'enregistrement ilz y ont formé opposition sur laquelle les parties ont esté appointées en droit, ce qui a fait une instance par l'evennement de laquelle les supplians espèrent que le dit sieur de Lully sera déboutté de l'effect des lettres par luy obtenues, et que celles accordées aux supplians seront exécuttées, à l'effect de quoy ilz ont esté conseillez d'en requérir l'enregistrement.

Ce considéré, Nosseigneurs, il vous plaise procédant au jugement de la dite instance débouttant ledit sr Lully de l'enregistrement des lettres par luy obtenues, ordonner que les lettres obtenues par les supplians soubz le nom dudit Perrin le vingt huistiesme juin 1669 seront enregistrées pour estre exécuttées selon leur forme et teneur, condemner ledit Lully en tous leurs domages et interrestz et aux despens de ladite instance, et vous ferés bien.

Signé: ALEXANDRE DE RIEUX ET DEFFONDANT, ET DU BOIS, procureur. Et plus bas est escrit: et jugeant soit signiffié le XXXe may 1672 et Signiffié ledit jour.

(Published by Etienne Charavay in the 'Revue des Documents historiques' 2e année [1874–1875] chez A. Lemerre et C. Motteroz, Paris, 1875, pp. 110, 111. A note states that although this 'requête' was undoubtedly printed, it cannot be found in the Bibliothéque nationale. It was copied from a manuscript found there – melanges 36 fol. 204.)

Appendix Thirty-Five

EXTRACTS FROM GUICHARD'S REPLY TO THE DEFAMATORY LIBELS OF LULLY AND AUBRY

A Messieurs les Gens tenans le Siège Présidial en la Chambre Criminelle de l'Ancien Chastelet de Paris:

. . . . . CET homme qui n'est petry que l'ordure et de boüë, regarde tout le monde du mesme oeil dont il se void luy-même, et comme ceux qui portent leur veüe sur quelques objets au travers d'un verre coloré, s'imaginent que ces objets en ont la couleur, quoy qu'ils conservent celle qui leur est propre; de mesme ce libertin de profession, dont la veüe qui s'est affoiblié par l'excez des débauches, ne porte pas plus loin que luy confond tout le monde dans la crapule et le libertinage qui luy sont particuliers . . . . .

Chacun scait de quelle trampe et de quelle farine est Jean-Baptiste: le Moulin des environs de Florence, dont son père etait Meunier, et le Bluteau de ce moulin qui a este son premier Berceau, marquent encore aujourd 'huy la bassesse de son origine. Quand un vent meilleur que celui se son Moulin l'eut poussé en France à l'âge de treize ans, peut-on dissimuler que le hasard jetta dans le Commun de Mademoiselle parmy les galopins? Ignore-t-on qu'il sceut adroitement se tirer de la marmite avec son archet? Les comptes de la Maison de cette Princesse ne font-ils pas foy qu'il fut peu de temps après valet des valets de sa Garde-Robe, puis petit Violon, puis grand Violon, et n'est-il pas bien plaisant après cela de vouloir apliquer faussement aux autres tout ce qu'on luy peut si légitément reprocher?

Voilà les titres honteux du personnage qui ose néanmoins dans sa Requeste se comparer *à ces grands hommes de l'Antiqué, que les Romains reçevoient dans le corps du Senat, quoy-qu'ils fussent estrangers, comme étans Nécessaires à la République!* Luy qui ne peut tout au plus prétendre qu'a la qualité d'Affranchy, après avoir porte celle d'Esclavé, et dont le vice qu'il a succé avec le laict de son Pays s'oppose au droit de naturalité qu'il a receu dans le nostre.

Le supliant ne pretend point entrer icy dans le détail des debauches infâmes et du libertinage de Baptiste; il ne veut pas souiller les oreilles des Juges par le récit d'une longue suite d'ordures et d'infamies *semblables à celles qui ont autrefois attiré le Feu du Ciel sur ces Villes entières,* et qui auroient fait infailliblement chasser ce libertin de la Cour peu de temps après qu'il eut commencé d'y paroître, si l'on avait crû trouver un jour dans son répentir de quoy justifier la grâce qu'on luy fit enfaveur de la Musique.

Il est vray de dire que cet Arion de nos jours doit son salut à son Violon, comme celuy de Lesbos fut redevable du sien à sa Harpe, qui le tira du naufrage. Le vent qui a receu les cendres de l'infâme Chausson dont le procez note Baptiste, a porté cette vérité si loin, que mesme les Gazettes Estrangères, au sujet d'un méchant Feu d'artifice qu'il avise de faire vis-à-vis sa maison en l'année 1674, publierent partout que *s'il n'avoit pas reussi dans* ce feu la, on reussiroit mieux à celuy qu'il avoit merité ce Grêve. . . . .

(From a collection of essays on the theatre n.d., but to all appearance printed in the XVII century. Bib: Nat: Cote Inv. 328–329. The entire 'reponse' occupies thirty-two pages of abuse similar to the extracts quoted here.)

Appendix Thirty-Six

EXTRACTS FROM THE PRIVILÈGE GRANTED TO GUICHARD
FOR THE ESTABLISHING OF AN ACADÉMIE DES SPECTACLES

LOUIS par la grâce de Dieu, Roy de France et de Navarre, à tous
ceux qui ces présentes lettres verront, salut.

Les spectacles publics ayant toujours fait les divertissemens les
plus ordinaires des peuples et pouvant servir à leur félicité aussy
bien que le repos et l'abondance, Nous ne nous contentons pas de
veiller à la tranquillité de nos sujets par nos travaux et nos soins
continuels, Nous voulons bien y contribuer encore par des divertissemens publics. C'est pourquoy nous avons agréé la très-humble
supplication qui nous a este faite par nostre cher et bien-amé Henri
Guichard, intendant des bastimens et jardins de nostre très-cher et
très-amé frère unique, le duc d'Orléans, de luy permettre de faire
construire des cirques et des amphi-thèatres pour y faire des carrousels,
des tournois, des joustes, des luttes, des combats d'animaux, des
illuminations, des feux d'artifice et généralement tout ce qui peut
imiter les anciens jeux des Grecs et des Romans.

A CES CAUSES, estant informé de l'intelligence et grande
connoissance que le sieur Guichard s'est acquisés dans la conduite
de ces actions publiques, Nous luy permettons d'establir en nostre
bonne ville de Paris des cirques et des amphithèatres pour y faire
lesdites représentations, sous le titre de *l'Académie royale des spectacles*
pour en jouir par lui, ses heirs et ayans cause, avec pouvoir d'associer
avec luy qui bon luy semblera pour l'establissement de ladite académie.
Et pour le dedommager des grands frais qu'il luy conviendra faire,
Nous luy permettons de prendre telles sommes qu'il jugera à propos, et
d'establir des gardes et autres gens nécessaires aux portes des lieux
ou se feront lesdites représentations. Faisant très-expresses inhibitions
et défences à toutes personnes de quelque qualité qu'elles soyent,
mesme aux officiers de nostre maison, d'y entrer sans payer; comme
aussy de faire faire lesdites représentations et spectacles, en quelque
manière que ce puisse estre, sans la permission par écrit dudit sieur
Guichard, à peine de 10,000 livres d'amende et de confiscation des
amphithèatres, décorations et autres choses, dont un tiers sera applicable à Nous, un tiers à l'hôpital général, et l'autre tiers au sieur
Guichard; à la réserve néanmoins des illuminations et feux d'artifice,
dont l'usage sera libre et permis comme auparavant nos présentes
lettres, et à la charge qu'il ne sera chanté aucune piéce de musique
auxdites représentations et que lesdits spectacles seront donnés
gratis à nostre peuple de la ville de Paris . . . . revoquant et annulant
par ces présentes toutes permissions et privilèges cy-devant donnés.

(*Lettres, Instructions, et Mémoires de Colbert par Pierre Clément, Paris, Imprimerie impériale
1868, Vol. V.*)

Appendix Thirty-Seven

CAMBERT IN ENGLAND

CONSIDERABLE doubt rests upon Cambert's activities once he had arrived in England. Sir George Grove in the first edition of his *Dictionary of Music and Musicians*[1] says that Cambert 'became a band-master to a regiment and then Master of the Music to Charles II'. This is repeated in later editions. French writers usually quote the latter appointment, but Cambert's name does not appear in the collected records of *The King's Musick*,[2] other than in two entries referring to 'Monsr. Combert' (*sic*).

'1674 July 4th . . . . Order that the twelve violins following doe meet in his Majesty's theatre within the palace of Whitehall on Wednesday next by seven of the clock, to practice after such manner as Monsr. Combert shall enforme them' (L.C. Vol. 774).

The second entry duplicates the first (L.C. Vol. 482). The names of the 'twelve violins' are the same in both cases. This suggests nothing more than that Cambert was a useful rehearsal-master and implies no official recognition or position. He certainly never was Master of the King's Musick.

Nearly every writer states that *Pomone* was performed here, some adding 'with indifferent success'; but there is no evidence of any kind to support the supposition. It appears to be an attempt to explain the disappearance of the manuscript from Paris, since Cambert might have brought it with him to London. Records show that *Ariane* was performed at the wedding of James, Duke of York, afterwards James II, and Mary of Modena in 1674. Earlier, Cambert had tried to form an English 'Academy of Music' with the aid of Monsieur Grabu, another Frenchman, whom Charles II had made Master of his Musick, in succession to yet another one, Nicholas Lanière (or Lanier). Grabu assisted in the production of *Ariane* by re-writing Perrin's text so that it applied to Charles II instead of Louis XIV, and by composing additional movements and substituting his own music for several Airs etc. written by Cambert.

The English Academy does not appear to have matured as no evidence can be found in any official record.

---

[1] 1878.   [2] H. Carte de Lafontaine.

Appendix Thirty-Eight

PLACET ADDRESSED TO THE KING BY JEAN LAURENT DE
BEAUREGARD[1] IN APRIL 1681

LE NOMMÉ Jean Laurent de Beauregard remontre que, depuis 1662 jusqu'en 1672[2], le feu sr Perrin a demeuré et vecu chez luy, avec un mulet.[3] Lequel sr Perrin s'estant appliqué à la composition des paroles de musique pour l'etablissement des opératz, il ne fit faire plusieurs repetitions es années 1667 et 1669, avec tant de succès, que le Roy, sur le recit qui luy en fut faict par des personnes des plus considérables de sa cour, qui les avoient venus dans le palais de sr duc de Nevers, luy accorda le privilége de la représentation, par lettres patentes données à Saint-Germain-en-Laye, le 8e jour de juin[4] 1669. La première s'en fit par l'opera de *Pomone*, le 4e mars[5] 1671 qui réussit sy advantageusement que les profficts eussent été capables d'acquitter dans trois mois toutes les dettes dudit sr Perrin, sy son emprisonnement et la révocation que fit Sa Majesté de son privilége, pour l'accorder audit Baptiste Lully, ne luy eust faict cesser les moyens. Cette disgrace a tourné à grande perte au suppliant, qui est un des créanciers dudit Perrin, pour l'avoir nourry, logé, et entretenu avec un valet, six années ou environ, et loge les musiciens qu'il avoit faict venir pour ledit etablissement, du nombre desquel sont encore présentement les srs Morel, Gillet Clédière et Miracle, qui sont de la musique de Sa Majesté; les autres font encore presentement valoir par leurs belles voix les ouvrages de musique dudit sr de Lully. Cependant, comme ledit Perrin est mort insolvable en la maison du suppliant, qui tient maison garnie et pensionnaires, et qu'il ne luy a laissé pour tout payement que quatre productions admirables de son esprit, qui sont quatre operatz intitulez; *Diasne amoureuse ou la Vendage d'amour*, *La Reyne du Parnasse ou La Muse d'Amour*, *Arriane ou le Mariage de Bacchus*, et *la Nopce de Venus*[6], tous ses rares ouvrages seroient admirez des plus beaux esprits du siècle et deviendront utiles au suppliant, qui est dans le necessité, luy estant de deub par ledit sr Perrin plus de 10,000 livres sy Sa Majesté veut ordonner audit sr Lully qui n'a point produict de nouveaux operas depuis longtemps, de les prendre et faire part au suppliante des profficts qui en reviendront, jusques à la concurrence de son deub, sy mieux n' ayme ledit sr Lully permettre au suppliant de les faire représenter à condition de luy donner pour la représentation desdits quatre operatz telle part que sa Majesté ordonnera.[7]

(Quoted in 'Les débuts de l'opéra' by Arthur de Boislisle, Paris, 1875.)

---

[1] Perrin's landlord.   [2] 1675.   [3] *sic* – valet.   [4] June 28th.

[5] Most authorities consider the date to have been either March 18th or 19th.

[6] Existing copies of these libretti have been renamed by someone with a caustic wit – *Arriane* becomes 'Arrignez ou La Matrage de Bagnolet', *Diasne amoureuse*, 'Diable amoureux', and *La Vendage d'Amour*, 'La Vengance de l'Amour'.

[7] Petitions were handed to the Secretary of State every Monday in the King's Antechamber. They were sorted and transcribed by clerks before going to the Ministers concerned. A large 'N' in the margin of this particular petition signifies 'réponse négative (du Roy)'.

Appendix Thirty-Nine

Satire on Lully by La Fontaine

LE FLORENTIN

Le Florentin
Montre à la fin
Ce qu'il sait faire.

Il rassemble à ces loups qu'on nourrit, et fait bien;
Car un loup doit toujours garder son caractère
    Comme un mouton garde le sien.
J'estoire avert l'on me dit: prenez garde;
Quiconque s'asseocie avec lui se hasarde:
Vous ne connoissez pas encor le Florentin;
    C'est un paillard, c'est un matin qui tout devore,
Happe tout, serre tout; il a triple gosier.
Donnez-lui, fourrez-lui, le gloût demande encore:
Le roi même auroit peine à la rassasier.

Malgré tous ces avis, il me fit travailler.
    Le palliard s'en vint reveiller
Un enfant des neuf Soeurs; enfant à barbe grise,
    Que ne devoit en nulle guise
Etre dupe: le fut, et le sera toujours.
Je me sens ne pour être en butte aux méchans tours.
Vienne encore un trompeur, je ne tarderai guere.
    Celui-ce me dit: Veux-tu faire,
    Presto, presto, quelque opera,
    Mais bon? ta muse répondra
    Du succés par-devant notaire.
    Voici comment il nous faudra
    Partager le gain de l'affaire.
Nous en ferons deux lots, l'argent et les chansons:
    L'argent pour moi, pour toi les sons.
Tu t'entendras chanter, je prendrai les testons;
    Volontiers je paie en gambades:
    J'ai huit ou dix trivelinades
Que je sais sur mon doigt; cela joint à l'honneur
De travailler pour moi, te voila grand seigneur.
Peut-être n'est-ce pas tout à fait sa hanangue;
    Mais, s'il n'eut ces mots sur la langue,
Il les eut dans le coeur. Il me persuada;
    A tort, à droit me demanda
Du doux, du tendre, et semblables sornettes,
    Petits mots, jargons d'amourettes

Confits au miel; bref il m'*enquinauda*.
Je n'epargnai ni soins, ni peines
Pour venir à son but et pour le contenter:
Mes amis devoient m'assister;
J'eusse, en cas de besoin, disposé de leurs veines.
Des amis! disoit le glouton, En a-t-on?
Ce gens te trompéront, otéront tout le bon,
Mettront du mauvais en la place.
Tel est l'esprit du Florentin:
Soupconneux, tremblant, incertain,
Jamais assez sur de son gain,
Quoi que l'on dise ou que l'on fasse.
Je lui rendis en vain sa parole cent fois;
Le b . . . . . avait juré de m'amuser six mois.
Il s'est trompé de deux; mes amis, de leur grâce,
Me les ont epargnes, l'envoyant ou je croi
Qu'il va bien sans eux et sans moi.

Voilà histoire en gros: le détail a des suites
Qui valent bien d'être deduites;
Mais j'en aurois pour tout un an;
Et je ressemblerois à l'homme de Florence,
Homme long a conter, s'il est un en France.
Chacun voudroit qu'il fut dans le soin d'Abraham.
Son architecte ey son libraire
Et son voisin et son compère,
Et son beau-père,
Sa femme et ses enfans, et tout le genre humain,
Petits et grands, dans leurs prières,
Disent le soir et le matin;
Seigneur, par vos hontés pour nos si singulières,
Delivres-nous du Florentin.

U

Appendix Forty

DEDICATION OF 'ARMIDE' TO THE KING

SIRE,

de toutes les tragédies que j'ay mises en musique, voici celle dont le public a temoigné estre le plus satisfait: C'est un spectacle ou l'on cour en foule et, jusqu'icy, on n'en a point vey qui ait reçu plus d'aplaudissements. Cépendant, c'est de tous les ouvrages que j'ay faits, celui qué j'estime le moins heureux, puisqu'il n'a pas encore eu l'avantage de paroistre devant Votre Majesté. Vos ordres, Sire, m'ont engage d'y travailler avec soin et avec empressement. Un mal dangereux, dont j'ay esté surpris, n'a pas esté capable d'interrompre mon travail et le désir ardent que j'avais de l'achéver dans le temps que Votre Majesté le souhaitait, m'a fait publier le péril ou j'estois exposé et m'a touché plus vivement que les plus violentes douleurs que j'ay souffertes. Mais que me sert-il, Sire, d'avoir fait tant d'efforts pour me haster de vous offrir ces nouveaux concerts? Votre Majesté ne s'est pas trouvée en estat de les entrendre. Elle n'en a voulu prendre d'autre plaisir que celuy de la faire servir au divertissement de ses peuples.

Appendix Forty-One

LEGAL AND SOCIAL ASPECTS OF THE ACADÉMIE ROYALE DE MUSIQUE

THE MEMBERS of the Académie royale de musique were spoken of as being in the Service du Roy. This had the benefit of conferring the Right of Sanctuary upon them and, in a world in which parental authority played a dominating role, they were immune from victimisation. The usual procedure for parents desiring to control or repress a recalcitrant child was to ask for a *lettre de cachet* which consigned the child to the Bastille or to any other prison of the parent's choice. Two courses were open to the child if he wanted to remain free. He could either enter the Army or join the Académie in some capacity or other. The parent had no right of appeal.

Curious situations sometimes arose which made the arrangement work in two directions. A certain application for a *lettre de cachet* was justified because a young man 'compromet l'honneur de sa famille en exerçant le mêtier de comédien'. This would not have been granted if the Académie had been involved. In another position an actor requested that his son be deported to the American Colonies 'parce qu'il refuse d'embrasser la profession du théâtre'. Parental authority in those days was something truly operative, but it should be remembered that the parent himself had suffered a similar discipline in his youth, and that the child in question would certainly exercise it himself in his turn.

Appendix Forty-Two

LULLY'S INFLUENCE IN ENGLAND

IT IS well-known that King Charles II of England, having experienced the artistic glories of Louis XIV of France, decided to reflect some of them in his own palace, and sent Pelham Humfrey (1647 – 1674) to Italy and France in 1664 in order that he might study the prevailing tastes and fancies; Humfrey returned to England in 1667. There is no record of his ever having been to Italy, and, apart from the line in Pepys' Diary[1] that he came back from France 'a veritable Monsieur', there is none of his having stayed in that country, nor is there anything to show that he ever studied under Lully or that he even met him personally. All that can be found is the acceptance of a request for more money. The evidence lies in what he brought back with him.

Some French writers state that he played the violin in Lully's orchestra, but this, if correct, must have been a courtesy arrangement, for Lully (as has been seen) used only French musicians. The certain evidence of his stay in Paris can be seen in the complete change which came over dramatic and church music as soon as he returned to London.

There are many experts who would do anything rather than acknowledge that English music owes any debt to French, but they are not in the least averse to acknowledging Italian and German influences. It is difficult to understand this refusal to face facts. Professor Sir Jack Westrup, in his masterly *Purcell*[2], is one of these. He maintains that Lully's was the music of frivolity and that up to that time he had composed 'only ballets'.[3] However, Lully had composed his great *Miserere* in 1664, and examination reveals that it was the origin of the style of the English church music of the Restoration Period.

This was but one of the many works which Lully wrote for the Chapelle Royale, over whose music he had complete control. Purcell was to occupy a similar position as one of the Composers to His Majesty's Chapel Royal – he was never Master of the King's Musick, this being an administrative and organisational appointment entailing a certain amount of conducting, but no 'official' composing.

Professor Westrup also maintains that the 'music of frivolity' could not have influenced Humfrey because the majority of Humfrey's anthems are based upon a 'dominant note' which is 'not frivolity at all, but a serious and sometimes pathetic melancholy'.[4] However, fifteen of these anthems are set to joyful words and it is surely not

---

[1] November 15th, 1667.
[2] *Master Musicians*, Dent, London, p. 201. See also *A History of Music in England*, Walker, O.U.P., p. 142.
[3] *Op. cit.*, p. 201 (but the footnote contradicts the whole theory).
[4] *Op. cit.*, p. 201.

maintained that a composer can be joyful only in the major mode. Even if this theory were correct, it would serve only to emphasise the impression which Lully's *Miserere* had made upon Humfrey. However, Lully also wrote 'joyful music' – *Magnificat, Laudate pueri, Exaudi Deus*, to say nothing of *Te Deum* (for double choir, like the *Miserere*).

The only credit given to Lully lies with the Overture, but Professor Westrup concedes this point somewhat grudgingly, and thinks that Humfrey 'may also by his own example have acquainted Purcell with the French type of instrumental Overture'. We may well ask how else Purcell could have found out about it, and how else Humfrey could have discovered its existence but at the source of its 'invention'. In 1658 Lully had composed the Overture to the Ballet *Alcidiane et Polexandre* in this style:

Ex.71

This was the first ballet for which he wrote the entire music.

In 1660 he composed an 'Overture et six entrées' for Cavalli's *Serse*, the Overture opening as follows:

Ex.72

As the year 1664 witnessed the beginning of Lully's collaboration with Molière, Humfrey might well have seen *Le Mariage forcé, L'Amour medicin* (1665) and *Le Sicilien* (1667), together with the pastorales *Les Plaisirs de l'Ile enchantée* (1664) and *Le Pastorale comique* (1667).

Overtures had become an established element of the theatre and since not all of Lully's have survived, it may be assumed that he used some previously written. It is not difficult to see how Purcell followed Lully's example when Humfrey returned to London, and how closely he followed the model, even in its embryonic stage. The influence, however, had spread from the same source to other composers, and in 1685 Grabu prefaced his *Albion and Albanius* with an Overture commencing thus:

Ex. 73

It was in this year that Lully's first opera, *Cadmus et Hermione* was performed in London. Of this work, Professor Westrup says that 'it is probable that he [Purcell] saw this performance or at any rate knew the music, if it was he who appropriated the instrumental 'Entrée de l'Envie' in the Prologue and used it for the dance that follows "Arise, ye subterranean winds" in "The Tempest".'[1]

Both these hypotheses are reasonable. It is certain that the musicians who had sat at the feet of Humfrey would not miss this opportunity of hearing the model opera and it seems equally certain that Purcell himself must have utilised Lully's tune, although it is impossible to understand why he did so.[2] The music is not so wonderful as to preclude any other composer from writing his own for a similar situation. This opera by Lully formulated Purcell's approach to dramatic music, just as Lully's *Miserere* influenced the church composers of the period.

The connection between the Overtures of Lully and Purcell may be seen by comparing the examples already quoted together with that from *Cadmus et Hermione*, with three by Purcell.

---

[1] *Op. cit.*, p. 111.
[2] Mr. Dennis Arundel suggests that this may have been inserted by someone else (*The Critic at the Opera*, Benn, p. 153).

The Overture remained comparatively insignificant until Rameau, Bach, and Handel made it musically important. It may truthfully be said that Lully's fugato sections pale before some of those by Purcell.

Certain characteristics of Lully's Airs find their reflection in many of Purcell's and also in those of his contemporaries. Of these, one of the most striking is the accent placed so often by Lully on the second beat of a triple measure. His word-painting was reflected in Grabu's *Albion and Albanius.*

WHEN' MOR-TALS LAUGH ————

On the other hand, tunes of the quality of the well-known 'Bois épais' from *Armide* (1686, see Ex. 51) find no English stylistic parallels.

Lully's dotted rhythms became almost clichés through their over-frequent usage. They can be found in the *Miserere*

MUL-TI-TU-DI-NEM MI-SE-RA-TI-O-NUM TU-A-RUM.

and were echoed by Grabu in *Albion and Albanius*, as seen in Ex. 75. They penetrated English Church Music in unexpected places, and were used constantly in the ritornelli and choruses.

CLOTH — ED WITH WHITE ROBES.

It was at such moments that the Royal Toe was able to move with the lilt of the music. Michael Wise (c. 1648 – 1687) got very near to writing a Galliard in 'Awake, Awake, put on thy strength, O Zion'.

HAL - LE - LU — JAH, HAL-LE - LU —— JAH, HAL -LE - LU — JAH, HAL-LE- LU —— JAH, HAL -LE - LU - JAH, HAL - LE - LU - JAH.

Taken slowly, this particular 'Hallelujah' has considerable dignity. John Blow (1649 – 1708), however, became skittish and undignified in 'I beheld, and lo, a great multitude'.

EX.79

HAL - LE - LU - JAH, HAL - LE - LU - JAH, — HAL — LE-LU - JAH, HAL — LE - LU-JAH.

while Purcell became quite absurd in 'O give thanks'.

Ex.80.

THAT I MAY SEE THE FE — LI

CI -TY.

Blow tried to go further in 'I was in the Spirit on the Lord's day' and nearly tied himself up into a rhythmic knot.

EX.81.

HAL - LE-LU-JAH, HAL - LE-LU — JAH, HAL - LE-LU-JAH, HAL — LE - LU — JAH.

(Was this a malicious attempt to confuse the royal reaction to the lilt?)

Most important of all was the *recitativo stromentato* which Lully tentatively introduced. There is not a very great gulf fixed between this extract from Lully's *Miserere*

EX.82.

AM - PLI -US, LA - VA ME AM - PLI -US, LA - VA

ME AB I — NI -QUI - TA - TE ME -A

and these from Humfrey, Wise, and Blow.

HUMFREY: HEAR, O HEAVENS

WISE: PREPARE YE THE WAY

Blow continues the strain in Ex. 83C with this piece of word-painting.

(Compare Ex. 54 and 98).

Church music became dramatic and the new type of Verse Anthem contained many instances of musical dialogue. The solemn admonition in Humfrey's 'Hear, O Heavens', administered by three voices to the words 'Wash you. Make you clean. Put away the evil of your doings' is a purely operatic reflection[1], while the following dialogue from Wise's 'Prepare ye the Way of the Lord' might have come straight from a *Tragédie-Lyrique*.

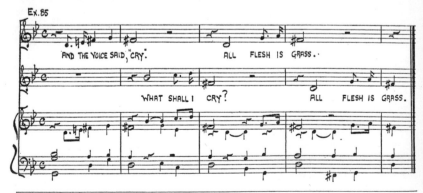

---

[1] It is too long to quote here.

The instrumental 'symphonies' delighted Charles II (whose mind was not always on the words of the anthems), and Purcell's 'Unto Thee will I cry' and 'O Sing unto the Lord' contain respectively four and five of these movements. Apart from Handel's 'Chandos Anthems' which are virtually genuine 'Cantatas', English church music showed nothing similarly elaborate until Samuel Sebastian Wesley (1810 – 1876) composed *The Wilderness.*

The English composers discovered what Lully never set out to find, namely, the value of expressive harmony and modulation as counterparts to expressive melody. The influence, therefore, lies solely in the manner; the matter is completely original. Secular music became more dramatic, sacred music more secular without losing its devotional characteristics. Church music found the additional element of dramatic expression; there was increasing contrast in style from one section to another and more variety through the use of contrasted voices. The gap between recitative and air began to close up so that it is sometimes difficult to distinguish between the two.

That Purcell headed the drift towards Italianism does not alter the argument that Lully through Pelham Humfrey indirectly re-volutionised English musical thought. One has but to compare the four-square writing of Dr. William Child (1606 – 1697) and his absurd attempts at gaiety with the word 'Hallelujah' to see why English music had to take in new blood. This was not always of the best quality, but it never circulated sluggishly or perfunctorily and never drowned the music's essentially English qualities, though these were later completely submerged for over a century by George Frederick Handel, and afterwards by Felix Mendelssohn-Bartholdy and Johannes Brahms. The genuine English spirit was not to re-appear and become established until 1922 when Vaughan Williams' *A Pastoral Symphony* finally set the seal upon aesthetics which went back even further than Henry Purcell.

Appendix Forty-Three

ACCOUNT BY BACHAUMONT OF THE OPENING NIGHT OF THE SALLE DES TUILERIES

L'OPERA s'est ouvert par 'Castor et Pollux', avec l'affluence qu'on presume. La garde était plus que triplée. La représentation a été des plus tumultueuses, et les brouhaha ont duré sans discontinuation pendant le premier acte et une partie du second. On a trouvé différents defuts à la salle: 1. Le parterre est trop élévé pour le théâtre; 2. les premières loges avancent de beaucoup et ne sont pas assez cintrées; 3. les sécondes loges sont ecrasées par celles-là, auzquelles on parait avour tout sacrifié; 4. le paradis est si reculé et si exhaussé qu'on y est dans un autre monde et qu'on n'y entend rien. En général on se recrie fort contre l'architecte, M. Soufflot. On est etonné qu'un homme connu par des talents aussi supérieurs ait fait des fautes aussi enormés. On le defend qu'il a été forcé de tout sacrificier à certaines loges de protection qui font un effet des plus désagréables et rendent le public fort mécontent du peu d'égard qu'on a pour lui.

(*Mémoires secrets (1762–1789) – London 1787–1789 – 36 vols.*)

Appendix Forty-Four

ACCOUNT BY BACHAUMONT OF THE SECOND NIGHT AT THE SALLE DES TUILERIES

AUJOURD'HUI, second jour de l'Opéra, il y avait très-peu de monde. Il est certain que le délabrement où il est par rapport aux sujets ecarté une infinite de gens. Le sieur Pillot fait Castor et le fait horriblement mal. Mademoiselle Arnould joue supérieurement le rôle de l'amante; l'actrice s'y developpe dans les plus grand jeu et dans la verité la plus parfaite des situations. Gelin est mediocre, mademoiselle Chevalier braille à l'ordinaire. Les ariettes que chante mademoiselle La Mière sont très-plates, quant aux paroles et quant à la musique même. On admire le dernier baller, qui vraiment est de genie. C'est le système de Copernic mis en action; il est très bien exécuté. Reste à savoit pourquoi le système de Copernic dans cet opéra! Vestris est absent. Heureusement mademoiselle Lany a reparu. Le premier jour, l'Opera avait fait 5,240 livres; il n'y a fait aujourd'hui que 100 louis.

(*Op. cit.*)

Appendix Forty-Five

LA SALLE DES MACHINES

IN 1789 the Théâtre-Italien was taken over by Leonard, Marie-Antoinette's hairdresser. He was ejected on October 6th of that year when the Royal Family returned (or was returned) to Paris. Leonard himself escaped the guillotine, although his father was sentenced and executed during the Terror. The trial of Louis XVI took place there. Napoleon I built the Chapelle and the Théâtre des Tuileries on the same site; these remained in existence until the 1871 Revolution, when the entire building was sacked and burnt to the ground, and the Palais des Tuileries disappeared for ever – as a whole, but in part its stones, gates, etc. can be found all over Paris. The Place de la Concorde was paved with them and relics can be seen in the courtyard of the Ecole des Beaux-Arts and elsewhere.

Appendix Forty-Six

DECREE CONTROLLING ADMISSION TO THE
SALLE DU PALAIS ROYAL

ORDNANNCE DU ROI. Sa Majesté fait très-expresses inhibitions et défenses à toutes personne du quelque qualité et condition qu'elles soient, même aux Officiers de sa maison, Gardes, Gendarmes, Chevau-légers, Mousquetaires, aux Pages de S.M., ceux des Princes et Princesses de son sang, des Ambassadeurs et à tous autres, d'entrer à l'Opéra sans payer. Defend S.M. à tous ceux qui assistent à ce spectacle, et particulièrement à ceux qui se placent au parterre, d'avoir le chapeau sur la tête pendants les entractes. Veut et defend S.M. qu'il n'y ait aucune préseance ni place marquée pour les carrosses, et qu'ils aient tous, sans aucune exception de distinction, à se placer à la file les une des autres au fur et à mesure qu'ils arriverant aux entrées des spectacles. Ordonne S.M. d'imprisonner les contrevants . . . .

Appendix Forty-Seven

THE OPERA BALLS

THE OPERA BALLS were held during two seasons, the first from November 11th until Advent, the second from Epiphany to Shrove Tuesday. On Sundays they lasted from midnight to six o'clock in the morning. On the occasions when there was no operatic performance, there was a *Concert Spirituel*. The price of admission was three livres, except at the end of the Carnival, when the charge was doubled.

The first successful function took place on January 2nd 1716 and it was decided to hold three Balls each week. On these occasions the theatre formed a floor eighty feet long. The boxes were decorated with multi-coloured carpets and hangings, while the stage lights were augmented by three hundred candles. The orchestra consisted of two bands of fifteen players each, placed at the opposite ends of the theatre. The combined orchestra gave a concert 'composé de grands morceaux de symphonie des meilleurs maîtres' for half-an-hour before each Ball opened – presumably they were united on one spot for this purpose.

The Balls were masked and acquired a bad reputation. They became the happy hunting ground of all the bad hats of Paris, pick-pockets, thieves, gamblers, and a brisk trade was done by the prostitutes of the neighbourhood. It was said that all the gods of beauty and pleasure received due honour except 'le dieu de l'hymnée' who was 'maltraité'. Members of the Court paid surreptitious visits and on one occasion Louis XV went incognito in order to see exactly what went on there. On another, Marie Antoinette was discovered there, and this simple escapade was held against her by her enemies. During this visit the Comte d'Artois knocked the elbow of the Duc de Bourbon, who promptly challenged the Comte to a duel. The King forbade his brother to fight, but honour required him to do so. The contestants fired token shots at each other, but the Comte d'Artois was hit in the arm. The fighters immediately went together to the Opera where Marie-Antoinette was waiting the result of the duel in a state bordering upon hysteria. When the adversaries entered arm-in-arm, the whole audience burst into loud cheers.

Appendix Forty-Eight

La Salle du Palais Royal

The foyer can still be seen as it forms the entrance to a restaurant. One enters by the original vestibule and climbs the original staircase, the only difference being that the old frontage has been replaced by a plate-glass window and door. The walls are decorated with engravings showing the disposition of the theatre, to say nothing of a Menu offering almost unlimited possibilities (with champagne) at the price of 1 franc 50 centimes, a charge which remained in force until 1914. The average daily clientèle at that time numbered 2,000 – the wonder is that it was not higher, at that price!

During the Consulate, Napoleon used the billiards room every evening. On one occasion he put his cue through the glass window. He immediately ordered that it be made to open outwards instead of inwards as the decree ordained. The proprietor of the Restaurant claims that this is the only instance in the whole of Paris, a 'Privilège' in fact – but the writer has noticed another in the Rue Saint-Honoré.

Appendix Forty-Nine

MADEMOISELLE SAINT-HUBERTY

THIS SINGER may have behaved badly, but she earned the approval of all who heard her. Among contemporary critics, Gunguéne is worth reproducing:[1]

> Le talent de cette sublime artiste prend sa source dans son extrème sensibilité. On peut mieux chanter un air, mais on ne saurait donner aux airs, aux recitatifs un accent plus emû, plus passioné. On ne peut avoir une action plus dramatique, un silence plus eloquent. On se rapelle encore son terrible jeu muet, son immobilité tragique, et l'effrayante expression de son visage pendant la longue ritournelle du choeur des prêtres dans *Didon*.[2] Quelqu'un lui parlait de cette impression qu'elle paraissait eprouver et qu'elle avait communiqué à tous les spectateurs. 'Je l'ai réellément eprouvée,' repondit-elle, 'des dixieme mésure, je me suis sentie morte!'

The Baron Grimm was equally enthusiastic:[1] 'C'est la Voix de Todi, c'est le jeu de Cleron, c'est un modèle qu'on n'a point en sur le théâtre, et qui longtemps en servira'.

She was sent on many Provincial tours. In Marseilles a *Fête Nautique* took place in which she took part, clad 'à la grecque'.

In Strasbourg, where she sang *Didon*, she caused a flutter in the heart of an artillery lieutenant named Bonaparte, who addressed her in verse:[3]

> 'Romains qui vous vantez d'une illustre origine,
> Voyez d'où dependait votre empire naissant:
> Didon n'eut pas de charme assez puissant
> Pour arreter la fuite ou son amant s'obstine;
> Mais si l'autre Didon, ornement de ces lieux,
> Eut été reine de Carthage,
> Il eut pour la servir abandonné ses dieux
> Et votre beau pays serait encore sauvagé!'

She remained prima donna at the Académie until 1790. She then fell in love with the Comte d'Entraigues and followed him to England, where they were married. They lived there until 1812 when they were both murdered by some assassins who wished to get hold of incriminating papers proving that they had been plotting against the Imperial Government of France.

---

[1] Quoted by Lasalle *op. cit.*, pp. 153, 154.
[2] By Piccinni.
[3] Lasalle, *op. cit.*, p. 155.

Appendix Fifty

THEATRES OCCUPIED BY THE OPERA

March	19*th*	1671	Jeu de Paume de la Bouteille (Rue des Fosses-de-Nesles [Mazarin])
November	15*th*	1672	Jeu de Paume de Bel-Air (Rue de Vaugirard)
June	17*th*	1673	Première Salle de Palais-Royal (Destroyed by fire April 6th 1763)
January	24*th*	1764	Salle des Machines des Tuileries (Destroyed by fire May 1871)
January	26*th*	1770	Deuxième Salle du Palais-Royal (Destroyed by fire June 8th 1781)
August	14*th*	1781	Salle des Menus-Plaisirs (Rue Bergère) (Destroyed by fire April 1788)
October	27*th*	1781	Salle de la Porte-Saint-Martin (Destroyed by fire May 1871)
August	7*th*	1794	Salle Montansier (Rue de la Loi [Richelieu]) (Demolished by decree February 13th 1820)

OFFICIAL TITLES HELD BY THE OPERA

June	28*th*	1669	Académie d'Opera [sic]
March	13*th*	1672	Académie Royale de Musique
June	24*th*	1791	Opéra
June	29*th*	1791	Académie de musique
September	17*th*	1791	Académie Royale de Musique
August	15*th*	1792	Académie de Musique
August	12*th*	1793	Opéra
October	18*th*	1793	Opéra National
August	7*th*	1794	Théâtre des Arts
February	2*nd*	1797	Théâtre de la République et des Arts
August	24*th*	1802	Théâtre de l'Opéra

Since the last date there have been fourteen other changes.

BIBLIOGRAPHY

BIBLIOGRAPHY

A: General

Works in English are listed separately at the end of this section

AEBISCHER, PAUL:

Trois Farces françaises inédites (*Paris, Champion, 1924*)

D'ALEMBERT, JEAN LE ROND:

Oeuvres complètes (5 vols.) (*Paris, Belin, 1821 – 1822*)
Eléments de musique théorique et pratique suivant les principes de Monsieur Rameau (*Paris, David, 1752*)
Mélanges de litterature, d'histoire et de philosophie (2 vols.) (*Berlin, Paris, Briasson, 1753; Amsterdam, 1759*)

D'ASSOUCY, CHARLES COYPEAU:

Aventures burlesques (*Nouvelle édition avec préfaces et notes par E. Colombey, Paris, Delahaye, 1858*)
Rimes redoublées (*Paris, Imprimerie de C. Nego, 1671*)
Poésies et lettres contenant diverses pièces héroïques, satiriques, et burlesques (*Paris, Loyson, 1653*)
Les Aventures d'Italie de M. d'Assoucy (*Paris, A. de Raffle, 1677*)
Le jugement de Pâris en vers burlesques (*Paris, Quinet, 1648*)
L'ombre de Molière et son épitaphe (*Paris, Loyson, 1673*)
Sur la mort imaginaire et véritable de Molière (*Paris, de Varennes, 1673*)
L'Ovide en belle humeur (*Paris, C. de Sercy, 1650*)

BARRAUD, HENRI:

La France et la musique occidentale (*Paris, Gallimard, 1956*)

BEAUCHAMPS, – :

Recherces sur les théâtres de France (*Paris, 1735*)

BELGODÈRE-JOHANNÈS, V.:

Histoire de la musique de l'antiquité à nos jours (*Paris, Laurens, 1947*)

BELLAIGUE, – :

Souvenirs de musique et de musiciens (*Paris, Nouvelle librairie nationale, 1921*)

BENSERADE, ISAAC DE:

Les oeuvres de Monsieur Benserade (2 vols.) (*Paris, C. de Sercy, 1697*)

BERLIOZ, HECTOR:

Gluck (*Paris, Gazette musicale, 1837*)

BOISLISLE, ARTHUR MICHEL DE:

Les débuts de l'opéra français à Paris (*Paris, Extrait du tome II des Mémoires de la Société de l'histoire de Paris et de l'Ile de France, 1875*)

BORDES, CHARLES:

Preface to *Esther* (*Paris, Schola Cantorum, 1920*)
Preface to *Athalie* (*Paris, Schola Cantorum, 1920*)

BORREL, EUGÈNE:

Jean Baptiste Lully – le cadre, la vie, l'oeuvre (*Paris, La Colombe, 1949*)

BRUNEAU, ALFRED:

La musique française – rapport sur la musique en France du XIIIe au XXe siècle (*Paris, Fasquelle, 1901*)

BRUYÈRE, ANDRÉ:

'Les muses galantes', musique de J. J. Rousseau (*Paris, Richard Masse – Les Carnets critiques, 1952*)

BUTI, L'ABBÉ FRANCESCO:

Ercole amante, tragedia representato por le Nozze della Maesta Christianissime. Traduite en français. Hercule amoureux, tragédie représentée pour les noces de leurs majestez très chrétiennes (*Paris, R. Ballard, 1662*)

CAPON, GASTON:

Les Vestris, le 'diou' de la danse et sa famille 1730 – 1808, d'après des rapports de police et des documents inédits (*Paris, Société de Mercure de France, 1908*)

CELLER (LECLERC), LUDOVIC:

Les origines de l'Opéra (*Paris, Didier, 1868*)
Les décors, les costumes et la mise en scène au XVIIe siècle (*Paris, Liepmannssohn et Dufour, 1869*)

CERF DE LA VIEVILLE, DE FRENEUSE, LE (DOM JEAN-PIIILIPPE)

La comparaison de la musique italienne et de la musique française (*Brussels, Foppens, 1704*)

CHABANON, MICHEL PAUL GUIDE:

Eloge de Monsieur Rameau (*Paris, Imprimerie Lambert, 1764*)

CHAILLEY, JACQUES:

Histoire musicale du Moyen-Age (*Paris, Presses Universitaires Françaises, 1950*)
La musique mediévale (*Paris, Editions du Coudrier, 1951*)

COHEN, GUSTAVE:

La Comédie latine en France au XIIe siècle (2 vols.) (*Paris, Les Belles Lettres, 1931*)
Mystères et Moralités liegoises du Moyen-Age d'après le manuscrit 617 du Musée Condé à Chantilly (*Paris, Champion, 1920; Brussels, Palais des Académies, 1953*)
Farces françaises inédites du XVe siècle (2 vols.) (*Cambridge Mass., Medieval Academy of America, 1949*)
La Passion des Théophiles (*Paris, Delagrave, 1947*)
Mystère de la Passion des Théophiliens (*Paris, Richard Masse, 1950*)
Le Miracle de Théophile (Transposition littéraire, transposition musicale par Jacques Chailley) (*Paris, Delagrave, 1933*)

Le Jeu de Robin et Marion (Transposition littéraire, transposition musicale par Jacques Chailley) (*Paris, Delagrave, 1935*)

Le Jeu d'Adam et d'Eve (Transposition littéraire, transposition musicale par Jacques Chailley) (*Paris, Delagrave, 1936*)

Ronsard, sa Vie et son Oeuvre (*Paris, Boivin, 1924, 1932, 1947; Paris, Gallimard, 1956*)

Ronsard. Oeuvres complètes, ed. critique, annotée G. Cohen (*Paris, Gallimard – Bib. de la Pleiade, Nos. 45 and 46, 1938*)

Le Livre de Conduite du Régisseur et le Compte des Dépenses pour le Mystère de la Passion, joué à Mons en 1501 (*Strasbourg, Librairie alsacienne, 1925; Paris, 57 rue de Richelieu, 1925; Oxford, O.U.P., 1925*)

COMBARIEU, JULES:
Histoire de la Musique, Vol. I (*Paris, Colin, 1913*)

COUSSEMAKER, EDMOND DE:
Drames liturgiques du Moyen-Age (*Paris, librairie archéologique de Victor Didron, 1861*)

CRUSSARD, CLAUDE:
Un musicien français oublié: M.-A. Charpentier (*Paris, Floury, 1945*)

DANGEAU, PHILIPPE DE COURCILLON, MARQUIS DE:
Journal de la cour de Louis XIV – 1684 à 1715 (*London, 1770; Paris, Xhrouet, 1807*)
Journal du Marquis de Dangeau (19 vols.) (*Paris, Didot, 1854 – 1860*)

DEBUSSY, CLAUDE ACHILLE:
Monsieur Croche, anti-dilettante (*Paris, Dorbon aîné – Les Bibliophiles fantaisistes, 1921*)

DIDEROT, – :
Le Neveu de Rameau (*Paris, Delaunay, 1821*)

DONNAY, MAURICE:
Molière (*Paris, Fayard, 7th ed. 1949*)

DROZ, EUGÉNIE:
Le Recueil Trepperel, I Sotties (*Paris, Droz, 1935*)

DUFOURCQ, NORBERT:
La musique française (*Paris, Larousse, 1949*)

DUKAS, PAUL:
Les écrits de Paul Dukas sur la musique (*Paris, S.E.F.I., 1948*)

DUMESNIL, RENÉ:
Histoire illustrée de la musique (*Paris, Plon, 1934*)
Histoire illustrée du théâtre lyrique (*Paris, Plon, 1953*)

ECORCHEVILLE, JULES:
Vingt suites d'orchestre publiées pour la première fois d'après un manuscrit de la bibliothèque de Cassel et précédées d'une étude historique (2 vols.) (*Paris, Fortin, 1906*)

FÉTIS, FRANÇOIS JOSEPH:

Biographie universelle des musiciens et biographie générale de la musique (*Brussels, Leroux, 1835 – 1844*)

Nouvelle édition, avec supplément et complément publiés sous la direction d'A. Pougin (*Paris, Firmin-Didot, 1878 – 1880*)

Histoire générale de la musique depuis les temps les plus anciens jusqu'à nos jours (5 vols.) (*Paris, Firmin-Didot, 1860 – 1876*)

FRANCOEUR, – :

L'opéra avant la Révolution (Recueil de textes sur l'opéra) (*Paris, Bib. de l'Opéra, n.d.*)

GARDIEN, JACQUES:

Jean Philippe Rameau (*Paris, La Colombe, 1949*)

GOFFLOT, L.–V.:

Le Théâtre au collège (*Paris, Champion, 1907*)

GOULAS, NICOLAS:

Mémoires de Nicolas Goulas publiées par Ch. Constant (3 vols.) (*Paris, H. Loones, 1879 – 1882*)

GRAMONT, ANTOINE III, DUC DE:

Mémoires du Maréchal de Gramont, duc et pair de France, données au public par le duc de Gramont (*Paris, David, 1716*)

GROS, ÉTIENNE:

Philippe Quinault, sa vie et son oeuvre (*Paris, Champion – Librairie Ancienne, 1926*)

GROUCHY, VICOMTE EMMANUEL-HENRI DE:

L'opéra pendant la dernière année de la monarchie (*Paris, La Nouvelle Revue rétrospective, No. 4 Octobre 1894*)

HALLAYS, ANDRÉ:

Racine, poète lyrique (*Paris, Schola Cantorum, 1899*)

HOROWICZ, BRONISLAW:

Le théâtre d'opéra (*Paris, Éditions de Flore, 1946*)

HUYGHENS, CONSTANTIN:

Musique et musiciens du XVIIe siècle – correspondance et oeuvres musicales – publiées par W. J. A. Jonckbloet et J. P. N. Land (*Leyden, Brill – Société pour l'histoire musicale des Pays-Bas, 1882*)

D'INDY, VINCENT:

Cours de Composition musicale Vols. I and III (*Paris, Durand, 1909, 1950*)

JACOB (LACROIX), PAUL:

Recueil de Farces, Sotties et Moralités du XVe siècle (*Paris, Delahaye, 1859*)

JACOBSEN, J. P.:

Essai sur les origines de la Comédie en France du Moyen-Age (*Paris, Champion, 1910*)

JOLY, GUY:

Mémoires de monsieur Joli [sic] conseiller au Parliament, contenant l'histoire de la Régence d'Anne d'Autriche et des premières années de la majorité de Louis XIV jusqu'en 1665 (*Amsterdam, Bernard, 1718*)

Mémoires de monsieur Joly, conseiller du Roi au Chatelet de Paris pour servir d'éclaircissement et de suite aux mémoires du Cardinal de Retz (*Rotterdam, Les héritiers de Leers, 1718*)

JUBINAL, ACHILLE:

Mystères inédits du XVe siècle (2 vols.) (*Paris, 1827*)

JULLEVILLE, LOUIS PETIT DE:

Histoire du Théâtre en France (*Paris, Cerf, 1885, 1886*); (*Les Comédiens en France au Moyen-Age, 1885*); (*Répertoire du Théâtre comique en France au Moyen-Age, 1886*); (*La Comédie et les Moeurs en France au Moyen-Age, 1886*)

KLEIN, ABBÉ FÉLIX:

Sept Comédies du Moyen-Age (*Paris, Spes, 1927*)

LABORDE, DE:

Essais sur la musique

LALO, PIERRE:

De Rameau à Ravel: portraits et souvenirs (*Paris, Michel, 1947*)

LALOY, LOUIS:

Rameau (*Paris, Alcan, 1908*)

LANDORMY, PAUL:

Gluck (*Paris, Gallimard, 1941; 16th ed. 1949*)

LAURENCIE, LA (LIONEL DE LA LAURENCIE):

Rameau (*Paris, Laurens, 1908*)

LINCY, LEROUX DE, AND MICHEL, FRANCISQUE XAVIER:

Recueil de farces, moralités, et sermons joyeux (4 vols.) (*Paris, Techener,* 1831 – 1838)

LORET, JEAN:

La muse historique ou recueil des lettres en vers écrites à son altesse Mademoiselle de Longueville par le Sieur Loiret [sic] (*Paris, Chenault, 1656*)

LUYNES, CHARLES PHILIPPE, D'ALBERT, DUC DE:

Mémoires du duc de Luynes (17 vols.) (*Paris, Didot, 1860 – 1865*)

MABILLE, ÉMILE:

Choix de Farces, Soties et Moralités des XVe et XVIe siècles (2 vols.) (*Nice, Gay, 1875*)

MARET, DOCTEUR HUGHES:

Eloge historique de Monsieur Rameau, lu, le 25 août 1765, par Monsieur Maret (*Dijon, Causse, 1766*)

MARMONTEL, JEAN-FRANÇOIS:

Oeuvres complètes (19 vols.) (*Paris, Verdière, 1818 – 1920*)
Mémoires (*Paris, Firmin-Didot frères, 1846*)

MASSON, PAUL MARIE:

L'Opéra de Rameau (*Paris, Laurens, 1930*)

MAUGARS, ANDRÉ:

Réponse faite à un curieux sur le sentiment de la musique d'Italie (*Paris, Claudin, 1865*)

MAZARIN, JULES, CARDINAL:

Lettres du Cardinal Mazarin pendant son ministère recueillies et publiées par M.A. Cheruel (9 vols.) (*Paris, Imprimerie Nationale, 1872 – 1906*)

MENESTRIER, LE PÈRE CLAUDE FRANÇOIS:

Des représentations en musique ancienne et moderne (*Paris, Guignard, 1681*)

MERSENNE, FRANÇOIS MARIN:

Harmonie universelle contenant la théorie et la pratique de la musique (*Paris, Cramoisy, 1636*)

MIGOT, GEORGES:

Jean Philippe Rameau et le génie de la musique française (*Paris, Delagrave, 1930*)

MOLIÈRE (POQUELIN), JEAN BAPTISTE:

Les oeuvres de Monsieur Molière (théâtre complet) (*Paris, Barbin, 1673; Amsterdam, Brunel, 1725*)

MONTPENSIER, MLLE ANNE-MARIE-LOUISE DE:

Mémoires (4 vols.) (*Amsterdam, Wetsein et Smith, 1735*)

MOTTEVILLE, MADAME FRANÇOISE BERTAULT DE:

Mémoires de Madame de Motteville pour servir à l'histoire d'Anne d'Autriche (5 vols.) (*Amsterdam, Changuion, 1723; Paris, Colnet, 11 vols., 1822 – 1823*)

MUSSET-PATHAY, VICTOR DONATION DE:

Histoire de la vie et des ouvrages de J. J. Rousseau, suivis de lettres inédites (2 vols.) (*Paris, Pelicier, 1821*)

NODOT, – :

Le triomphe de Lully aux Champs-Elysées (1687). Publication d'un manuscrit de la Bib. de l'Arsenal (*Paris, La Revue musicale, numéro spécial, 1st January, 1925*)

NOVERRE, JEAN GEORGES:

Lettre sur la danse et sur les ballets (*Stuttgart and Lyons, Aimé Delaroche, 1760*)

D'ORMESSON, OLIVIER LEFÈVRE:

Journal d'Olivier Lefèvre d'Ormesson et extraits des mémoires d'André d'Ormesson publiée par M. Cheruel (2 vols.) (*Paris, Imprimerie Impériale, 1860 – 1861*)

PARFAICT, FRÈRES CLAUDE ET FRANÇOIS:

Dictionnaire des théâtres de Paris (7 vols.) (*Paris, Lambert, 1756*)
L'Histoire de l'Académie royale de musique.

PAUPHILET, ALBERT:

Jeux et Sapience de Moyen-Age, texte établi et annoté par A. Pauphilet
(*Paris, Éditions de la Nouvelle Revue française, 1941 – Bib. de la Pleiade, Moyen-Age 3*)

PERRAULT, CHARLES:

Des hommes illustres qui ont paru en France pendant ce siècle avec leurs
portraits au naturel (*Paris, Dezollier, 1696 – 1700*)

PERRIN, 'ABBÉ' PIERRE:

Les oeuvres de poésie de Monsieur Perrin, contenant les jeux de poésie,
diverses poésies galantes, des paroles de musique, airs de cour . . . . etc.
(*Paris, Loyson, 1661*)
Paroles de musique pour le concert de chambre de la Reine (*Paris, Imprimerie
de D. Pellé, 1667*)

PHILIPOT, EMMANUEL:

Trois Farces du Recueil de Londres (*Rennes, Plihon, 1931*)

PICOT, ÉMILE:

Recueil général des Sotties (3 vols.) (*Paris, Didot, 1902 – 1912*)

PICOT, ÉMILE, ET NYROP, CHRISTOPHE:

Nouveau Recueil de Farces françaises des XVe et XVIe siècles, dans collection
de documents pour servir à l'histoire de l'ancien théâtre français (*Paris,
Morgand, 1880*)

POISOT, CHARLES:

Histoire de la musique en France (476 – 1860) (*Paris, Dentu, 1860*)

POUGIN, ARTHUR:

Les vrais créateurs de l'opéra français: Perrin et Cambert (*Paris, Charavay
frères, 1881*)
Jean Jacques Rousseau, musicien (*Paris, Fischbacher, 1901*)

PROD'HOMME, JACQUES-GABRIEL:

L'Opéra, 1669 – 1925 (*Paris, Delagrave, 1925*)

PRUNIÈRES, HENRI:

Lully (*Paris, Laurens – Les musiciens célèbres, 1910, 1927*)
La vie illustre et libertine de J. B. Lully (*Paris, Plon, 1929*)
L'Opéra italien en France avant Lulli (*Paris, Champion, 1913*)
Le ballet de cour avant Benserade et Lulli suivi du ballet de la Délivrance de
Roland (*Paris, Laurens, 1914*)
Nouvelle histoire de musique (*Paris, Rieder, 1934 – 1936*)

PURE, ABBÉ MICHEL DE:

Idées des spectacles anciens et nouveaux (*Paris, M. Brunet, 1668*)

RACINE, JEAN:

Préfaces (théâtre complèt) (*Paris, Barbin, 1676*)

RADET, – :

Lully homme d'affaires propriétaire et musicien (*Paris, Allison – Librairie de l'art, 1891*)

RAGUENET, ABBÉ FRANÇOIS:

Parallèle des Italiens et des François en ce qui regarde la musique et les opéra (*Paris, Moreau, 1702*)

RENAUDOT, THÉOPHRASTE:

Gazette de France: Recueil des gazettes, nouvelles, relations et autres choses mémorables de toute l'année 1632–1652) par Th. Renaudot (*Paris, Bureau d'Adresse, 1633 – 1653*)
Recueil des gazettes, nouvelles, ordinaires et extraordinaires, relations et récits de choses avenues toute l'année 1653 – 1671 par Théophraste Renaudot fils (*Paris, Bureau d'Adresse, 1654 – 1672*)

REVUE MUSICALE:

Ronsard et la musique (collaboration de L. Laloy, P. de Nolhac, H. Prunières, A. Suarés, C. van den Borren, A. Schaeffner, A. Coeuroy, M. Pincherle) (*Paris, La Revue musicale, numéro spécial, May 1924*)

Lully et l'Opéra Français (collaboration de L. de la Laurencie, H. Prunières, X. de Courville, A. Tessier, A. Levinson, Le Cerf de la Vieville, Nodot) (*Paris, La Revue musicale, numéro spécial, January 1925*)

ROLLAND, ROMAIN:

Musiciens d'autrefois (*Paris, Hachette, 1908*)
Les origines du théâtre lyrique moderne: Histoire de l'Opéra en Europe avant Lully et Scarlatti (*Paris, Thorin, 1895*)

RONSARD, PIERRE DE:

Les Elégies, Eclogues, et Mascerades (Oeuvres complètes, Vol. V) (*Paris, Garnier, 1923 – 1924*)
Sonnets pour Hélène (*Paris, Droz, 1947*)

ROUCHÈS, GABRIEL:

Inventaire des lettres et papiers manuscrits de Gasparo, Carlo, et Ludovico Vigarini conservés aux archives d'état de Modène (*Paris, Champion, 1913*)

ROUSSEAU, JEAN JACQUES:

Dictionnaire de musique (*Paris, Duchesne, 1768*)
Julie ou la Nouvelle Héloïse (*Amsterdam, M. M. Rey, 1761*)
Les Confessions (*Geneva, 1782*)
Lettre à d'Alembert sur les spectacles (Lettre de J. J. Rousseau à Monsieur d'Alembert sur son article Genève dans le 7e volume de l'encyclopédie et particulièrement sur le projet d'établir un théâtre de comédie en cette ville, 20 mars 1758) (*Amsterdam, M. M. Rey, 1758*)

SAINT-EVREMOND, CHARLES DE MARGUETEL, SEIGNEUR DE:

Oeuvres meslées (*Paris, Barbin, 1688 – 1692*)
Sur les tragédies, sur les comédies, de la comédie italienne, de la comédie anglaise, sur les opéra, à M. de Bouquinquant (Oeuvres meslées, Vol. II, tome 11) (*Paris, Barbin, 1684*)

SAINT-SIMON, LOUIS DE ROUVROY, DUC DE:

Mémoires du duc de Saint-Simon (6 vols.) (*Paris, Gide, 1818*)

SÉNECÉ, ANTOINE BAUDERON DE:

Lettre de Clément Marot à Monsieur de Sénecé touchant ce qui s'est passé à l'arrivée de J. B. Lully aux Champs Elysées (*Cologne, P. Marteau, 1688; Paris, La Revue musicale, numéro spécial, 1st January 1925*)

SÉVIGNÉ, MARIE DE RABUTIN-CHANTAL, MARQUISE DE:

Lettres (édition ancienne, pas complète) (*Paris, Janet et Cotelle, 1822 – 1823*)
Lettres (édition complète) (*Paris, Gallimard, 1953*)

TABOUROT (ARBEAU), THOINOT:

Orchésographie (*Paris, Vieweg, 1888*)

TIERSOT, JULIEN:

La musique dans la comédie de Molière (*Paris, La Renaissance du livre, n.d.*)

TILLET, TITON DU:

Description du Parnasse français exécuté en bronze suivi d'une liste alphabétique des poètes et des musiciens rassemblés sur ce document (*Paris, Goignard et fils, 1727*)

TOLDO, PIETRO:

Études sur le théâtre comique français au Moyen-Age (*Turin, Loescher, 1902*)

TRUINET (NUITTER), CHARLES, AND THOINAN, E.:

Les origines de l'opéra français (*Paris, Plon – Nourrit et Cie, 1886*)

D'UDINE, JEAN, (ALBERT COZANET):

Gluck (*Paris, Laurens, 1906*)

VALLIÈRE, LOUIS-CÉSAR, DUC DE LA:

Ballets, opéra et autres ouvrages lyriques (*Paris, C. J. B. Bauche, 1760*)

VIOTTI, – :

Mémoire au Roi concernant l'exploitation de privilège de l'opéra demandé par le Sieur Viotti (Recueil sur l'opéra) (*Paris, Bib. de l'Opéra, 1789*)

VOITURE, VINCENT DE:

Les oeuvres de M. de Voiture (*Paris, Mauger, 1691*)

VOLTAIRE, FRANÇOIS MARIE AROUET DE:

Commentaires dans oeuvres complètes (*Geneva, Cramer, 1761*)

BROCKWAY, WALLACE, AND WEINSTOCK, HERBERT:

The Opera: A History of its creation and performance 1600 – 1941 (*New York, Simon & Schuster, 1941*)

BURNEY, DR. CHARLES:

The Present State of Music in France and Italy (*London, T. Becket, 1771*)
A General History of Music (4 vols.) (*London, the author, 1776 – 1789*)

CAPELL, RICHARD:
Opera (*London, Benn, 1930, 1949*)

COOPER, MARTIN:
Gluck (*London, Chatto & Windus, 1935*)

DEMUTH, NORMAN:
A Course in Musical Composition, Vol. IV (*London, Bosworth, 1959*)

DENT, E. J.:
Opera (*London, Penguin Books – Pelican Special, 1940*)

EINSTEIN, ALFRED:
Gluck (*London, Dent, 1936*)

FULLER-MAITLAND, J. A.:
The Age of Bach and Handel (Oxford History of Music, Vol. IV) (*Oxford, Clarendon Press, 1902*)

GIRDLESTONE, CUTHBERT MORTON:
Rameau (*London, Cassell, 1958*)

GRAY, CECIL:
The History of Music (*London, O.U.P., 1928*)

GROUT, DONALD JAY:
A Short History of Opera (2 vols.) (*New York, Columbia University Press, 1947*)

HARGRAVE, MARY:
Earlier French Musicians (1632 – 1834) (*London, Kegan Paul, 1917*)

HAWKINS, SIR JOHN:
A General History of the Science and Practice of Music (5 vols.) (*London, printed for T. Payne, 1776*)

HUGHES, DOM ANSELM:
Early Medieval Music (The New Oxford History of Music, Vol. II) (*London, O.U.P., 1954*)

LOEWENBERG, ALFRED:
Annals of Opera 1597 – 1940 (*Cambridge, Heffer, 1943, in two vols., 1958*)

NEWMAN, ERNEST:
Gluck and the Opera (*London, Dobell, 1895*)

PARRY, SIR C. H. H.:
The Music of the XVIIth Century (Oxford History of Music, Vol. III) (*Oxford, Clarendon Press, 1902*)

PRUNIÈRES, HENRI:
A New History of Music (tr. Edward Lockspeiser) (*London, Dent, 1943*)

ROLLAND, ROMAIN:
Some Musicians of Former Days (tr. Mary Blaiklock) (*London, Kegan Paul, 1915*)

SCHOLES, PERCY:
A Miniature History of Opera (*London, O.U.P., 1931, 1949*)

SONNECK, OSCAR G.:
Catalogue of opera librettos printed before 1800 (2 vols.) (*Washington, Government Printing Office, 1914*)

STANFORD, SIR CHARLES, AND FORSYTH, CECIL:
A History of Music (*London, Macmillan, 1916*)

YOUNG, KARL:
The Drama of the Medieval Church (2 vols.) (*Oxford, Clarendon Press, 1933*)

B: Historical, Topographical, Sociological

Works in English are listed separately at the end of this section

BABEAU, ALBERT:
Le Théâtre des Tuileries sous Louis XIV, Louis XV, Louis XVI (*Nogent-le-Rotrou, Imprimerie de Daupeley-Gouverneur, 1895*)

BOYSSE, ERNEST:
Les Théâtres des Jesuites (*Paris, Vaton, 1880*)

BURNAND, ROBERT:
La Cour des Valois (*Paris, Hachette – De l'histoire, 1938*)

CALMETTE, JOSEPH:
Le Grand Règne de Louis XI (*Paris, Hachette – De l'histoire, 1938*)

CARRÉ, LT.-COL. HENRI:
La Marquise de Pompadour (*Paris, Hachette, 1937*)
Mademoiselle de La Vallière (*Paris, Hachette – Le rayon d'histoire, 1938*)
Madame de Montespan (*Paris, Hachette – Le rayon d'histoire, 1939*)

CASTELNAU, JACQUES:
La vie au Moyen-Age d'après les contemporains (*Paris, Hachette – De l'histoire, 1949*)

CAYLUS, MARTHE-MARGUERITE, COMTESSE DE:

Souvenirs de Madame de Caylus (*Amsterdam, M. M. Rey, 1770*)

CHAMPIGNEULLE, BERNARD:

Versailles, le château, les jardins, les Trianons (*Paris, Bordas, 1949*)
Versailles dans l'art et l'histoire (*Paris, Larousse, 1955*)

CHRIST, YVAN:

Le Louvre et les Tuileries (*Paris, Tel, 1949*)

COHEN, GUSTAVE:

Le théâtre en France au Moyen-Age (*Paris, Rieder, 2 vols., 1928 – 1931; Paris, Denoel, 2 vols., 1937; Paris, P.U.F., 1947*)
Histoire de la mise en scène dans le théâtre réligieux français au Moyen-Age (*Brussels, Imprimerie de Hayes, 1906; Paris, Champion, 1951*)

DESPOIS, EUGÈNE:

Le théâtre francais sous Louis XIV (*Paris, Hachette, 1874*)

D'ESPEZEL, PIERRE:

Le Palais-Royal (*Paris, Calmann-Levy, 1936*)

ESSARTS, NICOLAS-TOUSSAINT-LE MOYNE DES:

Les trois Théâtres de Paris ou Abrégé historique de l'établissement de la Comédie française, de la Comédie italienne et de l'opéra, avec un précis des lois, arrêts, réglements et usages qui concernent chacun de ces spectacles (*Paris, Lacombe, 1777*)

FARGUE, LEON-PAUL:

Les grandes heures du Louvre (*Paris, Les Deux Sirènes, 1948*)

FOURNIER, EDOUARD:

Le Théâtre français avant la Renaissance 1450 – 1550 (*Paris, Sanchez et Cie., 1872*)

GASSIES (DES BRULIES), GEORGES:

Anthologie du Théâtre français au Moyen-Age, Théâtre Comique; Jeux, Farces des XIIIe, XVe, et XVI siècles arrangés en français moderne (*Paris, Delagrave – Collection Pallas, 1925*)

GAXOTTE, PIERRE:

Préface de Gaxotte de l'ouvrage de *Ebeling*, J.B. 'Louis XV, extraits des mémoires du temps' (*Paris, Plon – l'histoire racontée par les témoins, 1938*)
Le siècle de Louis XV vu par les artistes (*Paris, 140 Faubourg St. Honoré, 1934*)
Le siècle de Louis XV (*Paris, A. Fayard, 1956*)

GOFFLOT, L. V.:

Le Théâtre au Collège du Moyen-Age à nos jours (*Paris, Champion, 1907*)

GOSSART, ANDRÉ-MARIE, AND FRAPPIER, JEAN:

Le théâtre comique au Moyen-Age (*Paris, Larousse, 1935*)

HAUTECOEUR, LOUIS:

Histoire du Louvre (*Paris, S.N.E.P., 1953*)

HILLAIRET, JACQUES:

Evocations du Vieux Paris (*Paris, Les Éditions de Minuit, 1951, 1952*)
Gibets, Piloris, et Cachots de Vieux Paris (*Paris, Les Éditions de Minuit, 1956*)

JULLEVILLE, L. PETIT DE:

Le Théâtre en France: (*Paris, A. Colin, 1889*)

LAFUE, PIERRE:

Louis XVI (*Paris, Hachette – De l'histoire, 1942*)

LASALLE, ALBERT:

Les treize salles de l'opéra (*Paris, Sartorius, 1875*)

LAVALLÉE, THÉOPHILE:

Histoire de la Maison Royale de Saint-Cyr (1686 – 1793) (*Paris, Furne, 1853*)

LEJEUNE, ANDRÉ, AND WOLFF, STEPHANE:

Les quinze salles de l'opéra (*Paris, Librairie théâtrale, 1955*)

LENÔTRE, G. (THÉODORE GOSSELIN):

Paris et ses fantômes (La petite histoire, Vol. III) (*Paris, Grasset, 1933*)
Versailles au temps des Rois (La petite histoire, Vol. IV) (*Paris, Grasset, 1934*)
Paris qui disparaît (La petite histoire, Vol. IX) (*Paris, Grasset, 1937*)
Existence d'artistes (de Molière à Victor Hugo) (La petite histoire, Vol. XI) (*Paris, Grasset, 1941*)

LINTELHAC, EUGÈNE-FRANÇOIS-LÉON:

Histoire générale du Théâtre en France (*Paris, Flammarion, 1910*)

MAZE, JULES:

La Cour de Louis XV (*Paris, Hachette – De l'histoire, 1944*)
Louis XVI et Marie-Antoinette: Les Coulisses de Versailles (*Paris, Hachette – Le Rayon d'histoire, 1941*)

NABONNE, BERNARD:

Les grandes heures de Saint-Germain-en-Laye (*Paris, Sfelt, 1950*)

NOLHAC, PIERRE DE:

Versailles et la Cour de France de La Reine Marie-Antoinette (*Paris, L. Conard, 1929 – 1930*)

REINHARD, MARCEL:

Henri IV ou La France sauvée (*Paris, Hachette – Le Rayon d'histoire, 1943*)

ROMAIN, COL. CHARLES-ARMAND:

Louis XIII: un grand Roi méconnu (*Paris, Hachette – Le Rayon d'histoire, 1934*)

SAUVAL, HENRI:

Histoire et recherches des antiquités de la ville de Paris (*Paris, Moette, 1724*)

SÉVIGNÉ, MADAME DE:

Lettres (*Paris, Janet et Cotelle, 1822 – 1823, incomplete; Paris, Gallimard, 1953*)

THAPHANEL, ACHILLE:

Le théâtre de Saint-Cyr d'après des documents inédits (*Versailles, Cerf et fils, 1876*)

TOESCA, MAURICE:

Les grandes heures de Fontainebleau (*Paris, Les Deux Sirènes, 1949*)

ANONYMES:

Henri IV; Paris; Le Palais du Louvre; L'histoire du costume; Louis XIV; Molière; Racine; Voltaire; Versailles (*Paris, Hachette – Encyclopédie par l'image, n.d.*)

GAXOTTE, PIERRE:

Louis the Fifteenth and his Times (tr. J. Lewis Mar) (*London, Cape, 1934*)

GIBBONS, A. O. (ED.):

The Trianon Adventure (*London, Museum Press, 1958*)

HARVEY, HOWARD GRAHAM:

The Theatre of the Basoche (*Cambridge Mass., Harvard University Press, 1941*)

LEWIS, W. H.:

The Splendid Century (*London, Eyre & Spottiswoode, 1953*).
The Sunset of the Splendid Century (*London, Eyre and Spottiswoode, 1955*)
Louis XIV (*London, Deutsch, 1959*)

MITFORD, NANCY:

Madame de Pompadour (*London, Hamish Hamilton, 1954*)
Voltaire in Love (*London, Hamish Hamilton, 1958*)
(ed.) Saint-Simon at Versailles (tr. L. Norton) (*London, Hamish Hamilton, 1958*)

PUTNAM, SAMUEL:

Marguerite of Navarre (*London, Jarrold, 1936*)

RITCHIE, R. L. GRAEME (ED.):

France – A Companion to French Studies (*London, Methuen, 1951*)

RODER, RALPH:

Catherine de Medici and the lost Revolution (*London, Harrap, 1937*)

ROWE, VIVIAN:

Royal Chateaux of Paris (*London, Putnam, 1956*)

STEAD, PHILIP JOHN:

The Police of Paris (*London, Staples Press, 1957*)

LIST OF RECORDED MUSIC

A few of the records listed below have been deleted from the official catalogues but may still be found in record libraries and among dealers' stocks. Records not readily available from distributors in Great Britain have not been included.

ALBERTUS PARIENSIS (12TH CENTURY):
Congaudeant Catholici (Codex Calixtinus) — H.M.V. History of Music HLP 4

BESARD, JEAN BAPTISTE (C. 1547 – ?):
En quelque lieu; Le voile la nacelle; Beaux yeux — Nixa WLP 5085

BLOW, DR. JOHN (1649 – 1708):
Venus and Adonis — Oiseau Lyre OL 50004

BOESSET, ANTOINE (C. 1585 – 1643):
Me veux-tu voir mourir? — Decca LW 5091
Cachez beaux yeux — Decca LW 5091

BONI, GUILLAUME (C. 1545 – C. 1594):
Rossignol, mon mignon — Oiseau Lyre OL 50027

BONNET, PIERRE (1538 – 1608):
Mon père et ma mère — Oiseau Lyre OL 50027
Francion vint l'autre jour — Brunswick AXTL 1048

BRULE, GACE (12TH CENTURY):
Je ne puis pas si loing fuir — H.M.V. History of Music HLP 3

CACCINI, GIULO (C. 1545 – 1618):
Amarilli — Decca LX 3113
Dolcissimo sospiro — Oiseau Lyre OL 50128
Och' Immortali — Decca LXT 2835

CAMPRA, ANDRE (1660 – 1744):
Air de Florise (Les Ages)
Air de Menalie (Alcino)
Air d'Hesione (Hesione) — Oiseau Lyre OL 50117
Festes Venetiennes — Vox STDL 500630

w

CAVALLI, FRANCESCO (1602 – 1676):
Musici della selva (*Egisto*)
H.M.V. History of
Music HLP 11

CERTON, PIERRE (C. 1510 – 1572):
Que n'est elle aupres de moi
Oiseau Lyre OL
50027

Psalm 130
Nixa WLP 5058

CHARPENTIER, MARC ANTOINE
(1634 – 1704):
Excerpts (*Medée ou Jason*)
Brunswick AXTL
1049

COLASSE, PASCAL (1649 – 1709):
Prologue (*Enie et Lavinie*)
Oiseau Lyre OL
50117

COSTERLEY, GUILLAUME (1531 – 1606):
Allons au vert bocage
H.M.V. History of
Music HLP 8

En ce beau moys
Oiseau Lyre OL
50027

Noblesse git au coeur; Mignonne allons voir
Brunswick AXTL
1048

Je voy di glissantantes eaux; Mignonne allons voir
Ducretet-Thomson
MEL 9007

DESMARETS, HENRI (1622 – 1741):
Air de Circé (*Circé*)
Oiseau Lyre OL
50117

DESTOUCHES, ANDRÉ (1672 – 1741):
Monologue de Callirhoe (*Callirhoe*)
Oiseau Lyre OL
50117

DUFAY, GUILLAUME (C. 1400 – 1474):
La belle se slet
London International
W 91116

Ce Moys de May
London International
W 91116

Pour l'amour de madouce amys
H.M.V. History of
Music HLP 6

GLUCK, CHRISTOPH WILLIBALD
(1714 – 1787):
Alceste
  Complete Work
Decca LXT 5273–9
  Overture
Decca LW 5144
  Divinités du Styx
Decca 45–71 100

Iphigénie en Aulide
  Overture
Decca LW 5144
  Vous voyez leur fureur extrême
H.M.V. History of
Music HLP 17

Orfeo	
Complete Work—German version	Deutsche-Grammofon DGM 18343–4
Italian version	RCA-Victor RB 16058–60
French version	Philips ABL 3359–60
Act II (abridged)	Decca LXT 2893
Che faro	Decca LW 5144
Che puro ciel	Decca LW 5225
Minuet and Dance	H.M.V. 7 ER 5052
Dance of the Furies, Dance of the Blessed Spirits	Deutsche-Grammofon DG 17062
Ballet Suite (Miscellaneous)	Decca LXT 5063
Paride ed Elena	
O del mio dolce ardor	Decca LX 3113
La Rencontre imprevue	
C'est un torrent; Un reuisselet bien clair	Decca LX 3113
Don Juan	
Pantomime Ballet	Nixa WLP 5028
GOUDIMEL, CLAUDE (C. 1510 – 1572):	
Amour me tue	Oiseau Lyre OL 50027
GROTTE, NICOLAS DE LA (16TH CENTURY):	
Quan je te veux raconter	Oiseau Lyre OL 50027
GUEDRON, PIERRE (1565 – C. 1620):	
Cette Anne si belle	Decca LW 5091
GUERRE, ELIZABETH DE LA (1666 – 1729):	
Air de Procris (*Céphale et Procris*)	Oiseau Lyre OL 50117
GUILLAUME D'AMIENS (13TH CENTURY):	
Ainsi doit entret en ville	Archive Production APM 14018
Main se levait Aelis	Archive Production APM 14018
Prendes-y-garde	Archive Production APM 14018
GUILLAUME DE DIJON (12TH CENTURY):	
Chanterai par mon coraige	H.M.V. History of Music HLP 3
HALE, ADAM DE LA (C. 1220 – 1287):	
Le Jeu de Robin et Marion	Archive Production APM 14018
Bergeronnete	H.M.V. History of Music HLP 4

HANDEL, GEORGE FREDERICK
(1685 – 1759):
March (*Occasional Oratorio*) — Columbia 33CX 1045

HUMFREY, PELHAM (1647 – 1674):
Hear, O Heavens — H.M.V. History of Music HLP 12

JANNEQUIN, CLÉMENT (C. 1475 – C. 1560):
Amour, la mort et la vie — Oiseau Lyre OL 50027

Au joli jeux — Archive Production APM 14042

Ce Moys de Mai — Brunswick AXTL 1048

Chant des Oiseaux (*Reveillez-vous*) — Archive Production APM 14042

Guerre — Archive Production APM 14042

Il estoit une fillette — Oiseau Lyre OL 50027

Las! pauvre coeur — Oiseau Lyre OL 50027

Ma peine n'est pas grande — Archive Production APM 14042

Petite nymphe folastre — Archive Production APM 14042

JEHANNOT DE L'ESCURIAL (13TH CENTURY):
A vous douce debonaire — H.M.V. History of Music HLP 5

JEUNE, CLAUDE LE (1528 – 1600):
Prince, la France le veut; Fiere cruelle — Oiseau Lyre OL 50027

Hélas, mon dieu; Revacy venir du printans; Tu ne l'entens pas — Brunswick AXTL 1048

LALANDE, MICHEL (1657 – 1726):
Sinfonies pour les soupers du Roy — London International TWV 91092

Concert de Trompettes pour les festes sur le canal de Versailles — Oiseau Lyre OL 50152
De Profundis (*Psalm 129*) — Vox PL 9040
Confitemini (*Te Deum*) — Oiseau Lyre OL 50153

LASSUS, ORLANDO DI (C. 1530 – 1594):
Bon jour mon coer — Brunswick AXTL 1048

Orsus filles, que l'on me donne — Archive Production APM 14055

Quand mon mary vient — Brunswick AXTL 1048

Un doux nenny — Archive Production APM 14055

LEONINUS (12TH CENTURY):
Judaea et Jerusalem (Responsory)

Archive Production
APM 14068

LITURGICAL DRAMA (*Anon.*):
Quem quaeirtis in sepulchro? (Lament
from *Daniel*)

H.M.V. History of
Music HLP 3

LULLY, JEAN BAPTISTE (1632 – 1687):
Dies Irae

Archive Production
APM 14100

Miserere

Oiseau Lyre OL
53003

Te Deum

Ducretet-Thomson
DTL 93043

Fanfares pour le Carrousel de Monseigneur

London International
TWV 91092

Marche des Mousquetaires du Roy
Marche des Mousquetaires gris
Marche du Régiment de Turenne
Le Bourgeois Gentilhomme (Complete)
Eight Excerpts (*Le Temple de la Paix*)

,, ,,
,, ,,
,, ,,
Decca LXT 5211–3
Oiseau Lyre OL
50136

Nocturne (*Le Triomphe de l'Amour*)
Alceste
(Act IV – Opening)

Columbia 33CX 1277

H.M.V. History of
Music ALP 11

(Air de Caron)
(Les Vents)
Amadis de Gaule (Air d'Arcabonne)

Decca LX 3112
Columbia 33CX 1277
Oiseau Lyre OL
50117

(Bois Epais)
Armide (Air d'Armide)

Victor RB 16127
Oiseau Lyre OL
50117

Cadmus et Hermione (Belle Hermione)
Thesée (Marche)

Decca LX 3112
Columbia 33CX 1277

MONTE, PHILIPPE DE (1521 – 1603):
Benedictus; Agnus Dei

H.M.V. History of
Music HLP 8

PERGOLESI, GIOVANNI (1710 – 1738):
La Serva Padrona
Complete Work
Stizzoso

Archive Production
APM 14064
Decca LW 5245

PERI, JACOPO (1561 – 1633):
A miel giorni fugaci

Decca LXT 2835

PURCELL, HENRY (1658 – 1695):
O sing unto the Lord

Archive Production
APM 14059

Rameau, Jean Philippe (1683 – 1764):
Castor et Pollux
Nature, amour   Decca LX 3112
Minuet from Prologue (Séjour de   Brunswick AXTL
l'eternelle paix)   1053

Dardanus
O jour affreux   Brunswick AXTL
     1053
Sommeil-Rondeau   Oiseau Lyre OL
     50194

Les Fêtes d'Hébé
Suite   Ducretet-Thomson
     DTL 93070
Volons sur les bordes de la Seine   Brunswick AXTL
     1053

Hippolyte et Aricie
Excerpts   Oiseau Lyre OL
     50034
Overture and Fanfare; Ballet figure;   Brunswick AXTL
Rossignols amoureux   1053

Les Indes Galantes
Suite   Oiseau Lyre OL
     50194
Clair flambeau   Brunswick AXTL
     1053
Invocation au soleil   Decca LXT 5269

Les Paladins
Ballet Suites 1 and 2   Oiseau Lyre OL
     50106

Pigmalion
Ballet   Archive Production
     APM 14302

Platée
Chantons Bacchus   Brunswick AXTL
     1053
Suite   Telefunken LGM
     65002

Zaïs
2 Gavottes   Oiseau Lyre OL
     50194

Zephyre
Sarabande   Oiseau Lyre OL
     50194

Rossi, Luigi (1598 – 1653):
Del silentio il giogo aigente   H.M.V. History of
     Music HLP 14

Rousseau, Jean Jacques (1712 – 1798):
Le Devin du Village
  Complete Work   Columbia 33CX 1503

Rudel, Jauffre (? – 1172):
  Lanquand li jorn   Archive Production
                                                   APM 14068
Sandrin, Pierre Regnault (16th century):
  Amour si haut   Oiseau Lyre OL
                                                   50027
Sermisy, Claudin de (c. 1490 – 1562):
  Au joly boys   Brunswick AXTL
                                                   1048
  Dictes sans peur   Oiseau Lyre OL
                                                   50027
  Hau, Hau, le boy   Brunswick AXTL
                                                   1048
  La, je m'y plains   Oiseau Lyre OL
                                                   50027
  Tant que vivray   H.M.V. History of
                                                   Music HLP 8
  Vivray-je tousjours en soucy?   H.M.V. History of
                                                   Music HLP 9

Vaqueiras, Raimbaut de
(c. 1155 – c. 1207):
  Kalenda maya (Estampida)   Archive Production
                                                   APM 14018
Ventadorn, Bernat de (c. 1150 – 1195):
  Lamcon vel la olha   Archive Production
                                                   APM 14068
  Quant val l'aloete mover   H.M.V. History of
                                                   Music HLP 3

INDEX

336 FRENCH OPERA